LOST

MUSCLE CARS

45 Stories of Hunting the Most Elusive and Valuable Muscle Cars

WES EISENSCHENK

CarTech®

CarTech®, Inc.
838 Lake Street South
Forest Lake, MN 55025
Phone: 651-277-1200 or 800-551-4754
Fax: 651-277-1203
www.cartechbooks.com

Edit by Bob Wilson
Layout by Monica Seiberlich

Author note: Many of the vintage photos in this book are of lower quality. They have been included because of their importance to telling the story.

ISBN 978-1-61325-225-3
Item No. CT551
Library of Congress Cataloging-in-Publication Data Available

Written, edited, and designed in the U.S.A.
Printed in China
10 9 8 7 6 5 4 3 2 1

OVERSEAS DISTRIBUTION BY:

PGUK
63 Hatton Garden
London EC1N 8LE, England
Phone: 020 7061 1980 • Fax: 020 7242 3725
www.pguk.co.uk

Renniks Publications Ltd.
3/37-39 Green Street
Banksmeadow, NSW 2109, Australia
Phone: 2 9695 7055 • Fax: 2 9695 7355
www.renniks.com

CONTENTS

DEDICATION

To the thousands of enthusiasts pursuing information on a classic car. It's the enthusiasts with whom I share this hobby and have led me to compile a number of these stories into a singular publication.

ACKNOWLEDGMENTS

Thanks to my wife, Michelle, and my two children, Elliott and Bailee. Their love and support has continued to allow me the opportunities to submerge myself in this hobby. One of my greatest joys in life is sharing it with them through car shows and cruises.

Thanks to my grandpas, Virgil Rettig and Maurice Eisenschenk. Without them the seed would never have been planted that old cars are cool. Thanks to my dad, Wally Eisenschenk. Burying the speedometer on his 1985 El Camino was a transitional period in my life. And finding the history on his 1969 Impala SS 427 convertible was one of the key components in confirming that these searches can be successful.

Thanks to my mom, Diane (1973 Javelin); brother, Keith (1969 Corvette;, and sister, Mary (1966 Mustang). The hobby runs deep in my family.

I have to thank CarTech for granting me the outlet to tell these stories. It's an honor and a privilege to call CarTech my place of employment.

And finally, I have to individually thank all of the contributors to this book. It would be foolish for me to think I'm the expert on every car in these upcoming pages. *They* are the ones more closely associated with these muscle cars, and their expertise, helpfulness, and graciousness have allowed these pages to be filled with some of the most bitchin' stories I've ever heard or read.

Those individuals are Corey Owens, Gary Emord-Netzley, Jim Cecil, John Foster Jr., Danny Reed, Dollie Cole, Mike Satterfield, Pat Smith, Kenny Gregrich, Daniel Fehn, Bret Mattison, Matt Hardigree, "Papa John" Schnatter, Richard Padovini, Dennis Manner, Richard Lasseter, Lance Marlette, Kevin Martin, Walt and Todd Trapnell, Peter Discher, Pierre and Patrice Moinet, Chuck Miller, Walt Czarnecki, Bradley Broemmer, Mike Galewski, Bill Cook, Chris Collard, Ron Johnson, Edward Ludtke, Rick Kopec, J. D. Feigelson, Geoff Stunkard, Lynn Wineland, Darryl Klassen, Allen and Hubert Platt, Ryan Brutt, Steve Reyes, Joel Naprstek, Chuck Conway, Doug Boyce, Richard Welch, Rusty Gilles,

Scott Hollenbeck, Bobby Schlegel, Bernard Durham, Ron Gusack, Thomas Benvie, Mike and Sharon Craig, Carl Ruprecht, Les Welch, Jon Mello, Michael Booth, Tommy Erwin, Bob Snyder, Charlie Morris, Richard McKinstry, Dennis Kincaid, Mark Meekins, Jeff Helm, Leon Dixon, Dana Hurt, Rick Nelson, Todd Werts, Roger Day, Ryan Weaver, George Kanavaros, Wade Ogle, Ola Nilsson, Scott and Joe Oldham, Jim Dunne, Kevin Marti, Andy Hack, Bob Snyder, Charlie Gilchrist, Jerry Hinton, Donald Surrett, Mike Dolence, John Emmi, Paul Hutchins, Barbara Hernandez, Marvin T. Smith, Carl and Char Hirst, Ken Stowe, Don Johnson, and Jay Sabol.

INTRODUCTION

Fifteen years ago I was conversing with a co-worker about the history of his 1966 Formula S Barracuda over a pile of base and casing at my father's stain shop. While restoring his car in 1988, he came across a gas receipt with a name on it. I asked him to bring it in so I could have a look at it. Eight years later I handed him the home address of the individual who purchased the Barracuda new.

We all remember Geraldo Rivera standing in front of Al Capone's long-lost vault with our eyes glued to our 24-inch Zenith televisions. Palms sweaty and mouths dry, we awaited the greatest discovery of the twentieth century. Surely gold bars, tommy guns, and dead bodies littering the floor would be found. Capone wouldn't have it any other way. Finally, after a continued buildup, a series of preset charges blasted dust and debris into the Chicago night. After the concrete chips and flying particles settled, there it was . . . *nothing*.

What Geraldo went through on that chilly April evening in 1986 is something that almost every muscle car hunter has gone through at least once, a crushing and emphatic automotive archeological defeat.

However, unlike Geraldo's vault, the dead end for a muscle car sleuth is just a wrong turn. Sure, that empty garage staring back at you feels like failure, but you can always find another source to talk to and another photo archive to thumb through. If Rivera were a car guy, he'd be back talking to the guy before the guy who led him to the dead end. And like a true enthusiast he'd be off and running toward the next unopened Capone vault.

To become an avid car sleuth, you have to be armed with a variety of talents, tools, and skills. The first skill is the ability to comprehend that patience is the key ingredient in any hunt. Dead ends are simply turnaround points, and long breaks without any news are simply just dramatic pauses in the grand scheme of things.

The tools for a muscle car hunter are not too different than those of a crime scene investigator. Thorough interviews need to be conducted and ample rehashing is to be performed over bits and pieces of information that may seem minute and trivial, but invaluable to connecting the dots. Photographs are examined like a hawk peering over a field for the movements of a rabbit with the researcher intent on finding that subtle tell that could release the floodwaters. Letters are mailed to the state DMV in hopes that historical ownership could lead to a promising new clue. Any and all paper trails are backtracked as far as humanly and digitally possible. And finally, the talents are in developing relationships with people that halt just before the threshold of annoyance is reached. An enthusiast has no shortage of avenues to go through to "solve" the case.

The abundance of truly spectacular lost muscle cars possibly still in existence is astounding. The list of legendary cars unaccounted for sounds like the roster at the Muscle Car & Corvette Nationals or the starting lineup for the 1927 Yankees. They're still out there. With names such as Z16, ZL1, and S/S AMX, from Hurst, Yenko, and Shelby, they are waiting to be rediscovered. They include famed promo/show cars, race cars, rare factory production cars, and celebrity-owned muscle. The total value of these lost muscle cars is potentially in the hundreds of millions of dollars. And yes, I have stories about Corvettes and Rancheros just to fire up the age-old debate as to whether sports cars and trucks are to be considered muscle cars.

Some of the stories included here do not include information on VINs, serial numbers, or other data. This is because many people didn't keep that information. Remember, at one time these cars weren't considered collectible. *Lost Muscle Cars* presents these cars in their last known configuration, location, and ownership lineage to the best of its owner's recollections. I'm calling on *you* to remember that badass Rebel Machine that used to roar through town or that 1969 Yenko that pulled its wheel out past the 60-foot marker at the local dragstrip. You could hold the keys to the last piece of information that could uncover the location of one of these missing beasts.

You don't have to be Jay Leno or Ric Gillespie to be a part of the next great discovery. Armed with this book, you're now a real automotive archeologist!

CHAPTER ONE

Concept/Promo/ Prototype Muscle

The muscle car era was truly the first time that American auto manufacturers had to build more than just beautiful cars. Racing had become a dominant sales tool and the homologation of factory production offerings changed the landscape of who was building what, where, and for whom.

The menacing stance of the Ford Super Cobra was enough to strike fear into anyone who happened upon it at a stoplight. Unfortunately, this was the last rendition of this body style. (Photo Courtesy Chicago Auto Show)

There were simply too many cars for the manufacturers to create themselves in the constantly changing muscle car wars. Outsourcing became a viable and successful tool in getting new cars to the market quickly.

Dodge used Creative Industries of Detroit and other sources to create Dream Cars like the Dodge Charger I and Dodge Charger II. Dodge also harnessed Creative's designers to develop cars for racing programs as done with the Dodge Daytona and its in-house nemesis used Creative to build the Superbird.

Ford was doing the same at Kar Kraft, creating the Boss 429 and Torino Talladega, required for homologation in NASCAR as well, and the Boss 302 cars for Trans-Am racing. Styline Customs typically handled preparation and customization for show cars for companies such

as Promotions Inc., but by 1969 they were waist deep in helping manufacturers create the Hurst Olds and the SC/Rambler, which needed to be produced for F Stock classification in the NHRA.

As much fun as it was creating cars for racing, manufacturers still had to focus on the general buying public, and they did so through auto shows.

Two of the biggest were the Chicago Auto Show and the Detroit Auto Show. At those venues, designers debuted their concepts and gauged public opinion and reaction. Other cars already slated for production were formally rolled out and introduced to the public for the first time.

The Mustang I made its debut at the U.S. Grand Prix race in 1962 held at Watkins Glen in upstate New York, but garnered much of its unfavorable public opinions from touring the auto shows. That sent Ford back to the drawing board, resulting in the design of the Mustang II. That car was received favorably by the public and became the blueprint for the development of the production models.

Unfortunately the survival rate for these promotional, concept, and prototype cars was fairly low. Some of them were cut up and parts were used for future endeavors while others were outright destroyed. With every production model, though, other cars were always created to re-start the design process.

Finding one of these cars and then working on verification of its authenticity can be daunting. Many of the designers who created these cars are no longer with us, which means that other types of historical documentation are needed. Hunting these cars is also difficult because some were never intended for public usage, and that means VINs and serial numbers were never part of the car.

Don't be discouraged, though. With hard work and some sleuthing you may open a barn door and be staring at one of these lost muscle cars.

By Wes Eisenschenk

Of all things to transpire after the 1968 Grand National (NASCAR) season, the defection of Richard Petty from Plymouth to Ford is perhaps one of the most overlooked separations in the history of motorsports. After nearly a decade of dominance, Petty, who had led the charge for Plymouth since switching from Oldsmobile during the 1959 season, was headed to the Blue Oval, and Plymouth had to go back to the drawing board.

In hindsight, 1968 wasn't that terrible of a year for King Richard and his Plymouth Road Runners. In fact, Richard closed the year with 16 wins (two in his 1967 Plymouth) and finished strong with 5 wins in his last 10 races. Throw out his DNF at Charlotte (third-to-last race) and his average finishing position over those last 9 contests was 1.88.

Creative Industries of Detroit grafted a new nose onto a 1969 Plymouth Road Runner to construct the Superbird and began the process of luring Richard Petty back to Plymouth. (Photo Courtesy Richard Padovini and Winged Warriors Car Club)

He started the 1969 campaign in his 1968 Road Runner and ended up 1st at Macon and 2nd at Montgomery, finishing behind Bobby Allison, also driving a Plymouth. So why would Richard want to leave the auto manufacturer with whom he had so much success and who had seemingly been offering him competitive equipment?

The Dodge Influence

The answer was happening over at Dodge. Before the 1968 campaign, Dodge had rolled out an all-new Charger. Aesthetically, the car looked unbeatable. Competitively, it was a turd. It was so bad aerodynamically that in mid-1968 Chrysler began to rework the body at Creative Industries of Detroit in order to make the car more competitive for 1969. By adding a flush nose (donated from the Coronet) and removing the sail panels from the roofline, the Chargers became more cooperative at the high speeds on the superspeedways.

Dodge would have to build 500 production copies to make the car eligible for competition in NASCAR for the 1969 season. Rumors persist that when NASCAR officials visited Creative to count how many cars were constructed, employees simply drove around the building and through the entrance again so they were counted twice. The final tally was 392 Charger 500s built with NASCAR apparently none the wiser.

Obviously, the willingness of Dodge to help make the Chargers faster while Plymouth sat on its hands didn't sit well with the Pettys. In truth, they weren't getting the factory support that they felt they needed, whereas it appeared the Dodge drivers were. For 1969, Plymouth had indicated to Petty that he would be campaigning the reworked Road Runner that he had driven in 1968. This proved to be the proverbial nail in the coffin for Richard and his days at Chrysler.

On November 25, 1968, Richard announced that he would be headed to Ford for the 1969 Grand National season. For 1969 Ford Motor Company planned to debut the new drop-nosed Talladegas and Cyclone Spoiler IIs.

Charger Daytona Debut

With an ever-increasing transition from dirt ovals to paved superspeedways in NASCAR's premier series, "aero" was the new term that everyone in the garage had to adhere to. Dodge began making the transition with the Charger 500 in 1968 but took things to a whole new level in 1969 because it just wasn't satisfied with its race cars.

In early 1969, Dodge began work on the Charger 500's successor, the Dodge Charger Daytona. The car was to debut in 1970, but plans changed when the Ford Talladega and Mercury Cyclone Spoiler II debuted at the Atlanta 500. This forced Chrysler to contract Creative Industries again to quickly begin production of the 503 copies for street use and NASCAR homologation.

In September at Talladega, the Charger Daytona debuted with its extended beak and grafted wing and with replacement driver Richard Brickhouse. Why Richard Brickhouse? Because 16 regulars, led by Richard Petty (head of the Professional Drivers Association), boycotted the race because of safety concerns.

With Brickhouse behind the wheel, the aero-sensitive machine ran laps consistently in the 197-mph range. The Daytona went on to win the race and ultimately ushered in Chrysler's dominance, placing Chrysler on the throne for the next season and a half.

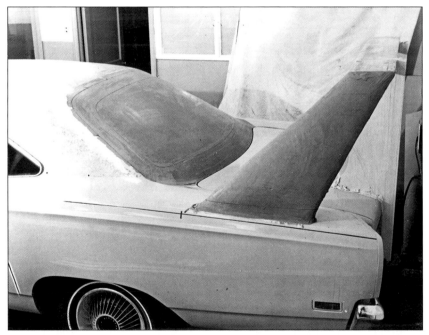

The prototype wing is applied to the rear quarter panels of the 1969 Road Runner at Creative Industries of Detroit. Similar to the 1969 Dodge Charger 500, a smaller rear window is also affixed to this Bird. (Photo Courtesy Richard Padovini and Winged Warriors Car Club)

Road Runner to Superbird Concept Car

In June 1969, Chrysler CEO Lynn Townsend began the changes that brought Richard Petty back to Plymouth by creating the winged car. Petty also requested that all of Plymouth's racing program go through Petty Enterprises. The deal was done and Petty signed a contract to return Plymouth after the 1969 racing season.

With a 1969, not a 1970, hardtop Road Runner donated by Chrysler, Creative Industries of Detroit began the task of building the Superbird. This donor car was either Alpine White or Sunfire Yellow based on the photos saved by Dick Padovini. Options appear to have included V7X Black Longitude Stripe, V1 Vinyl Roof, V21 Performance Hood Paint, G31 OS RH Manual Standard Mirror, C55 Bucket Seats, U64 F70-15 White Stripe Tires, W15 Deep Dish Wheel Covers, and M25 Wide Sill Molding.

The front clip featured a clay-molded nose with simulated fender scoops and what appears to be filled-in side markers, although the location isn't quite where the stock markers were. Out back, the

The clay is well massaged and smooth and braces provide stability for the new nose cone. The hood features pre-fabbed fender scoops. (Photo Courtesy Richard Padovini and Winged Warriors Car Club)

aero Bird's rear glass was removed and fitted with a smaller piece to make it more aerodynamic. The Bird's primitive, clay-molded rear wing wasn't adjustable and had to be braced for stability. The 1970 Superbird was a resounding success with Richard, who notched 18 total victories across 40 races, although he also competed in his Road Runner hardtop. It may have been a championship season for King Petty had he not been involved in a violent crash at Darlington that sidelined him for eight contests. The Superbird also notched key victories in superspeedway races at Talladega and Daytona, including a coveted win at the Daytona 500.

NASCAR eventually handicapped the Chrysler winged cars with engine-size restrictions, which rendered them uncompetitive. Today, Superbirds, especially those with the Hemi engine option, routinely sell for more than $300,000.

What happened to the 1969 Superbird concept car? Virtually nothing is known about its status. Whether it was destroyed,

Chrysler also called on Creative Industries of Detroit for the development of the 1969 Charger Daytonas. Note the Charger hoods and Daytona nose cones still lying around at Creative. (Photo Courtesy Richard Padovini and Winged Warriors Car Club)

Held up by bracing, the 1969 Superbird nose cone looks the part of an aero warrior. On the wall in the background are sketches of the prototype. I'll take one, please! (Photo Courtesy Richard Padovini and Winged Warriors Car Club)

converted back to 1969 Road Runner specs, or let loose to the general public remains a mystery. So, if you see a funky-looking 1969 Road Runner sporting a nose cone and a rear spoiler, don't mock the car or the owner. You might well be looking at one of the most important cars in the history of motorsports.

By Kevin Martin

Automakers have been creating special show cars (concept cars, idea cars, dream cars) since the 1930s to draw the buying public to their booths at the major annual car shows. Some of these cars were created to elicit the public's reaction to styling elements contemplated by the carmakers; others were teasers to show what was in store for upcoming production models.

Ford touted its 1969 show cars as the "Ford Better Idea Show." They weren't too extreme, but they were good props for shapely young go-go–booted hotties with come-hither patter. Ford's offerings were pretty tame this year because they were based on customized production models.

1966 Ford Fairlane GT A GO GO

When the words Ford, dream car, show car, and 1950s are mentioned in a single sentence, you can't be faulted if images of bubble-top gyroscopically balanced automotive concepts pop into your mind. Or vehicles that looked suspiciously like UFOs. That's not surprising

The Fairlane GT A GO GO was constructed to help call attention to Ford's revamped midsize model. It was designed by the Corporate Projects Studio and built in California by customizer Gene Winfield. (Photo Courtesy Chicago Auto Show)

because the chief of Advanced Styling for Ford from 1952 through 1963 was Alex Tremulis, the garrulous Greek who designed, among other lasting automotive monuments, the 1948 Tucker Torpedo. Some think that Tremulis was the greatest automotive designer ever.

George W. Walker, the designer of the 1949 Ford, brought Tremulis on board to inject some much needed pizzazz into another of Walker's creations, the Ford Corporate Design Center. The Corporate Design Center was Walker's response to Harley Earl's Art and Colour Section at General Motors, created in 1927.

Fairlane GT/GTA

By the early 1960s, Ford wanted to explore styling concepts that related more to what it wanted to build and sell rather than just to titillate the sci-fi crowd. So out with the Gyronaut and in with shrunken T-Birds. The first actual production car, rather than design element, which came out of this line of thinking was the 1964½ Mustang. It goes without saying that in 1966 Ford wasn't having any trouble moving Mustangs off the showroom floor, but its Fairlane GT/GTA was getting its butt kicked by just about every muscle car out there (except for the Buick Skylark GS). Sales were anemic (6,908 cars), as was the car's performance.

The Fairlane GT (the GTA was the automatic version) could barely get out of its own way let alone the likes of the Pontiac GTO and the Chevelle SS 396. The Fairlane's power was supplied by Ford's tried-and-true FE 390-ci 320-horse trailer-towing engine. On the street, it was well known that even a 4-speed 300-horse 327-ci small-block Impala left a Galaxie 390 in the weeds. The same went for the 325-horse 383-ci Dodge Coronet/Plymouth Satellite.

That's not to say that with some judicious tweaking, the FE 390 couldn't be persuaded to give a GTO a good run for its money. It could, and if you bought your new Fairlane GT from Tasca Ford in Providence, Rhode Island, the dealership probably had a package that could wake up your Fairlane 390 GT. But not every gearhead had a neighborhood high-performance Ford dealer named Tasca.

Backward Designing

Ford must have caught on that the Fairlane GT was a dog early in the sales year, because by the time the 1966 Chicago Auto Show

Automotive design guru Gene Winfield built the Fairlane GT A GO GO based on sketches supplied by Ford. This is one of the few color photos showing the vibrant blue interior. (Photo Courtesy Chicago Auto Show)

rolled around, Ford had an answer to pick up its lousy sales. It was called the Fairlane A GO GO. (Cue the laugh track.)

Ford, for what may have been a first in corporate history, created a show car in reverse. It took an arguably crisp and nicely designed 1966 Fairlane and added some styling features (such as eight fake chrome air intakes on the hood) that were bound to turn off its intended, performance-oriented market. As hokey as this styling element was, Plymouth picked up the idea for its 1967 GTX. And to pound home the performance theme, the A GO GO came with side-exit open exhausts controllable by the driver, known as cutouts. Drive to the dragstrip with the exhaust routed through conventional mufflers, hit a switch, and still get beat by everyone, only make more noise.

The real showstopper, however, was the interior, which featured acres of shiny blue metalflake vinyl. Fortunately, this design element never found a place in production car interiors, but was a big favorite in ski boats, choppers, and banana seats on kids' bicycles. To finish this all off was a metallic white paint job with a metallic blue center stripe.

The show car transformation took place at Ed Winfield's custom shop in California.

Ford's Ranchero Scrambler concept car didn't offer much conceptually that was new. However, it gave people their first look at the new logo that was featured on its newest car, the Maverick. (Photo Courtesy Bill Cook Archive)

1969 Ford Ranchero Scrambler

Today, it's extremely difficult to find any information on any factory show car and the 1969 Ranchero Scrambler is no exception. For tax reasons, most show cars were sent to the crusher once they had served their purpose on the car show circuit and rarely lasted more than a year. About all we have left now are a handful of photographs.

It's rumored that Larry Shinoda styled the Ranchero Scrambler; his earlier influence can be seen in the C1 and C2 Corvettes and the 1965 Corvair. By today's standards it's a rather mild custom. Even by the standards of its day, it's still a rather conservative makeover.

The wheels, Kelsey Hayes Magstars, were production options on a wide range of hot factory Fords at that time. The engine, a 428 Cobra Jet, was the top-of-the-line offering for a variety of Mustangs, Fairlanes, and Torinos. Even the body-colored bumpers (without parting lines) were yesterday's news, having debuted the previous year on the Pontiac GTO. Although the hidden headlights did not appear on the Torino until the following year, they had been on Thunderbirds since 1967 and the LTD since 1968.

So what was new? What presaged the future? One tiny detail: The chrome Longhorn in the center of the grille appeared the following year as the emblem for the restyled Falcon, otherwise known as the Maverick.

1969 Mercury Super Spoiler

The Super Spoiler was evidence that someone, with emphasis on "one," was calling the esthetic shots at Ford styling for what the public was told were the better ideas for the 1969 show cars. As with the Ranchero Scrambler, the Super Spoiler had hidden headlights and a body-colored molded-in front bumper. In fact, both the Ranchero and the Super Spoiler look as though they were styled by the same person who designed those wacky custom add-ons only available in the AMT Styline model car kits.

But the Super Spoiler went a bit further than the Ranchero. Based on a Montego Cyclone coupe, the A-pillars were chopped and the windshield header removed, as well as the roof set as far back as the C-pillars. What remained of the roof and the C-pillars were molded into what Ford termed an integral roll bar. The interior featured four bucket seats with gold brocade fabric. The engine in this stylistic tour de force was said to have been a 351 Cleveland or Windsor, but in either case, it was probably there for show and not go.

This Mercury Cyclone Super Spoiler concept car was about as extravagant as they came with its plush seats, chopped windshield, and shaved door handles. Very little information remains on this car. (Photo Courtesy Kevin Martin Archive)

The Super Cobra featured a 2-inch body drop, slanted back window, and an 8-inch nose extension. Much like the Ranchero Scrambler, a Shaker hood scoop adorned the mighty 428 Cobra Jet concealed beneath. (Photo Courtesy Bill Cook Archive)

Very few, if any, factory show customs ran or could be driven. In the parlance of the design studios, they were design studies only. It can be argued that the 1970 Cyclone production car was far wilder than the Super Spoiler show car.

1969 Ford Super Cobra

Proving that Ford was aware that colors other than pearlescent/metalflake brown existed, the carmaker daringly coated and massaged this Fairlane with a candy apple red exterior. Complementing this daring exterior color choice was an interior stitched in candy murano and hot red. To combat the Fairlane's chronic stubby exterior appearance, the nose was stretched 7 inches and the top was chopped by 2 inches. Powering this static styling exercise was Ford's answer to any question asked that year: 428 Cobra Super Jet!

Where Are They Now?

And so the go-go 1960s era came to a close. People drove 4,500-pound coupes because gas was only 32 cents per gallon. Eight miles per gallon was tolerable as long as we had interiors slathered in gold hot stamping and faux heraldic badges. Then this pesky thing called OPEC intruded without invitation and suddenly Detroit's answer, specifically Ford's, was the ugly antithesis to the Super Cobra, the Mustang II. The Malaise era began.

The grand question remains: What happened to the Ford show cars? That's not an easy question to answer for a number of reasons. Some of the cars were nothing more than glossy design exercises, known as styling bucks, built from fiberglass or heavily modified production sheet metal, without engines or running gear. Once they had served their purpose, which dictated a short life span, they were old news, just gathering dust and taking up space. This was probably the fate of the Ranchero Scrambler and the Mercury Super Cyclone.

The Fairlane GT A GO GO, based on a production car, presented a different set of problems. The first was tax liability, which would have come due as soon as any show car of this type ceased to serve its original purpose. The second was product liability. These cars were sent to outside contractors for modification. They were totally torn apart for repainting, custom bodywork/features, and interiors. During that process, certain parts critical to safety, emissions, or day-to-day function may have been removed and not replaced.

No one kept track of these items, but Ford and the other automakers were not blind to this fact and couldn't risk one of these cars actually being driven, especially on public roads. Combined with the tax liabilities, this usually meant a one-way trip to the crusher.

But every year, show car barn finds surface; some were hidden by the designers who worked on them; some were just stored and forgotten long ago. Some collectors specialize in show cars. So not all disappear; we just can't see them anymore.

By Wes Eisenschenk

By 1970, the Hurst Corporation was large and in charge of the performance shifter market industry for muscle cars. Known mainly for its 4-speed transmissions, Hurst was one of the few businesses with whom Ford, General Motors, Chrysler, and AMC allied themselves in an effort to maintain an edge in the marketplace. Lagging behind in salability was Hurst's line of automatic shifters. What the company needed was something to create awareness of its all-new shifter for 1970. Inside the corporate offices, a plan was developed for just that purpose. Hurst planned to give a 1970 SS Nova to the lucky person who came up with a clever name for its new automatic shifter.

And the Winner Is

Walt Trapnell was a salesman for M&H in 1970, selling racing slicks in Cleveland, Ohio. One day, he came across a Hurst display that was asking the public to get involved in naming the new Hurst shifter. Walt, a father of two boys, jotted down four separate entries

Todd Trapnell, the three-year-old Hurst-A-Matic Nova giveaway winner, salutes the cameraman with the V-for-victory sign, which he learned courtesy of Linda Vaughn. (Photo Courtesy National Dragster)

for each member of his family. On his son Todd's slip, he wrote "Hurst-A-Matic." Thinking nothing more of it, Walt went back to work and let the contest slip out of his mind.

A few months later, he received a phone call from Hurst corporate notifying him that he was one of 147 entrants who had submitted the name Hurst-A-Matic in the Hurst Nova giveaway contest. From the pool of 147, Hurst had conducted a drawing to whittle those down to 25 contestants. The gentleman on the phone told Walt that they were going to be conducting a final drawing and if he won, he would be receiving a call back in 15 minutes.

About 10 minutes later the phone rang in the Trapnell house. Walt eagerly answered it and was told that he, or rather *Todd*, was the winner of a brand-new Hurst-equipped 1970 Nova SS 396.

A Trip to the Nationals

Not only had the family won the Nova, but they also won an all-inclusive trip to the 1970 U.S. Nationals held in Indianapolis, Indiana. Todd and Walt were invited to partake in all of the festivities surrounding one of drag racing's premier events. They were excited to receive such an amazing gift, but they were disappointed when Hurst informed them that the flight included for the trip to Indy was for only two individuals.

The Trapnell family felt that they had won as a team and wanted to celebrate as a team. An agreement was made so that Walt drove instead of flying so the whole Trapnell family could enjoy the festivities in Indianapolis. Walt went on to reveal that Hurst was first class in taking care of the family. Todd, just three years old, was the star of the weekend. The Trapnells were going to be rubbing elbows with all of the top names in drag racing, from Garlits and Prudhomme to Sox & Martin. Most notable of all was that Miss Hurst Golden Shifter Linda Vaughn was going to be Todd's personal host.

One event they attended was the pre–U.S. Nationals gala. When it was time for a Hurst representative to take the podium and talk about the successful ad campaign, and to announce the winners of the giveaway Nova, Vaughn scooped up Todd and made her way to the podium.

As Linda spoke about the guests of honor for the weekend, Todd flashed the V-for-victory sign that Linda had taught him, giving everyone in the crowd a chuckle. Walt went on to say that when

Linda handed young Todd back to his mother he overheard Todd exclaim, "Mom, she's squishy!" The U.S. Nationals went down to the wire in the Top Fuel division with Don Prudhomme barely inching by Jim Nicoll in the finals. The event is well known for what happened after Nicoll crossed the finish line: His clutch exploded, ripping the dragster in two.

Prudhomme, with perhaps the best seat in the house, watched in horror as Nicoll's dragster disintegrated and he saw the front half of the car (with its engine) shoot past him with no sign of Jim. By a stroke of luck, Nicoll had flipped on the chute just before the explosion.

The opened chute lifted the driver and his cage/cockpit up and over the wall, setting Nicoll down in the grass. He sustained only a concussion and a swollen foot.

Home Again

After the finals, the Trapnell family returned home to Cleveland, with the Nova following shortly thereafter. Hurst had removed most of the graphics on the car, leaving it with just the gold striping and a few decals on the rear quarter panel.

The Hurst Nova, without its giveaway graphics, tackles the quarter-mile at Thompson Drag Raceway in the early 1970s. This is the last known photo of the car before it slipped into oblivion. (Photo Courtesy Charles Gilchrist Collection)

We'd all like to imagine that Walt stored the Nova away in the corner of the garage for young Todd to receive on his 16th birthday, but that is pure fiction. Walt drove the car for the rest of the summer but found out quickly that a Posi-Traction 396 big-block with 350 horses underfoot and icy Ohio roads don't go well together. Soon Walt had purchased an old Tempest to handle the winter duties and parked the Nova until spring.

The union between the Trapnell family and the Hurst Nova soon ended; the car was listed for sale. A middle-aged couple purchased the car with the intention of going Powder Puff racing on the east side of Cleveland. Thompson Dragway photographer Charles Gilchrist captured the Nova before the car vanished from the public eye.

In Cognito

The website Yenko.net is highly regarded as one of the best sources on the Internet for discussing all things Chevrolet muscle. In 2007, a thread was created questioning the whereabouts of the Hurst Nova. A series of promotional photos featuring Todd and the car were posted along with (perhaps) the last known photo of the Nova campaigning at Thompson Drag Raceway. As far as almost everyone is concerned, the car has simply vanished without a trace.

During discussions with the Trapnell family, they disclosed all the information they had on the Hurst Nova. Ironically, they'd never been approached until I located Todd in late 2014. The Nova had been painted Hurst White and included gold striping similar to the 1969 Hurst Olds. It's unclear what ultimately happened to this car, although it could have continued without any later owners knowing its history. With just a couple of gold stripes for reference, perhaps no one was any the wiser to the history of the car.

By Peter Disher

The plans to move Shelby American to Ford began early in 1967. Several things factored into this decision; among them was that Ford desired more control over the manufacturing process of the Shelby Mustangs. Shelby was plagued by problems with fiberglass suppliers and running production changes were common, and with the end of the lease at its Los Angeles airport facilities coming to an end, the opportunity arose for such a move.

In July 1967, plans were being finalized for the new model year of Shelby Mustang production. Pictures of the new 1968 Shelby Mustang models had to be released before actual production began so Shelby built two pre-production photographic cars. These two "1968s" were actually built from Shelby's 1967 engineering fleet. One was a convertible (GT500) and one was a fastback (GT350).

AO Smith

By the time the 1968 model year began production in September 1967, all Shelby personnel had reported to Ionia, Michigan. Along with the transition of personnel, the famed "Cobra" nameplate also

Adorned in Sunlit Gold, this Shelby GT350 must have been an impressive sight at the Paris Auto Show in 1967. (Pierre Monet Photo)

became the property of Ford. The Milwaukee, Wisconsin, company, AO Smith, had a plant in Ionia, Michigan, and offered Ford standardization on the assembly lines and promised larger production numbers than in previous years.

Smith was well known in the automotive industry and had a long history with the Big Three auto manufacturers. Original plans included production of some 8,000 Shelbys (4,450 were actually built). They also included plans for producing fuel-injected cars and supercharged versions that unfortunately never materialized. AO Smith's first job was to build four "pilot" cars. They would not be released to the public, but would be used for testing and evaluation. All four cars were painted Sunlit Gold with each one representing a model (GT350, GT350 convertible, GT500, and GT500 convertible). Interestingly, one of these vehicles was referenced on a piece of factory paperwork with the notation as the Paris Show Car.

A GT350 for a GT500

Earlier in the summer of 1967, the Ford GT40 had scored its second consecutive win at Le Mans. Ford had dethroned Ferrari in 1966 and had backed it up with another dominating performance. In Europe, Ford of France was eager to display the new 1968 Shelby Mustangs and capitalize on Shelby's name recognition. The following telegram dated September 28, 1967, was sent by George Merwin to B. Valton of Ford Motor Parts (France):

"GT 500 due to arrive Orly airport 1900 hours Saturday, September 30. Vehicle being sold to Ford of France. Will arrive freight collect. Copy of the invoice along with waybill number has been forwarded to A. Bordereau. Color of car is gold, new 1968 color. Copy of press packet is being forwarded. Brochures and specification sheets have not yet been printed. Regards."

The telegram detailed the request for a new GT500 to be displayed at the Salon de l'Automobile, the prestigious Paris Auto Show. These records also show that a GT350 was substituted as a last-minute replacement. This car was delivered to Aéroport de Paris-Orly on September 30, 1967, with the Shelby Mustang to be showcased at the 54th Paris Auto Show, which was held October 5 to 15, 1967. Those dates are important because only a handful of cars had been built prior to this period.

Chassis 1?

Among the scarce information on this car was an article found on a French car forum. It is dated November 1967, just a couple of weeks after the Paris Auto Show. The English translation tells you everything you need to know about a car described as "chassis 1":

"Arriving specially by plane, carrying the chassis number 1, this 1968 Shelby has an engine of 5 liters (302) developing 310 hp, weighing 1.325 kg (2,920 pounds), maximum speed 220 km/h (137 mph). The general features differentiate it even more from that of a Mustang; in fact, a car with prestige, that can be equipped like this one, has an automatic transmission and air conditioning (additional $639). The brakes are reinforced. It sells for ƒ46,500 [$8,485.00 in 1968] by Inter-Sport, which also announces marketing a convertible Shelby GT500. The U.S. base retail price for a GT350 fastback was $4,117."

It's interesting that the car was described as "chassis 1." The 1968 Shelby with serial number 00001 has been located and it does not appear to be the same car. According to information recently uncovered, the car serialized as number 00001 was a 4-speed car without air conditioning. That car was built after September 1967. The car that appeared in Paris may have been the first Shelby in France, but it was not chassis number 00001.

Most likely, the Paris Auto Show car is in fact, serial number 8T02J110578-00339, which was the first 1968 GT350 hardtop built. This car meets all the physical characteristics of the Paris Auto Show car. It was also the only GT350 in Shelby's inventory during the time. Interestingly, paperwork on this GT350 between Ford Motor Company and Ford of France indicates that this particular car was sold to the latter.

A New Home

As unreal as it may sound, this Shelby may have ended up in the Central African Republic (CAR). The country was going to be celebrating 10 years of independence and had ordered eight presidential limousines, and a diplomat in CAR requested a free Shelby Mustang from Inter-Sport. Interestingly, Inter-Sport handled marketing the Shelby in magazines for the 54th Salon de L'Automobile.

By Wes Eisenschenk with Denny Manner

We've all heard the old wives' tales about one-of-one factory-built muscle cars. For years, people have chased these mythical machines in an effort to uncover history and possibly own the most rare of the rare. One truly is the loneliest number when dealing with factory prototypes and that's why you rarely come across single factory-built specimens. That's why rumors of a factory-built Buick GSX sporting the ultra-rare Stage 2 package were just that, rumors, for the longest time. That is, until Buick engineer Denny Manner set the record straight.

During the pinnacle of the muscle car era, Denny Manner and his other Buick Engineering cohorts designed what may have become the most wicked factory production car of all time. Much like the S/S AMX, WO23 Coronet, and Hurst Hemi Dart, Buick designed a power-plant exclusively for off-road use.

This formidable engine sported special heads with enlarged and raised exhaust ports designed for use exclusively with headers, 11:1 forged pistons with low-tension rings, an Edelbrock B4B intake adorned with an 850 Holley carburetor, and the most imposing hood

This is the only known photograph of the mighty Buick Stage 2 GSX as constructed by Dennis Manner and Buick Engineering. Sadly, the car was dismantled a short time later. The hood survived and is currently on the Reynolds Buick GS, another car that received Stage 2 components. (Photo Courtesy Dennis Manner)

scoop this side of the 1968 Hemi A-Bodies. The Buick Stage 2 engine was intended to dominate NHRA Super Stock, and only a scant few cars were ever so equipped.

Factory-Built Stage 2

The prototype Stage 2 engine found itself residing between the fenders of an Apollo White Buick GSX at Buick Engineering. So was this technically a factory-built Stage 2 Buick GSX? The story goes, as told by Denny in the July/August 2013 *GSX-TRA* newsletter, "In early 1970, we factory-built a prototype 1970 GSX Stage 2, which the Buick sales and public relations departments used to promote Buick GS performance with both magazines and dealers through Bill Trevor at the GM training center in Burbank, California."

Yes folks, the *factory* built a prototype Buick GSX Stage 2. This car wasn't outsourced to Creative Industries of Detroit, Hurst, or any other of the performance builders in Detroit. It was built at Buick, by Buick engineers.

So what ever happened to this fabled Buick? For years rumors swirled that this factory-built Stage 2 caught on fire and was either destroyed or was residing somewhere ominous. Fortunately for automotive archeologists, Denny was able to put the rumors to bed in the December 2012 issue of Hemmings' *Muscle Machines*: "I don't know how the story ever got started about the prototype car ever catching on fire, which was not true, and I have been trying to correct that statement ever since.

"In addition to the Stage 2 development car I used as a workhorse at Buick Engineering, we built a prototype GSX car in Flint in Buick Engineering and sent it out to California for exposure and evaluation for the dealers, the racers, and the magazine writers.

"Upon its return to Michigan long after we had decided to not factory produce the package and we were about to retire the vehicle, one of our Buick engineers missed a shift driving it at our GM proving grounds and put a rod through the side of the block. It did not catch fire.

"We then disassembled the car and scrapped it out, but the special hood was donated to the Jones/Benesick Buick drag car they raced in California."

So there it was, the hunt for the elusive factory-built Buick Stage 2 was over. A guy missed a shift and lunched the fabled prototype. Or did he?

Other Stage 2 Recipients

Well, yes, the story of the factory-built Buick Stage 2 had a not-so-happy ending, but what about the other cars supplied with Stage 2 components? Two confirmed cars that received these engines for testing purposes were the Pops Kennedy–Jim Bell car campaigned out of Reynolds Buick in West Covina, California, and the Dave Benisek–Dave Jones 4-speed car. Both have survived and have been accounted for.

Also in development at the time of the Stage 2 program were experimental four-bolt main bearing cap blocks and cylinder heads that featured the Stage 2 exhaust ports with an enlarged intake port that had a steep tube inserted in the port for the pushrod to go through. They became known as the "tunnel port" heads.

Tony Branson campaigned a 1969 Buick GS out of Burlington, North Carolina, and was selected by Denny to evaluate these heads and the four-bolt main block. Other Stage 2 parts were sent as well. With a specially fabricated high-rise intake manifold and dual quads, Tony was able to catapult the Buick to a best time of 9.17 in the quarter-mile. The Buick was very successful and the only competition that gave him trouble was the purpose-built Race Hemi A-Bodies.

Among the few Buick racers that received Stage 2 components was Tony Branson of North Carolina. Branson campaigned this 1969 Buick with the experimental four-bolt main bearing cap block. (Photo Courtesy Dennis Manner)

The undisputed king of Buick performance may well have been this experimental four-bolt main block with enlarged intake port heads and Stage 2 exhaust ports. Adorning this monster is a custom high-rise intake fabricated by Tony Branson. (Photo Courtesy Lance Marlette)

In 2006 at the Buick performance meet and race in Ohio, Tony's heads and intake made an appearance, garnering much attention and confirming speculation. The speed parts were no longer with the car. A couple of years later, over dinner with Denny, Tony related that his Buick had been stolen. Unfortunately Tony passed away in March 2008, taking prized information on his Buick with him.

Tony Branson's stolen 1969 Buick GS is still missing, along with the four-bolt main Buick Engineering block. These prized pieces of Buick history need to be located and recovered so that their story isn't lost forever. If you have information on the missing Buick and engine, please contact the authorities. The Buick community will be eternally grateful.

By Bradley Broemmer

You can't talk about the Sonic 'Cuda without also talking about the RTS 'Cuda. Both were built by legendary custom car builder Chuck Miller at his shop in Detroit, Styline Customs. Stylist Harry Bradley designed both cars.

As the years have passed, the lines separating these two cars have blurred dramatically, so much so that some Mopar fans still speculate they were the same car and it was just modified a bit during the course of a couple of years. However, Chuck Miller himself said they were entirely separate cars. The RTS 'Cuda was built and paid for by Plymouth directly and the Sonic 'Cuda was built and paid for by Promotions Inc., the company that ran the International Show Car Association (ISCA) World of Wheels custom car shows.

Miller's Mods

The Sonic 'Cuda was built first and started life as a 383 Barracuda. It had a flat hood, basic black interior, console automatic, and

Stance is everything and this fish has it in spades. The 'Cuda made its rounds in the summer of 1974, including a stop in July at the Minnesota State Fair Grounds. (Photo Courtesy Mike Galewski)

no-frills basic black-on-black paint. The body modifications on all of Chuck's cars were done with fabricated steel, including the nose treatment on the grille.

The Sonic's engine remained the stone-stock 383 4-barrel the car was born with, but because Cragar was also a sponsor of that car's build, the company included a complete blower assembly along with a Fueler-style "bug catcher" unit and all the belts and pulleys. Chuck gutted this unit and mounted it atop the stock iron intake, hiding the 4-barrel and linkage underneath it all. It really looked functional, but it was just for looks.

Chuck said, "We hardly modified an engine back then for any of the show cars (other than dressing them up) because they were touring: They had to be dependable and easy to drive. Get 'em up on trailers and move them from town to town." Chuck explained that he always tried to start with black cars because that way, they had black paint everywhere inside and out and if they didn't have to modify an interior, black went with everything.

In photos the Sonic looks white with stripes all over, but that car wasn't white: It was very very light pink. Promotions Inc. opted to

Among the many stops for the Sonic 'Cuda on the Rapid Transit System caravan was at the New York Auto Show. An interesting design concept was the wheelie bars hanging through the exhaust ports. (Photo Courtesy Bob Snyder Collection)

make the Sonic 'Cuda into its grand prize giveaway car for the 1973 show season, and it was won by noted custom builder Jerry Pennington, who had won ISCA's Ridler Award in 1972 with a custom known as *The Scorpion*. He won that award again in 1973 with a bizarre custom named *The Devilish*.

Trail of Owners

Along with the Ridler Award in 1973, Pennington was handed the keys to the aging Sonic 'Cuda and became the car's first real owner. Chuck talked to Pennington's son and was informed that Jerry actually drove the Sonic 'Cuda for a few months after receiving it in 1973. Pennington then sold it to Treatment Products Limited in Chicago, Illinois, makers of The Treatment Silicone Car Wax. The company used it for promotions at car shows after lettering it "The Treatment." The company used it as a promotion vehicle across the upper Midwest perhaps as late as 1976 or 1977.

Chuck has heard reports that it eventually ended up as a street rod in Arizona, New Mexico, Nevada, Michigan, and maybe even in Oregon. A former worker for Treatment Products called Chuck and informed him the company had stored the 'Cuda in a warehouse for years and it had become quite dilapidated simply from neglect and disuse. The company's owner eventually sold the car just to get rid of it because of its sad shape, possibly for as little as $800 to $1,500. Even this is word of mouth from a former employee, because the earth seems to have swallowed up the Sonic 'Cuda somewhere around 1977.

Steven Juliano (noted Mopar collector) chased the car for a while just out of curiosity and was informed it was last seen painted black years ago in Lake Orion, Michigan, but nobody has seen it in ages. Because the Sonic 'Cuda began life as a plain-Jane 383 Barracuda, it's unlikely anyone would've restored it back to stock configuration. Presumably, it's still there in hiding and waiting to be rediscovered.

If you know anything solid about this car, please pass the info along to Chuck; he'd love to know what became of it.

By Wes Eisenschenk

In 1959, custom car builder Robert Larivee and his brother, Marvin, founded Promotions Inc. It was the Larivees' joint venture into the world of showing cars, which was a very popular hobby throughout the 1950s. In 1962, Promotions Inc. moved from the cozy confines of Michigan to sunny California, where Bob could network with SoCal's blossoming show car scene.

By 1963, Bob had formed the International Show Car Association (ISCA) in an effort to have better judging for the ever-expanding genre of show cars. One series of shows that Bob created was the International Champion Auto Show (ICAS). These two were and are often confused with each other.

With a character car, you're allowed to have a little fun. The famous running-bird logo featured on 1969 cars was enlarged and flanked part of the door and fender on both sides of the car. Beautiful women stretched out on the decklid came standard on the Road Runner Probe. (Photo Courtesy Chuck Miller Collection)

The tail section of the 1968 Road Runner Probe featured recessed tail lamps, an aluminum spoiler, and a full-length red stripe. The car wore Turbine Bronze paint from the factory. (Photo Courtesy Chuck Miller Collection)

Envisioned by Gene Baker and constructed by automotive design artist Chuck Miller, the Road Runner Probe was the giveaway car at the International Champion Auto Show. Terry Taylor of McLean, Illinois, was the top builder with his immaculate 1957 Chevy named Fire Chief, *and so won the Probe. (Photo Courtesy Chuck Miller Collection)*

Prepping the Giveaway Car

During the 1960s, Bob Larivee had developed a working relationship with the auto manufacturers in Detroit. As a grand prize giveaway for winning the ICAS, each year Bob had a car customized as a reward to the top builder. For the 1969/1970 ICAS show circuit, he had worked out a deal with Chrysler to give away a 1968 Plymouth Road Runner.

This Road Runner was shipped to Styline Customs where renowned fabricator Chuck Miller and designer Gene Baker worked on it. This wasn't the first venture between Promotions Inc. and Styline Customs. Over the years, Bob hired Chuck to work on other custom car projects; the most notable was *Red Baron.*

Chuck remembered that the car was delivered in white, a color that gave them a blank canvas. With Gene's vision of the car in place, the task of fabricating the Road Runner began. The car received a new, beautiful Candy Tangerine paint job. On the tops of the fenders, doors, and quarters, Chuck blended the paint to a deep coat of silver. The contrast was striking. Down the middle of the car, he added a Candy Tangerine stripe, visually dividing the car in half.

The 1968 Bird received a series of fabrications, including raising the fresh-air hood scoop at a 45-degree angle with the filler plates facing each other. Cosmetically the car received a set of Cragar S/S wheels, Goodyear GT wide-tread tires, Hurst shifter, roll bar, Thrush mufflers, and Stewart Warner tachometer. Chuck added a rear spoiler and Cibie headlights.

A large, brazen road runner ran across the bottom of the door and fenders, as seen on the 1969 models. The words "road runner," in lower case, as on the 1969s, were scripted with a box outlining them. The word "Probe" appeared in cursive lettering under the box. Other than the tach and roll bar, the interior remained stock.

The Winner Is

Terry Taylor of McLean, Illinois, won the Road Runner Probe for the conversion of his 1957 Chevy. The car, named *Fire Chief,* featured a tilting front end and a chromed 292-ci Chevy powerplant. Terry also won a seven-day trip to Los Angeles.

It's unknown how long Terry owned the Probe. He passed away some years ago, and his relatives have no information on the car.

Plymouth Road Runner-Probe

• Body & Paint By Chuck Miller   • Designed By Gene Baker
• Cragar s/s Wheels   • Goodyear GT Wide Tread Tires
• Hurst Shifter & Roll Bar   • Thrush Mufflers
• Cibie Headlights   • Ditzler Paint
• Stewart-Warner Tachometer.

This wonderful color shot of the Road Runner Probe really accentuates the creativity in color blending on the car. Of the noted fabrications, the fresh-air hood treatment, the custom roll bar, and the recessed headlights really stand out. (Photo Courtesy Chuck Miller Collection)

Fortunately, the car would be recognizable if discovered, unless it was converted back to its stock appearance. Very little information on this car exists other than a few clippings from a magazine article and these four photographs.

If you have any information on the Road Runner Probe, contact either Chuck Miller or Wes Eisenschenk.

By Wes Eisenschenk

It's hard being a manufacturer that holds onto the past when others are moving on to bigger and better things. That described AMC when Pontiac rolled out the GTO in 1964. Shortly thereafter Ford, Mercury, Chevrolet, Buick, Oldsmobile, Dodge, and Plymouth all unveiled performance models in their midsize and compact offerings while AMC watched from the sidelines. Late to the party, AMC dipped its toes into the pool with a 343-ci 280-hp Rambler with the mandatory 4-speed in 1967. The plan was to begin the transformation of its "Little Nash Rambler" in an effort to keep up with its competitors that were offering L79-equipped Novas and 383-powered Darts.

AMC's walk-off shot with the Rambler was the formidable 1969½ SC/Rambler. Almost all of the elements of the prototype found their way onto the production model. (Photo Courtesy Chuck Miller Collection)

GTO as Inspiration

In 1968, after testing the waters with the 343 Rambler, AMC dove head first into the pool. It unveiled new models with the AMX and Javelin that sported 390 cubes and 315 horses of AMC power. With muscle car offerings now in both the pony and sports car market, AMC began the process of phasing out its prized little compact, and it wasn't going to go quietly.

Enter Hurst Performance and Styline Customs.

Legend has it that Dave Landrith of Hurst was chatting with Pontiac GTO godfather Jim Wangers at Hurst headquarters on a fall day in 1968 when the two schemed up an AMC version of the 1964 GTO. Dave took this concept to AMC brass who had gathered to discuss the S/S AMX program.

The idea then made its way to Walt Czarnecki (formerly of Hurst) at AMC. He pitched the idea to the engineers, who needed to confirm that stuffing the 390 into the Rambler worked structurally. (The 1967 343-powered Rambler had a history of blowing out its rear glass because of chassis flexing during launches, which is why engineering's approval was so important.) The engineers went to work on making the Rambler chassis stronger.

The SC/Rambler was based on the Rogue chassis, which included connectors between the front and rear subframes and staggered rear shock absorbers modified to accept the V-8. A plate needed to be riveted into the trunk pan for the upper mount of the driver-side shock. Torque links were also installed, connecting the top of the rear leaf-sprung axle to the subframe. These reinforcements created the strength the SC/Rambler needed for hard launches at the dragstrip.

From Sketches to Reality

Hurst handled the components of the car while Gene Baker at Styline Customs, one of Detroit's premier automotive customizing shops, created the cosmetic design. "Gene sketched the SC/Rambler," noted Styline's founder and chief artist Chuck Miller. It was these sketches that changed the whole dynamic of AMC's image. "They had used the red/white/blue scheme in the Trans-Am race series, but had never offered it on a production model." With the chassis improvements and the design concepts approved, it was time to begin creating the SC/Rambler.

The prototype SC/Rambler featured unique taillights along with a transparent blue stripe that traveled across the rear glass. Neither was affixed to production models. (Photo Courtesy Chuck Miller Collection)

The Rambler delivered to Styline Customs was painted white with a 390 and a Hurst 4-speed already in place. With Gene's sketches, Chuck began the process of transforming the plain Rambler into the iconic image you see on posters and in books.

The bold red paint was shot and outlined with a black pinstripe. The recognizable blue stripe that traverses the hood, roof, and decklid was hand painted by Chuck (production versions had vinyl tape). The prototype also featured a transparent blue stripe applied to the rear glass; the folks at AMC ultimately vetoed it (a transparent gold stripe was also applied to the 1969 Hurst Olds and was also nixed). Frenched taillights also didn't make it into production. Otherwise, all of the styling cues that Gene drew up and Chuck applied were accepted.

Debut and Success

When the prototype was completed, it was sent to AMC and displayed on the third floor of the company's Detroit headquarters. The car definitely had an aura about it. Sure, the Javelin and AMX were impressive cars, but for little old AMC to stuff its largest engine into its smallest car was a shocking departure. Longtime AMC employees and buyers were surprised.

The response from the buying public and the support from AMC dealerships are a true testament to how successful this move was for the Rambler; 1,512 copies, 1,012 more than initially forecast, were shipped from Kenosha.

Walt Czarnecki and Chuck Miller both credit Dave Landrith with bringing the SC/Rambler to fruition, even though they all had a hand in creating this F-Stock weapon. Their lasting legacy is seen routinely at car auctions. Restored SC/Ramblers often sell for north of $50,000. Their visions and design elements created one of the most flamboyant and potent compact cars of the muscle car era.

All great muscle cars have a prototype, concept, or mule that were the basis of the production versions. For the SC/Rambler, all 1,512 cars owe their lives to the prototype envisioned by Dave Landrith and created by Gene Baker and Chuck Miller. This car ultimately changed how AMC cars were viewed in the printed media and at the stoplight. With Group 19 parts bolted on, SC/Ramblers dove into the low-12s at the dragstrip.

Rumors abound that have the protype AMC residing in a collector's garage in Florida. However, no one has contacted Chuck Miller to verify the car.

I wonder what became of this first Hurst SC/Rambler. . . .

CHAPTER TWO

Rare Muscle Cars

I n muscle car terminology, the word "rare" is usually associated with increased value. As with coins, stamps, artwork, etc., the fewer examples in the marketplace, the greater the value. Rare muscle cars are no different.

When the Big Three began building American iron, rare wasn't a word cared about or associated with preserving a vehicle. If it had been, Chrysler would have a warehouse full of 1971 Hemicuda convertibles aging like a fine wine. Rare came to mean that not enough people could afford one, knew about the dazzling array of options available, or even wanted one.

Some cars were built in extremely low volume due to increased costs. Convertibles typically fall into this category. Ordering a 1969 Trans Am added $725 to the bill of your Firebird. Add the convertible option on your order and it could reach $1,500 over the base price of a standard Firebird. Add another $500 in creature comforts and your base $3,000 Firebird checks out at the register at $5,000. Although these amounts don't sound like much today, it would be equivalent of adding $20,000 worth of options on a $30,000 vehicle. In the end, the ultimate Trans Am was never constructed, as none of the eight convertible buyers checked off the Ram Air IV powerplant.

A base 1969 Road Runner could be had for less than $3,000. Add the Hemi and the components paired with it and you've just added $1,000 to your bill. Around 84,000 1969 Road Runners were built, fewer than 900 with the Hemi.

Another aspect of low sales volume is the lack of sales staff knowing an option even existed at the time. In 1969 Chevrolet built more than 86,000 Chevelle SS cars. Of those, just 400 units came with the L89 aluminum head option. These cars are rare simply because factory literature at the time didn't list the L89 as an option. Without it on the sales sheet, sales staff couldn't "upsell" it to customers.

The survival rate of rare factory-built muscle cars typically exceeds that of their regular production counterparts. Convertibles have always been perceived as special. Hence of the eight 1969 Trans Am convertibles produced, all eight are well documented and accounted for.

Seafrost Green is a rare color for any Chevy muscle car, let alone an L78 1968 Nova SS. With just 667 L78 copies made, it's safe to say that Seafrost Green on this car makes it unique. (Photo Courtesy Mike Dolence)

By Wes Eisenschenk with Joe Oldham

In the heyday of the muscle car wars, few people had a better job than Joe Oldham, if you want to call it a job. Joe was an automotive journalist and his "job" was to beat the crap out of cars and then write reviews for *Hi-Performance Cars* magazine and other automotive publications of the day. It was a tough job, but somebody had to do it. Joe was living out every muscle car enthusiast's dream: drive, street race, cruise, and drag race every muscle car. He didn't have to spend money to do this; he was *paid* to do it. Of course, then he had to sit down and write articles about these cars, but it was a lot better than unloading trucks at a warehouse.

In 1968, one of the cars Joe tested was a 1968 Baldwin-Motion Phase III Camaro. If you've been living in the Amazon with the indigenous people, I can forgive you for not knowing what a Motion Camaro is or what Baldwin-Motion was. Otherwise, you should sit down in front of your computer for a couple of hours and Google Baldwin-Motion.

The car Joe tested was the company's 1968 demonstrator. After the test, Joe had to have one. And with the new season just around the

The Oldham Baldwin-Motion Camaro makes its debut at the 1968 Thanksgiving weekend hot rod show held in the New York Coliseum. It's difficult to believe that this was one of its only public showings. (Photo Courtesy Joe Oldham Collection)

corner, it would be a 1969. Remember, this is the guy who drove everything from Hemi Road Runners to Royal Bobcat Firebirds to 440-powered Barracudas to 428 Cobra Jet Mustangs. Joe had experienced (for free) everything the muscle car wars had to offer, and he decided to actually buy a Baldwin-Motion Camaro with his own money.

Joe's Special Camaro

Because the Camaro had to serve as daily transportation as well as his recreation, Joe ordered the car at Baldwin Chevrolet as an SS 427 rather than the balls-out Phase III model. Under the hood was a relatively stock L72 427/425-hp engine, not the Phase III's L88. Hooker headers, chambered exhaust, 4.10 rear end, breakerless ignition, and a 3-speed Turbo 400 Hydramatic transmission completed the powertrain.

Joe was the first 1969 Camaro owner to have a Tuxedo Black ride. But wait, you say, black wasn't an option on early Camaros in 1969. And you're right. Folks, when you write reviews of cars for a living, it's best not to poke a bear with a stick. So if Joe Oldham wants a black 1969 Camaro right at the start of production, the guys at Chevrolet manufacturing find a way. Because black was an option for Novas, and both Novas and Camaros were made at the Norwood, Ohio, assembly plant where Joe's car was being constructed, then hey, let's get some black plant over to the line when Joe's car comes by.

Other aesthetically pleasing features included a black interior, black vinyl roof, the Super Sport package, VE3 body-colored bumper, Motion fiberglass scooped hood, hood tach, and 15 x 8 Keystone Kustomag wheels with G70-15 (front) and L70-15 (rear) Mickey Thompson rubber. In the cabin, the car had the optional center console with power windows. Motion Performance added Sun gauges under the radio. For a more stealthy and clean look, Joe ordered the car without spoilers and had Motion remove the white Super Sport hockey stripes. The final effect was a very imposing machine.

Motion Performance owner Joel Rosen was also smitten with the car. He asked Joe to showcase the SS 427 in the Motion Performance display at the 1968 Thanksgiving weekend hot rod show held in the New York Coliseum.

Before the SS stripes were removed, Rosen had the car photographed extensively for Motion's 1969 advertising campaign. Part of the ad series was the now-famous "Wanted" poster ad featuring an Old West–style print with burnt edging and wording that described the outlawed weapon. To this day, the poster is often re-created and is a staple with muscle car memorabilia collectors.

Stolen After All

It would be great to tell you here that Joe was one of those fortunate original owners who held onto his car, and that years later he pulled it out of mothballs to resume his love affair with the Camaro, right? Well, thieves had another plan.

Only a few months into ownership, Joe opened his garage door one morning to witness a couple of crooks attempting to hijack his Camaro. As one guy finessed a piece of wire through the weather stripping above the glass, another stood lookout. Joe quickly took in the scene and charged. He was able to take them both down and land a couple of shots into the face of one of the perpetrators. He was then clocked over the head with something heavy and went groggy. The two would-be thieves bolted into the street without the Camaro.

For the next couple of months, Joe was on high alert, checking on his Camaro several times nightly. As good as he was at keeping an eye on the car, the thieves were one step better and finally nabbed it on a spring morning in 1969. Joe's beloved Camaro went MIA. The thieves, probably the same ones from the first attempted heist, had succeeded in stealing the car. This one-of-one 1969 Baldwin Motion SS 427 Camaro was gone and has not been seen since that day.

Oldham made the requisite visit to the NYPD to report the Camaro stolen. However, the police could do little about it. Cars such as this were often stolen and parted out because it was impossible to re-title them or

Joe Oldham takes delivery of his 1969 Baldwin-Motion SS 427 Camaro. Not even a rainy day could keep him from cracking a smile. (Photo Courtesy Joe Oldham Collection)

have them registered without tipping off the insurance companies or police. And speaking of insurance, the company finally paid Joe's claim several months later, but of course, the payment was thousands short of what he had paid for the car. "That's depreciation for you."

Now, 45 years later, and with lots of help and support from Summit Racing Equipment, Joe and his son Scott have re-created this prized car. But that is as close as he has come to owning his Baldwin-Motion SS 427 Camaro again. In 2013, the tribute car made an appearance at the Muscle Car & Corvette Nationals.

The Search Goes On

So what can be done to find Joe's old Camaro? For starters, it was a special paint car and had the code "- -" on the cowl tag. Tuxedo Black became a factory paint code for the 1969 model year, but it was not an option at the time Joe's car was built. It also wore a vinyl roof and was coded as such with a "B" in the upper body part of the cowl tag's paint code. Because this Camaro was built at the Norwood, Ohio, facility, it had "NOR" coding in the plant location on the tag. Of course, all of this is contingent on the car retaining its original cowl tag.

Other possibilities are that it spent its life (or still exists) as a cut-up race car needing no titling, licensing, or registration, or it has been scrapped. All of these are ominous and obviously not happy endings.

Another scenario is that someone who participated in the theft would be doing the muscle car community a huge favor by anonymously disclosing what happened to it. This one is a long shot to be sure, but according to Joel Rosen, the statute of limitations has long since expired. This means that, criminally, nothing can be charged against the perpetrator(s).

If you know its whereabouts or have information on Joe's old car, please contact Scott Oldham.

By Wade Ogle

As a young man, Morgan (last name omitted for privacy) was involved in a terrible accident and was paralyzed from the waist down. As part of his insurance settlement, he decided to buy a new car. With money to spend and a new lease on life, his new car had to be fast and had to be a convertible.

Because of economic, safety, and environmental concerns, by 1971, the muscle car era was waning and convertibles were fading into obscurity, so Morgan's prospects were thin. Chrysler no longer offered convertibles on its new B-Body line, and for this year Dodge chose to limit the engine size on its E-Body Challenger convertibles to 383 ci. In terms of ultra-performance, this left just one option: the vaunted Hemi engine in a 1971 Plymouth 'Cuda convertible.

Sure to bring your blood pressure up . . . This is what it looks like discovering the last missing 1971 Hemicuda convertible. (Photo Courtesy Wade Ogle Archive)

The Order Specs

Morgan went to Bill Luke's Chrysler Plymouth dealership in Phoenix, Arizona. He discussed his physical situation with the sales manager, who agreed to install hand controls for him to operate the gas and brake pedals on his new car. Satisfied, Morgan ordered a code BS27 'Cuda convertible with the stout 727 TorqueFlite automatic transmission.

As part of the 'Cuda package, Morgan's car was automatically equipped with chrome hood pins, dual exhaust, and chrome exhaust tips. He chose FE5 Rallye Red for his new ride, along with a V3X black convertible top. He loaded the order sheet with convenience options, including Power Steering, Console with Slap-Stik shifter handle, six-way adjustable driver's seat, black leather interior with bucket seats, power top, Light Package Group, AM/FM Multiplex Stereo, undercoating, tinted windows, and V5X vinyl side moldings.

For optimal performance he selected the top-of-the-line A34 Super Track Pak axle package that included power front disc brakes, the Maximum Cooling package, Hemi suspension, and 4.10 gears in a bulletproof Dana 9.75-inch housing with Sure-Grip differential.

And last, of critical importance, he upgraded from the 383 to the top-of-the-line E74 engine option. By selecting this box he had equipped his bright red 'Cuda with the most powerful engine ever installed in a convertible pony car: the 426-ci 425-hp Hemi. This included the menacing Shaker hood, a Hemi-only F60-15 Goodyear Polyglas GT tires, and other Hemi-specific accoutrements.

One of Seven

Chrysler's production figures reveal that for U.S.–ordered cars in 1971, only six other individuals made this same E74 selection in the BS27 'Cuda convertible. Of these seven prized vehicles, two 1971 Hemicuda convertibles were equipped with 4-speed transmissions and five others, including Morgan's, were supplied with automatics.

Because the 1972 model year saw Chrysler's discontinuation of both the 'Cuda convertible and the Hemi engine option, these seven pinnacle U.S.-shipped cars, along with five others exported to Canada and Europe, were the last and arguably greatest cars ever produced during the muscle car era.

Even when ordered, the guys at Bill Luke's dealership knew it was a special car. They had never ordered anything like it before, and it was a huge event when the transporter finally arrived. The dealership team installed the requisite hand controls and Morgan was off on his first short trip, which was literally across the street, where the car was immediately fitted with headers, traction bars, and mag wheels.

From Weekender to Lost

To the chagrin of Bill Luke's service team, the car, now equipped with Arizona license plates (PTE-971), became a fixture at the dealership on Monday mornings. Morgan generally picked up his car on Friday and proceeded to tear it up over the weekend. Monday morning, like clockwork, he brought it back for some sort of warranty repair, often with the interior filled with empty beer cans. By Friday the cycle started all over again.

This punishment didn't last long, and in early 1973 the 'Cuda was sold to its second owners, Bill and Bob Graham, for $1,700. They had wanted a Corvette convertible and couldn't find one, so they settled for this car instead. The first thing they did was to remove the hand controls. The original transmission was having problems and they took it back to Bill Luke for warranty repair, but the dealership said no. The dealership had had enough of this car, so the Grahams performed the swap themselves.

During one long, overheating trip from Phoenix to Reno, the Graham brothers accidentally left the Shaker bubble at a gas station. They later decided to fill the gaping hole in the hood with a homemade tunnel ram setup. They put dirt tires and high-lift leaf-spring shackles on the rear and turned their 'Cuda into a desert dune buggy of sorts.

Just two years later, the Graham brothers traded the four-year-old 'Cuda for a 1967 tri-power Corvette convertible, finally fulfilling their dream. Less than a year later, the 'Cuda was for sale again, this time for $1,900. The Grahams considered buying it back, as it looked the same except for a hole in the rear convertible window, but they couldn't come up with the cash.

And poof! For the next 30 years the car disappeared into oblivion.

Search Leads

Fast forward to the spring of 2005. By this time the value of these rare cars was in the stratosphere, literally in the millions, after having experienced price doubling each of the previous five years. As this happened, all of the 1971 Hemicuda convertibles had surfaced, except this one. Because Chrysler's U.S. production numbers were fairly well documented, it was known that seven of these cars were manufactured for the United States, but only six were accounted for. One equipped with an automatic was still missing.

The hunt for this "missing" car was on. Rumors were flying that this car had been shipped to England. Another rumor was that it had been a race car in the Midwest. No stones were left unturned. Because the seven-digit VIN prefix for all 1971 Hemicuda convertibles is the same, all these VINs start with BS27R1B. People with resources used this partial info to scan DMV and National Insurance Crime Bureau (NICB) records, trying to be the first to find this car. Without a specific VIN number, these efforts were fruitless. Everybody dreamed about finding this renegade car in a barn somewhere, but by now hope was waning, and in the back of everyone's minds, they suspected that this car's life had ended in the crusher long ago. With prices so high, what other explanation could there be?

Phoenix Karma

That's not to say that the whereabouts of this elusive machine were a total secret. As with any well-kept secret, of course, some people are in the know. Two of these individuals were Dave Blake and Charlie Grant, both from Phoenix.

From the mid-1970s through the early 1980s, Dave Blake had the foresight to hunt out and buy as many Hemicuda and Challenger convertibles as possible, going so far as to place want ads in *Hemmings Motor News*. After years of hunting, Dave was eventually successful; by the mid-1980s he claimed five prized examples, including a 1970 Hemi Challenger convertible, three 1970 Hemicuda convertibles, and a 1971 Hemicuda convertible.

At the beginning of Dave's mission, production totals were not publicly known, and hunting for cars nationwide was difficult. During these early efforts, Dave came to one critical realization: He knew these cars were far more rare than the general public thought, because try as he might, he simply couldn't find one to buy.

This early effort led to an unbelievable chance meeting in Phoenix in 1977. On one side was Dave Blake, a young man actively scouring the nation for a Hemicuda convertible. And on the other side was Bill Graham, previous owner of one of these rare automobiles. These two guys were both street racers, and on this day they bumped into each other on the hot Phoenix asphalt. Car chatter ensued and eventually Dave brought up his quest for a Hemicuda convertible. Bill's reply? "Oh, I used to own one of those."

Dave was in shock. Could this be true? Or was this more bench-racing talk? Dave's doubts forced Bill to prove his point. Bill sped off and shortly returned carrying an old insurance slip. Sure enough there it was, the magical BS27R1B VIN prefix along with serial number 337604 suffix proving the car's existence. Dave had been unsuccessfully combing the world for one of these unicorns only to find out there was one right in his own backyard the whole time!

As a fun side note, this discussion led Dave and Bill to become friends, and Dave introduced Bill to his sister. So the car's legacy laid the groundwork for them to become brothers-in-law.

A 30-Year Secret

Dave, now armed with the car's VIN, went straight to the Phoenix DMV. This was 1977, before any privacy concerns, and for the princely sum of $2 Dave received a comprehensive printout detailing the car's current ownership. The current owner was Charlie Grant, right there in Phoenix. What were the odds?

Turns out, Charlie had been the buyer of this 'Cuda just one year earlier, shortly after the Graham brothers had turned it down. Charlie had the original Hemi engine for the car, but it was damaged and sitting on a stand in his garage. The early years had not been kind, and after another year on the road under Charlie's watch, the car was beginning to show its age. With only 20,000 miles showing on the odometer, Charlie placed the car into long-term hibernation in 1977, planning to restore it someday.

And of equal importance, Charlie was a very private individual and didn't want anybody to know about his hidden treasure. But Dave Blake knew, and beginning in 1977, he tried for years to buy the car, to no avail. Still, this secret was safe. Charlie was extremely private, and Dave had nothing to gain by revealing this hidden treasure. This unspoken secret alliance lasted for nearly 30 years.

And a Revelation

During the spring of 2004, Dave and his father took their most prized possession, their 1971 Hemicuda convertible, to the Spring

Fling car show in Van Nuys, California. Dave had been following the recent surge in prices and had already turned down huge offers for his car. But this day was different.

Two special people were in attendance, Bill Wiemann and Charlie Grant. Charlie had come to see what all this fuss was about, knowing that sitting in his garage was the "missing" car everybody was looking for. And Bill Wiemann? Well, at this time Bill was both a successful businessman and a Hemi convertible buyer extraordinaire, at this moment being the owner of 3 of the 12 1971 Hemicuda convertibles ever produced. And on this day, Bill had his sights set on Dave's 1971, to add a fourth to his stable.

In exchange for Dave's pinnacle car, and in full public display, Bill dropped the bomb. He offered Dave $2.5 million *and* a P-51 Mustang fighter plane. Dave and the rest of the world were floored, because at that very moment they had all just witnessed the price for these rare 1971 Hemicuda convertibles double yet again.

The Earth shook, and everybody felt it. Most important, onlooker Charlie Grant felt it, and Dave now knew that there was no way he would ever be able to buy Charlie's car. Dave's secret was no longer valuable, and it was finally time to let the rest of the world in on it. Dave politely rejected Bill's offer, but as a consolation he told Bill his secret: the existence and whereabouts of the "missing" 1971.

As you can imagine, this sent Bill into a tizzy. Bill, like a bull in a China shop, stormed up to Charlie demanding answers. This strategy backfired, and a subdued Charlie flatly denied all existence of the car. But Bill now knew the truth, and acting like a rabid treasure hunter, he was not deterred. For the next year, Bill hounded Charlie, all to no avail. Bill even went so far as to do a property ownership search on Charlie, and then flew his private helicopter over Charlie's properties trying to catch sight of this elusive machine. Charlie still kept quiet, to Bill's frustration.

Lost No More

The day finally came in early 2006. Bill, also now living in Phoenix, had driven his fleet of Hemi ragtops to the local Pavillions car show. Charlie Grant was on site as well and saw how well Bill cared for his cars. Charlie also recognized that although he owned this fantastic vehicle he would not have the means to restore it with the care and attention it required. It was time.

Charlie met with Bill and told him that yes, he did in fact own the "missing" 1971, and it was at his shop in town. No time was wasted, a deal was struck, and the last of the U.S.–ordered Hemicuda convertibles finally returned to the public eye after 33 years of hibernation.

A few years earlier, I had purchased a different car from Bill Wiemann, and that transaction had gone smoothly by both parties, so I felt comfortable contacting him again.

Having owned the car only for a few weeks, Bill was understandably still riding the high because of his new find, but he could be persuaded. He had agreed to publicly debut the car at the Chryslers of Carlisle show in just two months and was frantically rushing to get the car ready. I agreed to honor his commitment, and we struck a deal. The "missing" Hemicuda convertible was now mine, and the debut at the Carlisle show was a resounding success.

The hunt for the last known 1971 Hemicuda convertible had finally come to an end.

Restored to its "as-original" condition, this 1971 Hemicuda Convertible is on the very short list of most coveted muscle cars for collectors. (Wade Ogle Photo)

By Ryan Weaver

*J*enks is lost and I want to find her. She is a 1969 Chevelle SS 396. I refer to the car as female for two reasons: I have always referred to any coveted mechanical device of great power and grace in the feminine gender. I can reminisce about my parents taking my brother and me to buy our first new bicycles and remember everyone commenting after one of us said "she" is a beauty. The second reason is that *Jenks* was sponsored by Jenkins Beauty Shop, owned and operated by B. Carol Jenkins.

I want to find this particular Chevelle because out of the 86,307 SS 396 cars produced by Chevrolet, this car is one of 8,486 (or 9,486, depending on the source) with the 375-hp 396-ci V-8, often referred to as the L78. Adding further to her rarity, and really the main reason I am looking for *Jenks*, is that she came with the rare RPO L89 aluminum cylinder heads.

Only 400 cars and trucks (El Caminos) were built with this option, making this rare Chevelle worth quite a bit more than a standard L78 car. Unless you used the now well-known Central Office Production Order (COPO) system to get an RPO L72 (425-hp 427), the L89 was the top engine choice from the order sheet at the dealer for your new Chevelle in 1969.

This rare and desirable Chevelle is one of only 400 copies built by Chevrolet featuring aluminum heads. It's adorned in code 76-76 Daytona Yellow. (Photo Courtesy Jerry Hinton)

The 400 L89 engines were split among five Chevelle body styles: Malibu (hardtop), Malibu (convertible), two-door sedan pickup (El Camino), 300 Deluxe Sport Coupe (hardtop), and 300 Deluxe Coupe (post sedan). The bulk of the 400 L89s are the Malibu hardtop body style like *Jenks*.

At the Dealer

In the spring of 1970, James (Jim) Jenkins and his stepson, Joe Hinton, went to DeNooyer Chevrolet in Battle Creek, Michigan, to purchase a car expressly for drag racing. A yellow Chevelle sat on the showroom floor with only about 6,000 original miles on the odometer. The original owner had the car for about a year and then traded it in at DeNooyer. Its color was the SS-only Code 76-76 Daytona Yellow, which was an extra cost.

The car featured a black D96 side stripe and black bench-seat interior but was ordered without a vinyl roof. The manual transmission was a closed-ratio M21 4-speed that was a perfect fit for drag racing. The rear-end gear was more of a road gear setup, likely 3.55s. However, because the car was trailered to and from the track for drag racing, the gears were quickly swapped to 4.88s and then 5.13s.

As an aside, Joe remembers that also on the showroom floor that same day in 1970 was a brand-new 1970 Chevelle SS 454 LS6 450-hp 4-speed car, blue with black stripes and a black bench-seat interior. He remembers vividly the 454-/450-hp sticker on the cowl induction breather assembly. Knowing the current LS6 prices, Joe wishes he had purchased that blue car and kept it.

Previous Owner

Joe remembers Jim getting in touch with the original owner before buying the car to see if he had had any problems with it. The original owner shared that the car had not had any problems and that it had not been beaten in any street races. Joe's mother financed the car through Clark Equipment Credit Union. Joe is not sure if the original title was in the name of B. Carol Jenkins, or her husband's name, James Jenkins. The salesman's name was Carl Simonoff; he had sold cars to Carol Jenkins from the 1960s to the 1990s. Carl unfortunately passed away a few years ago and had taken any information on the Chevelle with him.

The dealership is still in business but has moved a few miles away to Kalamazoo, Michigan; Heritage Chevrolet is now in the old location. I have contacted DeNooyer several times and my request for information and some history was forwarded to the management team and dealer principle.

Carol had also reached out to one of the original salesmen at DeNooyer, who still transports vehicles for the dealership from time to time, to see if he remembered anything about this car. Unfortunately no one remembers the vehicle, and all those records were thrown away long ago.

Life with Jim and Joe

The car was lettered up as *Jenks,* named after Joe's stepfather Jim Jenkins and paying homage to the beauty shop. Joe remembers the L89 getting bored 0.030 over by Doug Nash and having a "cheater" Lunati camshaft added. The costs came to the tune of $1,200. Joe mentioned that they purchased and installed some trick rear control arms from Mr. Gasket, which improved the launch of the car.

Jim raced it in B Stock at U.S. 131 Motorsports Park in Martin, Michigan. He recalls the car being a little outclassed because of the aluminum heads and thinks that it could have been more competitive in the C Stock category with cast-iron heads. The Chevelle ran consistent 12.50s in the quarter-mile, which, at the time, was roughly a second off the national record.

Joe said, "You could race for trophies or race for money." Jim raced *Jenks* for trophies and earned a few. They campaigned the car for two seasons and then she sat idle for a year or so, beginning to acquire Midwest rust. Jim then installed a small-block engine and registered the car for the street.

By 1974, the lettering was removed from the car and it was sold with the engine separate. The last thing that Jim and Joe found out was that the car went to Marshall, Michigan, near where Wattles Park Road and Michigan Avenue intersect. The Chevelle sat in a garage just 10 miles from the dealership where it was first sold in 1970.

To this day, Joe drag races cars and stepson Jerry restores them. If I find this L89 Chevelle, I've offered them first chance to buy her back, although they've said that they do not wish to purchase the car. They said they'd be very happy if I find it and purchase it myself; they feel very confident I will take great care of her.

Joe's One and Only

As I research and learn more about muscle cars, I am increasingly drawn to the history and great meaning that these cars have to the owners who care for them. At current value, a 1969 Chevelle may be more popular and worth more than a 1972 Camaro. But to a car guy who had both back in the day, one is a clear favorite. Every car guy (or gal) has a favorite that is kept forever; or they wish they had kept it.

Joe bought a 1972 240-hp Camaro SS350 in January 1972, during his senior year in high school. He owned it until 1979, when he and his wife started their family. Do you see why this car is the one that got away?

Joe drove this car back and forth to work some of the time and street raced it when he could get away with it. Joe remembers this car being about a 14.4- or 14.5-second quarter-mile car. It makes him feel like a kid again just thinking about it. This is the car that Joe has dreamt about finding.

Joe's Camaro received a little front-end damage during his ownership and he replaced the sheet metal and painted the car black. He had removed the SS badges so it was a sleeper. He sold the car in 1979 and remembers it going to Muskegon, Michigan.

Let's help Joe find his old 1972 Camaro. The car's VIN is 1Q87U2N150908.

- 1 = Chevrolet
- Q = Camaro
- 87 = two-door coupe
- U = SS 396 LS3 240 hp
- 2 = 1972
- N = Norwood
- 150908 = the sequential number of the car (numbers started at 100,001)

It was built in November 1971 and had an automatic transmission. The exterior was painted Midnight Bronze, and the interior was code 778 Tan. The car had no spoilers and came with Rallye wheels. He remembers the car having gauges in the dash, but it did not come with air conditioning.

By Wade Ogle

Collectors of Pontiac muscle cars are very fortunate for two key reasons. First, Pontiac has the Pontiac Historical Services (PHS). Second, Pontiac's muscle cars are cool.

Data Preservation

Throughout the muscle car generation, the practice of General Motors was that its factory records were not centralized; each of GM's divisions was individually responsible for maintaining its own records. Over time, some divisions have been more fortunate than others in the preservation of this valuable information. For Chevrolet and Oldsmobile, although overall production figures are generally known, very little additional information has been preserved by these divisions.

If you are a Chevrolet enthusiast, for example, to document a rare car you need to have the tremendous good fortune of having an original window sticker, build sheet, or other original documentation. As can be expected, this leads to some unscrupulous folks mocking up paperwork. This is an unfortunate issue that has become prevalent in today's collector world of top-tier muscle cars.

Compared to the lack of vehicle-specific factory production records from Chevrolet and Oldsmobile, both Buick and Pontiac have

Lost no longer! 223679N105354 was the last of the eight 1969 Trans Am convertibles to be unveiled to the public. Amazingly, all eight cars have survived the test of time. (Scott Tiemann Photo)

preserved the records for any individual car, thanks to tenacity and luck.

In Pontiac's case, the efforts of Jim Mattison and the PHS team recognized early on the historical significance of these microfiche records, which identified options for each individual car by VIN. Through the preservation of these records, for an extremely reasonable fee, Pontiac enthusiasts can now order the PHS history for any muscle car–era Pontiac. They will receive, among other things, the third-party assurance as to exactly how that particular car was originally configured. This confidence has allowed Pontiacs to reach a very high level of collectability.

Muscle Design

We all know about the GTO, Pontiac's hugely successful offering, and most people consider it to be the first true muscle car. The premise of the muscle car is a large engine in a small body. The GTO is not an enormous car, but Ford was the first to exploit this small-body high-performance concept with the introduction of the 1964 Mustang.

In direct kinship with Chevrolet's Camaro, Pontiac's answer to the Mustang was the Firebird, first released in 1967. Production of these first-gen Firebirds lasted for only three model years. Available in either coupe or convertible form, these monsters followed the classic long-hood/short-deck proportions that most of today's muscle car enthusiasts hold in such high regard. Throughout this three-year production span, the top-of-the-line 400-ci Firebird powerplant increased in both name recognition and horsepower, culminating with the 1969 Ram Air III (RAIII) and Ram Air IV (RAIV) versions, delivering 335 hp and 345 hp, respectively.

In addition, although the 1968 Firebirds received only subtle design changes to the initial version, the 1969 Firebirds and their Camaro cousins saw one-year-only refinements. Today, many consider these 1969-only designs to be General Motors' ultimate achievement in the muscle car theme.

Midway through the 1970 model year, the Firebird received a radically new design. Among a host of other changes for this new model, the badging of our fine-feathered-friend now had a "wings up" stance, compared to the "wings down" design unique to first-gen Firebirds. Continuing through 1981, while both sleek and aggressive, the dramatically new second-gen Firebird supported only the coupe body style. Pontiac enthusiasts had to wait another 21 years, well into the car's third-gen design, before another factory-built Firebird convertible became available. By the end of the Firebird run in 2002, horsepower ratings had finally crept back to the glory days of the muscle car era, further emphasizing what mighty cars the early 'Birds really were.

The Trans Am Option

As we look back, these early circumstances conspired to produce the most powerful, admired, and what many regard to be the most esthetically muscular Firebirds ever made. This, the 1969 version, could, fortunately, still be ordered in convertible form. The stage had been set for the most rare of combinations. And when this combination came forth, it was like a sledgehammer.

During this same banner year, at the very peak of its muscle car design and raw horsepower output, Pontiac unveiled the most significant Firebird ever produced, the 1969 Trans Am. On December 8, 1968, at the Riverside Raceway in Riverside, California, Pontiac introduced the new Trans Am option, accompanied by a new GTO packaged as *The Judge*. Although initially panned by many unappreciative critics, and with little corporate fanfare (for advertisement support Pontiac only released two magazine ads and one single-page sales brochure insert throughout 1969), the Trans Am went on to serve as Pontiac's flagship car for 34 years.

On the eve of the 61st annual Chicago Automobile Show in March 1969 the Trans Am Performance and Appearance option made its public debut. The Trans Am option WS4, RPO 322, started with the base Firebird equipment and then added a host of option-specific body upgrades. These included a special ducted steel hood with fiberglass scoop inserts, a blacked-out grille, functional front-fender air extractors, a front spoiler, and a rear pedestal-mounted airfoil.

The suspension and drivetrain were further optimized through the use of front disc brakes, quick-ratio power steering, F70-14 tires on 7-inch rims, heavy-duty springs and shocks, 3.55:1 Safe-T-Track 10-bolt differential, and an oversized 1-inch-diameter front stabilizer. Other visual appointments included a simulated wood-grain steering wheel, chrome valvecovers, and a chrome oil filler cap. Although the interior could be ordered in any standard Firebird color, all 1969

Trans Ams were uniquely cloaked in Cameo White with full-length Tyrol Blue body stripes and blue tail panel accentuated by "Trans Am" decals on the fenders and rear spoiler.

Only two of Pontiac's most premier 400-ci powerplants were available when the Trans Am option was specified, either the potent 335-hp RAIII or the optional 345-hp RAIV. The 3-speed manual was standard and a close-ratio 4-speed or a Turbo-Hydramatic automatic were available also. Cost for the Trans Am option alone (in addition to the base price of the Firebird) was just over a grand, which included a $5 licensing fee paid by Pontiac to the SCCA for use of the Trans Am name.

Unlike typical optional items, the WS4 "option" was really a comprehensive package, combining both appearance and performance features to define an entirely distinctive car. As such, the Trans Am Firebirds easily eclipsed the base models. For its inaugural year, only 697 of these pinnacle Trans Ams were produced, a fairly modest beginning for a car that went on to achieve such legendary status. And from these humble origins rose the most exclusive of them all, eight Trans Am convertibles.

The Droptop Eight

All eight of these droptops were ordered with the base RAIII engine, but the combination of rarity, uniqueness, performance, and desirability sets them apart, even from their rare hardtop siblings. As such, they rivaled the most revered cars produced by any manufacturer throughout the entire muscle car era. Many consider these eight Trans Am convertibles to be the most significant cars that the Pontiac Division produced during its 85-year history. That's saying something!

Unbelievably, when new, these Trans Am convertibles were so expensive many dealers couldn't sell them. PHS records indicate that many of these cars originally went unsold and were returned to Pontiac for redistribution, often multiple times, before eventually finding a home.

Because the Trans Am package was initially an option, rather than a distinctive model, the VIN prefixes do not uniquely identify these cars within their Firebird family. Fortunately, through PHS documentation records, along with Pete McCarthy's book, *Pontiac Musclecar Performance 1955–1979*, we have a full account of these one-year-only first-gen Trans Ams, including the eight convertibles. In addition to knowing that these eight ragtops were equipped with RAIII engines, we also know that four were ordered with 4-speeds; the other four were automatics. All eight were ordered with the optional Rally II wheels. Three of the eight were sold new in Canada.

PN 223679N105354

The whereabouts of seven of these cars are well known, and fortunately they have been fairly well cared for. But one remains missing. The missing car is one of the 4-speeds that was sold new in Canada. Moreover, it is one of just two equipped with the ultra-desirable Rally Gauge Cluster package that included the tachometer, clock, and the stacked-gauge setup.

For 45 years, details were sketchy about this missing convertible. Rumors long existed that this car was located in a garage somewhere in western Canada, although no real evidence has ever surfaced supporting this claim. It is known that the car was originally sold new to General Motors of Canada, but then the trail became cold.

One rumor was that many decades ago two Trans Ams were following each other on the streets of western Canada. That's when a horrific fire erupted from the engine compartment of the front car, this very same convertible. Everyone watched in horror as the poor ragtop literally burned to the ground right in front of them.

Another rumor was that this car made its way back into the United States, settling somewhere in the Illinois area. Unfortunately, no concrete evidence has been provided.

Not unlike with UFOs, a number of sightings of this car have been reported, likely due to the prevalence of clones (standard 1969 Firebird convertibles dressed up to mimic one of these prized eight), but no one publically came forward with real proof. Naturally, some were concerned that this car no longer existed, having met its fate with the crusher years ago.

In October 2015 these rumors finally came to an end. Enter Rick Mahoney, a muscle car collector extraordinaire with an affinity for Pontiacs. Rick's resume includes having owned one of the other 4-speed 1969 Pontiac Trans Am convertibles, VIN #223679N104810. Like most muscle car treasure hunters Rick had been in hot pursuit of this unicorn for decades. His title searches eventually led to an owner in Michigan. Discussions lasted for more than a year, but in

October 2015 Rick was finally able to purchase the car. A concours restoration has already been commissioned with Pontiac authority Scott Tiemann of Supercar Specialties.

It is interesting to note some similarity between the rumors and the facts. As Rick learned, while in Canada the car was in a serious front-end collision, and ended up at a salvage yard in Vancouver, British Columbia, in the early 1990s. Earlier history is still unclear, although it is known that several years prior to this collision the car lived some of its life in upstate New York.

In 1994 a U.S. resident purchased the car from the Canadian salvage yard, and took it to Michigan where it was titled in 2000. Throughout this period a wealth of parts were collected toward the car's eventual restoration. It was this titling that eventually gave Rick the clue he so critically needed, closing a major chapter in lost muscle car history.

After decades of searching, the lost Trans Am convertible was unveiled in October 2015 to have been discovered by Pontiac enthusiast and collector Rick Mahoney. Renowned restorer Scott Tiemann is handling the restoration. (Scott Tiemann Photo)

By Leon Dixon

It was the beginning of the 1960s and I often found myself hanging out on North Woodward Avenue during balmy summer nights. It was a magical automotive mecca in those days. Night after night, there was endless cruising and street racing. This was all interspersed with stops at various drive-in restaurants that dotted the thoroughfare.

We didn't need a car show in those days because we already had one at nearly every traffic light and certainly at each drive-in. Hoods were often raised and races were set up right there amid the window trays, waitresses on roller skates, hamburgers, and chocolate malts.

Few places on earth were cooler than the Detroit car scene in 1968. Especially when you lived minutes from Woodward Avenue and you could go hunting for prey in a 1968 Royal Bobcat GTO convertible. (Photo Courtesy Leon Dixon Archive)

Somewhere on I-75

I quickly decided that Ted's Drive-In restaurant near the corner of Square Lake Road and Woodward Avenue was *my* favorite haunt. The coolest cars (and girls) always seemed to turn up there. And eventually there was an added benefit that only the kids who hung out there knew about: a special secret quarter-mile raceway, just for us.

In those days, the rear (or side) entrance to Ted's emptied out onto Square Lake Road. If you hung a right and traveled just a bit east, you came to a barricade that led to the unfinished I-75 interstate highway. It was easy enough to simply drive around the barricade to find yourself on a beautiful, deserted stretch of pristine concrete roadway. From this point going south, the pavement on I-75 was completed, but it only went on for a mile or so before ending at a huge pile of dirt. At night, there were no lights and no traffic. But, best of all, no cops. For those of us who street raced on North Woodward, it was a dream come true.

One night, somebody showed up with a can of white paint and measured off a quarter-mile on the unfinished I-75. Regulars at Ted's chipped in and bought a flashlight and a six-pack of beer and gave it all to the guy who served as the flagman. And so it came to pass that, for a while, I-75 became known, unofficially, as North Woodward dragway.

In my early days on North Woodward, I made the rounds with my buddy Conce in his 1955 Chevy Bel Air hardtop. It was in mint condition with a 265 Power Pack V-8, dual exhausts, and more. Before long, I had graduated to my very own 1963 Ford XL convertible. It was triple black with a big 390 V-8 and Police Interceptor performance package.

Then something really wild happened. Another friend bought a new 1964 GTO. It was a stunning car. A few months later another friend bought a new 1965 triple-black GTO convertible. It was loaded with everything imaginable, even a record player. I decided that the GTO was one of my new favorites, and maybe someday I would buy one.

Military Life

I had to postpone dreams of buying a new GTO when my father became ill and ultimately died. I was on my own and I had just too many expenses and responsibilities then. So I held onto my XL and took a job working for Ford. For a time, my gleaming black beauty and I cruised the haunts of North Woodward and even won a few street races. But then came the letter from Uncle Sam and the dreaded military draft. In an instant, it was all over and my Ford XL went into deep storage. I found myself in a U.S. Army uniform, and from that moment forward, everything changed. Cool cars and Woodward Avenue quickly became a fond, yet distant, memory.

GENERAL MOTORS DISTRIBUTORS MILITARY SALES PROGRAM

HEADQUARTERS VIETNAM REGIONAL EXCHANGE

APO 96243

CHEVROLET — PONTIAC — OLDSMOBILE — BUICK — CADILLAC

Delivery Point _____ Delivery Date _____

Name _____ Rank _____

Military Address : _____ Stateside Address : _____

Car Line *GTO* Model *Convertible* Year _____

Color _____ Trim _____ Top _____

Description	Rpo ※	Price	Special Instructions :
Basic Unit		2739.18	
Auto - Trans		207.72	
Synchro Trans			
Power Steering		83.08	
Power Brakes		36.93	
Tinted Glass.		30.47	
Radio		53.55	
White Walls			
Airconditioner..			
Positraction..			
Console		60.01	
Rally II wheels		73.86	
New Car Service		70.00	
Processing		15.00	
D & H or EOH..		163.00	
Total Price			
Destination Charge. ..		10.00	
TOTAL DELIVERED PRICE		3562.81	

Total Delivered Price $ _____

Less Deposit _____

Balance due $ _____

Finance Company _____

Amount financed $ _____

Here is the original purchase form from Vietnam for the 1968 GTO convertible. I purchased the car in Detroit, but Royal Pontiac in Royal Oak, Michigan, "Bobcatted" the GTO for me. (Photo Courtesy Leon Dixon Archive)

After several months of training I found myself in the jungles and central coastal area of the war in Vietnam. It was 1967. Of course, it was an extremely difficult existence with not a lot of occasions for anything resembling joy. For the most part, life there proceeded one day at a time. First, you were happy to wake up alive. Then you made it though a day and hoped that you survived through the coming night. And so it went.

I was luckier than many out in the field. After some very extensive schooling, I had succeeded in becoming a communications specialist, which was a rather elite job in those times. I found myself in a great unit with good men. Of course constant danger was all around and it was a brutal and unforgiving environment. Some of us didn't survive to come home. Others were wounded. But one way or another, we somehow made it through each day and did our jobs. Despite all this, at times the talk drifted back to the relative comfort of cars and even North Woodward Avenue memories.

One night on guard duty in a perimeter bunker, one of my buddies asked me if I had seen the new GTO with the "invisible" front bumper. Huh? Nope. I told him I had not seen it and was dying to know all about the car with the mysterious new bumper. He told me that he had a magazine article clipping back at our tent and promised to show me when we returned the next morning.

Turns out that my friend's dad back in Texas had made him a fabulous incentive offer. He said that if my buddy just made it home alive, he'd give him a brand-new 1968 GTO with that "invisible front bumper."

My buddy was due to return stateside months before I was (he'd been in Vietnam long before I arrived). Sure enough, I received a letter from Texas a few weeks after he left for home. I opened the envelope and a photo of a bright Solar Red GTO fell out. "It was waiting in the driveway when I got home!" he wrote. Wow. That started my fires burning and I resolved that one way or another I was going to survive the war and buy myself a new 1968 GTO.

An XL for a GTO

Then something else happened. On a visit to our rear base camp in the muddy central highlands, I discovered that we actually had a post exchange (PX) store. It was a kind of glorified tent covered in red mud that was constantly soaked from the monsoon rains. That day, a guy wearing fatigues inside was offering stupendous deals on new cars for soldiers. It turned out that you could buy a new car at deep military discount via the PX. And General Motors had a special overseas purchase program for soldiers in Vietnam. Ohhh! The news was getting better and better. Could I order a new GTO? Of course I could. Hot diggety!

The fellow in the fatigues pulled out an order form and started to fill in the blanks. All he had to show me was a waterlogged, musty-smelling page from a brochure that was stained from the red mud. But I held it in my hands as if it were gold and continued to give the guy my wants. I ordered a new 1968 Pontiac GTO convertible, in the middle of Vietnam and the war.

When I returned home, I traded in my Ford XL for the new GTO. Again came more surprises. When I arrived at the Detroit dealership, I discovered that I could order loads of additional features I didn't know about. I quickly decided that I wanted more, so the dealer offered to sell me a loaded car he already had in stock. This car had Hideaway Headlamps, Rallye II wheels, Hood Tach, AM/FM, 8-track tape deck, and the almighty 360 HO (rated somehow the same as the Ram Air) engine among the goodies.

I signed the papers and rolled my new GTO up next to the 1963 Ford XL as the salesmen made fun of me for being so sappy over two cars. Finally, I was off to new adventures as I sadly turned over the Ford's keys and drove away.

Mirrors, Splitters and Bobcatting

I still had friends back at Ford, and about the time I bought my GTO, one of them called to talk cars. I told him that the door-mounted mirror on the GTO just didn't look right to me. "Wait 'til you see the new mirrors coming out on Mustang for 1969!" he said. "They got this new model coming up called Mach I and it has streamlined body-color racing mirrors. We got a pair of prototypes that we're gonna toss in the trash. You want 'em?" Ohhh. What the heck did he say that for? Of course I wanted the mirrors!

They arrived in gray primer and I quickly took my new racing mirrors to Packer Pontiac on Livernois Avenue. The body shop painted them to match my yellow Mayfair Maize GTO, and I was out on the street with the twin racing mirrors long before the Mustang was. I often pulled up to a red light and people in other GTOs rolled the windows down and asked about my cool mirrors. I toyed with them. "Oh? You mean, yours didn't come with these? I thought they all did!"

I took to visiting the ultimate GTO paradise: Ace Wilson's Royal Pontiac in Royal Oak, Michigan. There I came to know Pontiac performance guru Milt Schornack and asked him about ways to squeeze more performance out of my car. In the end, I wound up bringing my GTO in one morning to leave in Milt's capable hands. By the time I got it back, it had been "Bobcatted."

The Royal Bobcat treatment was based on years of Pontiac racing heritage and guaranteed you a car that would blow the doors off anything stock on Woodward. Royal did things such as cams, jetting, blueprinting, etc. A set of Mylar stickers came with the treatment. For 1968, Royal either positioned these insignias on your doors or gave them to you. I never installed them, opting for "sleeper" status.

One final thing: Ever since I saw the 1964 and 1965 GTOs that my buddies bought years earlier, the one appearance goody I wanted was the cool double exhaust tips that Pontiac called exhaust splitters. These were stainless twin pipes that stuck out at angles sideways just aft of the rear wheels. I thought they were great! I was crushed to discover during the ordering process that splitters were no longer available as of the 1968 model year. They had been replaced with exhaust trumpets, which kind of looked as if they were from a 1965 Mustang GT. But I wasn't having any of it.

When I mentioned my disappointment about the exhaust tips to Milt at Royal, he simply said, "Well, that's all show stuff and I prefer *go* stuff, but let me see what I can rig up for you." When I got my car back, sure enough exhaust splitters were poking out behind the rear wheels, just the way I imagined them. As as far as I know, I had the only new 1968 GTO on Woodward with exhaust splitters and those wild racing mirrors. My car was extremely popular on the Street of Dreams and I was quizzed at every other traffic light. And yes, it ran like a, well you know.

Life Moves On

I soon found myself back in college studying full time. The abysmal gas mileage combined with stratospheric insurance rates on muscle cars at the time pushed me to sell the GTO and I bought a little sports car. I consoled myself by thinking it was a sensible, practical move. But I was still in love.

Sadly, as I watched the new owner drive off in my beautiful GTO Bobcat, I noticed a taillight bulb must have blown. As he reached the corner and the turn signal flickered oddly, my GTO seemed to be saying a sad, tearful goodbye to me.

I last saw my Ford XL in 1969, battered and beaten, covered in Bondo, with the top in tatters, with a barbarian at the wheel. I couldn't bear to look at it.

And the GTO? Last I heard it was in the Carolinas, wrecked with a seized rear axle. It was only a rumor and that was in the 1970s. Despite my best efforts, I assume the car is lost forever.

To this day, I still have that original order form, the original letter from Pontiac Division congratulating me on my purchase, Royal license plate frames, Bobcat stickers, Protect-o-Plate, and more.

But so many times I have dreamed about my beautiful Mayfair Maize GTO Bobcat convertible. And I often still wonder . . . whatever became of that incredible piece of my life?

A 1968 GTO painted in Mayfair Maize with a black convertible top and black interior made for a striking combination. **Motor Trend** *named the GTO its car of the year, and rightly so. Note the exhaust splitters and hood tach. The prototype racing mirrors were actually for a 1969 Mach 1 Ford Mustang. (Photo Courtesy Leon Dixon Archive)*

By Roger Day

Back in 1969, I knew nothing about COPO cars or how they were ordered. But on August 19, on my way to work at around 8 a.m., a bright Monaco Orange Chevelle with black hood stripes caught my eye on the showcase section of Bill Allen's dealership lot. I pulled in to have a look, and the salesman, Charlie Fieden, didn't waste any time tracking me down. He hit me with the key points about performance mods made at Dick Harrell's shop. My eyes were riveted to the Harrell MSRP document on the driver-side window.

It made me smile just thinking of the possibilities of an L72 between the fenders of a muscle car. My aging 1966 SS396 Chevelle, purchased new in May 1966, had more than 105,000 miles on the clock.

A couple of hours later, I drove the Harrell-modified 1969 COPO Chevelle off the lot and to work.

My car rolled off GM's "KAN" assembly line in Kansas City, Missouri, during the third week of July and near the end of the 1969 model year. Bill Allen Chevrolet ordered the car via the COPO process. After modifications at Dick Harrell's shop, it was delivered to and marketed by the dealership as a Harrell performance

It doesn't get much more potent than this stunning 1969 Dick Harrell COPO Chevelle. The fine folks at Dick Harrell's shop applied the hood stripes, hood locks, and emblems you see here. (Photo Courtesy Roger Day Archive)

NEW CAR SALES INVOICE

CUSTOMER'S COPY

BILL ALLEN CHEVROLET, INC.
101 ARMOUR ROAD   GRAND 1-4770
NORTH KANSAS CITY, MISSOURI

Nº 12115

DATE August 19, 19 69

SALESMAN Feiden

SOLD TO Roger Day
ADDRESS Route 2
Plattsburg, Missouri

MAKE	SERIAL NO.	MOTOR NO.	KEY NO.	TYPE	MODEL	COLOR	PRICE
Chevrolet	136379K470099	T0409 MP	8K25 6120	69 Malibu spt cpe spec. paint	A2010		2765 75

OPTIONAL EQUIP. 427-450 HP spec. 3 spd. turbo HM positract. rear end 4.10 ration, dual exhaust system, spec. purpose suspension, HD cooling syst. chrome valve covers, hood locks, large power disc brakes, spec. wide stance whls. 14x7 wide oval tires spec. striping.   1664 30

INSURANCE COVERAGE INCLUDES
- [ ] FIRE AND THEFT
- [ ] COLLISION ____ AMT. DED. ____
- [ ] P.L. & P.D. ____ AMOUNT ____

INSURANCE
PAY TO   tachometer   68 00
LICENSE   AM radio   61 00
SALES TAX

OPTIONAL EQUIPMENT AND ACCESSORIES

DESCRIPTION	PRICE

1500.00
1927.83
3427.83

2020.83
93.00
1927.83 10 days?

3266.64 13 pmts
1179.02
2087.02
155.25 ins.
4.53 late chgs
2246.80 ins rebate
93.00 unit rebate
1927.83 Payoff

DELIVERED PRICE   4559 15

SETTLEMENT

CHARGE
CASH ON DELIVERY
DEPOSIT

USED CAR Chevelle SS   1859 15
YEAR 66 STOCK NO. A2010A
SERIAL NO. 138176K180883
MOTOR NO. ____
NOTES GMAC 36098.88 begn. 10-2-69   2700 00
VF life 106.77 VF A&H 135.24
TERMS:

TOTAL   4559 15

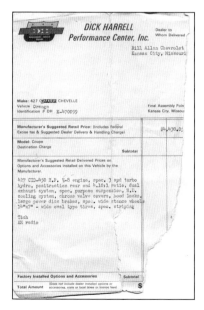

DICK HARRELL
Performance Center, Inc.

Dealer to Whom Delivered

Bill Allen Chevrolet
Kansas City, Missouri

Make: 427 CAMARO CHEVELLE
Vehicle Orange
Identification # DH K-470099

Final Assembly Point
Kansas City, Missouri

Manufacturer's Suggested Retail Price: (Includes Federal Excise tax & Suggested Dealer Delivery & Handling Charge)   4,830.05

Model: Coupe
Destination Charge
Subtotal

Manufacturer's Suggested Retail Delivered Prices on Options and Accessories installed on this Vehicle by the Manufacturer.

427 CID-450 H.P. V-8 engine, spec. 3 spd turbo hydro, positraction rear end 4.10:1 ratio, dual exhaust system, spec. purpose suspension, H.D. cooling system, chrome valve covers, hood locks, large power disc brakes, spec. wide stance wheels 14"x7" - wide oval type tires, spec. striping

Tach
AM radio

Factory Installed Options and Accessories   Subtotal
Total Amount (Does not include dealer installed options and accessories, state or local taxes or license fees) $

I held onto the original paperwork for my Chevelle. Without it I would have never been able to successfully track down my beloved car. (Photo Courtesy Roger Day Archive)

Here is some awe-inspiring reading material: Dick Harrell's invoice for the performance mods on the 427-equipped COPO Chevelle conversion. (Photo Courtesy Roger Day Archive)

car. This magical alignment made it one of only three known KAN-built 1969 COPO Chevelles. Like any great keeper of the records, I saved the original Harrell MSRP document and the Bill Allen customer invoice from the day I bought the car and tucked them away for safekeeping.

A Bit of Racing

During that first winter in 1969, I was never left behind at a streetlight. On the few occasions I raced in the flats locally, I was unbeaten. My first race with my friend John Carter was in early December 1969 on Highway 33 near Plattsburg. He had a hot SS 396-ci 350-hp Chevy Nova. John smoked his tires while I screamed to the turnaround. It was a hollow victory because my engine scuffed a cylinder wall and the block was replaced under GM's warranty at Bill Allen's shop days later.

Late in the summer of 1970, the Chevelle tackled one of its strongest competitors in a test of Dodge versus Chevrolet. This race was just outside my wife Karen's hometown of Gallatin, Missouri, shortly after we were engaged. Karen and her friend Janel Reynolds were riding around with me that summer evening when we were invited to race by Ben Houghton, a friend of theirs. He had a strong-running Challenger R/T 440 six-pack.

Another friend, Junior Burke, set it up on Highway 13 between Gallatin and Hamilton. Ben smoked his tires. I eased off the line and then hammered the gas pedal, building up steam toward the end of the quarter-mile. I blew Ben's doors off in round one, but flashing red lights in the distance halted a rematch.

Search and Success

My wife and I often talk about our first meeting at a Memorial Day gathering in 1970, our romance and subsequent engagement that summer, and the Monaco Orange 1969 Chevelle that was so much a part of that time. We were having one of those conversations in October 2008 when I decided to embark on an all-out, do-or-die effort to find the car. The original engine had scuffed a cylinder wall at about 12,000 miles in December 1969; thanks to the GM warranty the short-block was replaced. The second engine starved for oil at about 35,000 in October 1970 because the oil pick was not spot welded to the oil pump. For this, the GM warranty allowed for repair but not replacement of the short-block, so on October 19, 1970, I traded it in for a new Camaro RS.

In December 2008, I successfully tracked down and talked to the fellow who owned the car in the mid-1980s. He knew all about the car's heritage and told me the Dick Harrell emblem on the trunk lid had been removed the day he sold the car at auction, which virtually erased this super car's history.

After talking with him, bits and pieces of information fell into place. He also mentioned another owner who had contacted him

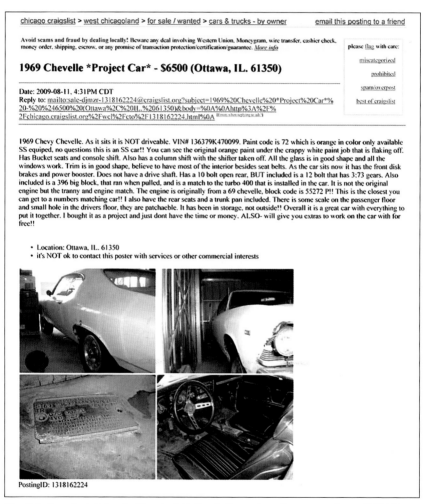

So this is what it feels like to hit the lottery. I rediscovered my COPO Chevelle thanks to this Craigslist ad. Nope, that's not a typo in the price. (Photo Courtesy Roger Day Archive)

about the car in 2005. I followed the trail to the 2005 owner and was told it had been sold for scrap and crushed a couple of years back. My spirits were also crushed when I heard that report, but I didn't fully give up hope. So, in May 2009, Karen and I drove to the farm, only to find that all of the old cars were gone. I pored over Internet sites and asked for help to find my long-lost Chevelle. I actually gave up hope several times over 12 years, only to pick it up and start back at it again. Loose ends remained and I just couldn't quit the search without real answers.

In May 2009, I received an intriguing email. "Roger, by chance was your car's VIN 136397K470099?" asked Dan. Was it a scam or was my car perhaps really out there? How did someone other than myself (or a previous owner) know the Chevelle's VIN? Dan's email rekindled my fire; it was the spark I needed. I emailed Dan three times, but he never responded. In late July, I left a voice mail for him and he returned the call but couldn't remember details about the ad that he'd seen back in May.

I expanded my online search and just a few days after I spoke with Dan, I found an expired Craigslist ad from Illinois with the correct VIN. It was inactive, but I kept reentering the VIN in Google, hoping that the seller might relist. He did, and on August 12 shortly after 6 a.m., I found his relist from the day before. I sent several emails to the seller and he finally responded and by mid-afternoon we connected via telephone. We agreed to meet the next morning at 7:30 a.m. at a storage rental in Ottawa, Illinois.

The next morning, at the appointed time, I was ready and waiting. After he arrived and we exchanged pleasantries, he opened the overhead door to reveal a white Chevelle. I spotted a mid-1980s Missouri inspection sticker, and he handed me a clear Illinois title and Missouri DMV envelope. Inside was an old title application from the same mid-1980s Missouri owner I found in 2008. Money changed hands, papers were signed, and I took ownership (again) of my old 1969 Chevelle.

A Dream Come True

Restoration began immediately, and by December 2010 the frame, body, and paintwork were complete. The detailing portion of the project took place in Texas, and piece-by-piece everything began to go back together just as it was in 1969. On Memorial Day weekend

2011, Karen and I took our "anniversary" run around the block. It was 41 years ago that weekend that I took her home in this very same car the night we met!

On June 7, 2011, bright and early, we left for Chevellabration. Twelve hours later, we were at the Best Western in Goodlettsville, Tennessee. It was great to be back again, but this time we had a car to show, hopeful that it would be well received. Hundreds of beautiful Chevelles were parked on the grassy field at Moss-Wright Park, where everyone could look them over. The cars judged by participants are divided into year and by class: stock or modified. We were honored to receive the Peoples Choice award (what some call Best of Show).

To cap off the amazing first year back in the Chevelle, we then took off on a two-day road trip to Rosemont, Illinois, to attend the Muscle Car & Corvette Nationals, the premier car show of its kind in the world. We just couldn't believe how many truly great muscle cars were in attendance. Our Chevelle was in the COPO Invitational section. How could it get any better?

Our Dick Harrell–prepped Chevelle was entered for the Concours Day 2 judging event. The judges spent what seemed like hours looking over, under, inside, and outside our car. Then they came over to review the results. I simply couldn't believe the final tally: 994 out of 1,000 possible points. It was gold!

Finding this Chevelle has been an answered prayer. It feels like a miracle that I found my old car and was able to bring it back from the depths of obscurity. Every time I climb behind the wheel of my 427 COPO, it makes me feel like that young man who stared dumbfounded at the MSRP window sticker back in 1969.

By Todd Werts

D uring the summer of 1965, my uncle cruised the streets of the Virginia Beach area in his 409 tri-powered Cherry Red 1957 Chevrolet Bel Air convertible. He'd always loved fast cars and gladly took on all comers in the Hampton area cruising scene. Leaving the Bel Air in the trusted care of his girlfriend at the time, he was off to the U.S. Army and it wouldn't be long before the only thing he was driving were mud-laden jeeps through the jungle terrain of Vietnam.

After a virtual eternity in combat, Uncle Don's tour was finally up and he was hungry to return to his beloved Bel Air and the local street scene he'd longed for every night in the jungle. After arriving home, he headed straight for his Cherry Red Tri-Five only to find out that his ex-girlfriend had moved and the car had been left behind and lost to whomever moved in after she moved out. Uncle Don had a pocket full of money saved up from his time in the army and was hungry to replace the 1957 with a new, fast car.

L72 or ZL1

It was late in the summer of 1969 in Newport News, Virginia, when Uncle Don strolled into Casey Chevrolet looking for a loaded Z/28 he'd been hearing so much about. Test driving that Z was a dream compared to driving the jungle jeeps of just a few weeks prior and he raved at its power and handling. As some often are wont to do, the salesman informed Uncle Don that "if he liked the Z, he should try out one of the Camaros in the showroom."

On the showroom floor sat two 1969 Camaros equipped with high-performance 427 engines, one car finished in silver and one in blue. Uncle Don remembers that blue Camaro was "special." Equipped with a plain black interior, 4-speed transmission, 4:10 Posi-Traction rear, and the potent 427, the car just called Don to take it out for a spin. Two seconds into the test-drive, feeling power he'd never felt before, he knew he had to have it.

His memory recalls a sizeable down payment, leaving $4,700 to be financed through GMAC. Although the VIN has yet to be discovered, Uncle Don insists the engine was an all-aluminum block used on 1969 ZL1 COPO Camaros. General Motors built just 69 of these rare beasts in 1969. Also important to note, however, is that Uncle Don also remembers removing the valvecovers and seeing the words "hi-perf" stamped into the heads. This made *Blue Beast* an L72 car because the ZL1 heads did not have such a stamp. Whether it was an L72 or ZL1, the car was definitely a COPO and irrefutably a bona fide street machine.

Street Racing

Having spent most of his cash, Uncle Don upgraded only the ignition system and took to the streets, driving the car hard, picking up every street race he could and, according to his memory, only losing one. He campaigned the car throughout the Virginia Beach area and it wasn't long before word spread and takers faded away.

To every problem, a solution can be found, and he soon convinced a friend to procure a 307-ci twin for his *Blue Beast* and thus began the "bait-and-switch" campaign. When he hung out at the diner with his buddies and the 307 Camaro, they lined up race after race. He recalls his conquests, including a yellow Yenko Camaro, a 1969 Z/28, Mustang, and a multitude of Challengers, Chargers, and 'Cudas.

As an interesting side note, Uncle Don says, "It could have been the drivers, but the Z/28 stayed way closer than the Yellow Yenko." He recalls one particular 440 R/T losing in the quarter-mile, and then "from 100 on." The guy simply refused to believe he could lose to that little Camaro.

On one particular evening, Uncle Don remembers a fellow walking into the diner and challenging anyone there with his 440 dual 4-barrel 'Cuda. Uncle Don obliged and they agreed to meet on the

A favorite of street racers was using the old bait-and-switch method when word got out about a certain car's success. Here Don's 427 COPO is parked with his friend's 307-prepped and visually identical Camaro. (Photo Courtesy Donald Surrett)

flats in Poquoson, Virginia, where they often settled horsepower wars. Showing up on a trailer, the Mopar was tubbed with drag slicks.

For the first time, Uncle Don felt a little uneasy and pored over the 'Cuda. Sure enough, the 'Cuda hooked up perfectly while Uncle Don sat and spun. Eventually gaining traction, Uncle Don poured it on, and to his best recollection, he was tearing past the 'Cuda at the line as if it were standing still. But still, it was a loss, and a second-chance request wasn't accepted. That one blemish was all that stood between the COPO and a perfect record. As summer faded into fall, and fall into winter, Uncle Don was racking up the traffic violations all around Virginia Beach. He succeeded in eluding "the fuzz" on multiple occasions by high-tailin' it out of there and hiding behind bushes, buildings, or whatever he could find, but failed no fewer than seven times between the fall of 1969 and the spring of 1970. As insurance companies often do, Uncle Don's coverage on the car was canceled in the spring of 1970 as a result of those speeding violations.

Thieves Swoop In

It was also during the early spring of 1970 that the car began to revolt to the commands of Uncle Don's heavier than normal right foot. On various occasions the timing went "out of whack" and valve issues began to emerge. One fateful day, while traveling on Route 64 in Hampton, the car overheated massively in front of the Hampton Coliseum. Pulling immediately to the side of the road, Uncle Don locked his COPO and left it alongside the road and traveled on foot to the nearest service station to secure a tow truck to retrieve *Blue Beast*.

Upon arriving back at the scene where the car had been parked, however, two solid black skid marks were all that was found. Despite filing stolen vehicle reports with both the Hampton and Virginia State police, *Blue Beast* has never been located. The state police informed Uncle Don of an active car thief ring from New York stealing and stripping muscle cars from the area.

Uncle Don also suspected one particular character of having a hand in the theft as he had tried to buy the car on multiple occasions. It had been rumored that this guy was known for stealing and stripping fast cars for their engines and burying them in his back yard until the heat faded away. This was also never proven. Either way she was gone and never seen again.

Search Leads

Although it is unclear without the VIN if Uncle Don had a real COPO ZL1, or an L72-equipped COPO, one thing is sure: He still misses his *Blue Beast*. After purchasing the Camaro, he did eventually track down his Cherry Red Bel Air, sitting outside of a local gas station, stripped of most of its hardware.

We (his family) are currently sourcing any documentation and/ or information that could possibly still exist in an effort to locate his COPO Camaro. Should anyone have any knowledge regarding *Blue Beast*, even if it is just stories about taking her on in the streets of Virginia Beach, please contact Todd Werts at twertsy@gmail.com or 570-510-3604.

By Dana Hurt

In 1967 Don Yenko, along with others, changed the muscle car game forever with his creation of the Yenko 427 Super Camaro. As an accomplished race car driver and enthusiast, Yenko wanted to create a car with optimal performance for both on and off the track. Taking a page out of Carroll Shelby's book, Don began the transformation of the much-loved Chevy Camaro into a viable performance car, making every Camaro drag racer's dream come true.

The popularity of the 1967 Yenko carried over to the 1968 model year with Don Yenko's creation of the Super Camaro. Experts say Don only made approximately 65 copies of these L72 427- to 450-hp beauties, making them extremely coveted and desirable to all Chevy

Only people who truly love old cars can fully imagine the transformation from a disassembled, dented hulk to a beautifully restored Yenko Camaro. With the help of Muscle Car Restoration & Design, that vision became a reality for me.

lovers. It has been reported that only 15 or 16 of these Super Camaros exist today, in turn making them rare, desirable, and exclusive. What makes this car even more spectacular is its features.

These special Camaros were ordered through the GM central office production order division that later came to be known as the COPO program. For 1968, the 9737 COPO Camaro was only available to Don Yenko and, in fact, Yenko was considered the manufacturer of these 1968 Yenko Camaros.

Most people tend to think the high-performance aspect of the COPO program hit its stride in 1969. However, this COPO package was added in 1968 per Don Yenko's request to RPO L78 SS Camaros that were equipped with the 396-ci 375-hp big-blocks. The COPO 9737 designation added cooling, suspension, and brake upgrades along with a 140-mph speedometer, heavy-duty springs, a larger anti-roll bar, an M-21 close-ratio 4-speed transmission, and a 4.10 posi rear differential.

Yenko Mods

The 9737 COPO 1968 Camaros were delivered from Chevrolet to Yenko's dealership in Cannonsburg, Pennsylvania, with the RPO (regular production order) L78 396/375-hp engines. Yenko's mechanics then removed the L78 396 engine and installed an L72 427 short-block. The original L78 396 heads, aluminum intake, and carb were then installed on the 427 short-block.

Yenko also added Pontiac 14 x 6 Rally II wheels with a special "Y" for Yenko in the center caps, wide-oval red-stripe tires, and a unique fiberglass hood. Also added were Stewart Warner interior gauges and Yenko emblems along with 427 emblems on the exterior, and one Yenko emblem on the glove box.

One of the identifiable features needed to unlock the past of this 1968 Yenko resides on the rear bumper: the "Go NAVY" decal. (Photo Courtesy Dana Hurt)

Desert Rat Backstory

Sometime around 2004, a friend of mine who hunts a lot of rare cars told me that a man in the high desert of California had a 1968 Yenko Camaro under a tarp in his yard. He knew that the car needed to be restored, and it was real. He told me it was not for sale, but I might be able to see it. It took several months to make the owner comfortable enough for me to have a look at it. He had owned it almost 20 years and very few people had laid eyes on it.

I pursued the purchase of the car for more than a year with no luck. One day, out of the blue, the owner called me and wanted to meet for lunch. We met and struck a deal. It sounds easier than it was, and during the next several months, I exchanged funds and scoured his property for all of the parts that went with the car.

I asked him how he came across the car and this is what he told me: "Two young men saw a parked tow truck with this old Camaro strapped down on the back. They moseyed over and looked at it closer and noticed some odd emblems on the fender and tail panel and realized they had seen those emblems in a magazine article not too long before. They thought this might be a Yenko Camaro and searched out the driver of the hauler.

"The driver told them he had picked up the car near San Diego and he was taking it to the wrecking yard, where, for a few bucks in his pocket, it would most likely be crushed for metal. This was not going to be a good ending for this fabled muscle car, so the young men made the driver an offer on the car and purchased it right then and there.

"Next they sought out advice from a Camaro expert who lived in the desert. Being a Camaro guy, he never forgot that car. Some time later the two owners of the Yenko again called the Camaro expert when one of their cars broke down and they needed transportation to get to work. They did not have any money, but they did have a trade-in. The Camaro guy traded them a 1967 Ford Mustang with a six-banger, straight up, for, you guessed it, the Yenko."

That was in the mid-1980s. And that is where it had been sitting until I dislodged it in 2006.

When I purchased the car, it had a "Go Navy" sticker on the rear bumper and a sticker for military parking on the rearview mirror. It was originally ordered and sold through Jay Kline Chevrolet in Minnesota, one of the Yenko network dealers. It did not have a lot of rust, which gave me the feeling that it came out West pretty early in its life; slumbering in the upper desert of California. It was nick-named *Desert Rat*, and I thought that was funny because I found a rat living in the trunk.

The car carries the Yenko number YS 8011, but I researched it thoroughly before purchasing to make sure that I was dealing with a verified Yenko super car. It still wore the original faded Fathom Blue paint (which helped because the trim tag had a "--" instead of a num-ber for paint code, meaning that it was a special order paint car). It also had the original Special Order Yenko trim tag, Yenko doorjamb tag with Yenko serial number, original 140-mph speedometer, orig-inal large front sway bar, and all VINs, including the hidden ones, were intact, including more clues that sealed the deal.

Restoration Results

This car is on the Yenko VIN list and shows up in several docu-ments proving its lineage. The VIN matches the YS number; no issues there. After it was pulled out and cleaned and documented, I had it transported to Illinois for a complete makeover by well-known mus-cle car restorer Rick Nelson of Muscle Car Restoration and Design (MCRD). Finally, it would get the attention it deserved.

To say this was a no-expense-spared restoration would be a gross understatement. Even though the restoration cost well into six fig-ures, it was the attention to detail by Rick and Ann at MCRD that sets this car apart. Only GM parts, NOS or restored, were used wherever possible. Noted painter Tom Scholz told me this is the best paint job he has ever done.

In November 2011, it was ready to make its first debut since 1968. *Desert Rat* was asked to be one of five special cars to be unveiled at the prestigious Muscle Car & Corvette Nationals in Chicago, Illinois. None other than Dr. Lynn Yenko Zoiopoulos, Don Yenko's daughter, was on hand to help with the cover removal for the first time since the work was done. The look on people's faces was evidence of the job that MCRD did on this fine car.

The vehicle took the Gold in 2011 and returned to the Muscle Car & Corvette Nationals in 2012 and scored 992 out of 1,000 points to take Gold again. It took home a sponsors' trophy as well. This car now has on- and off-trailer miles and is ready to compete in any con-cours or judged event.

By Ola Nilsson

Hemicuda. The name alone generates curiosity, commands respect, and strikes fear in other muscle cars and their caretakers. Since its inception, the Hemicuda has been a top-notch contender to compete with all of the other makes and models. It is viewed by many as one of the ultimate muscle cars.

Chrysler Corporation designated the new-for-1970 Plymouth Barracuda series body style as the E-Body. Plymouth offered three models built on the Barracuda series car line. The base model was the Barracuda with a prefix of BH in the VIN. The upscale luxury model was the Gran Coupe with a prefix of BP. The sport model was the 'Cuda with a prefix of BS.

Plymouth offered the E-Body for sale in three distinct markets: United States (U.S.), Canada, and Export. The U.S. version received a

This 1970 Hemicuda convertible appeared in the October 1969 issue of Popular Science *magazine. Most likely a pilot car, it appeared in numerous magazines, assisting in launching Plymouth models for the 1970 sales season. (Photo Courtesy Jim Dunne)*

designation code of Y05. Canada cars received a designation code of Y07. The Export version had a designation code of Y09. These codes were generated at the factory designating the origination region of the initial order form.

Here I focus on the U.S.–specification Y05 cars. The Canada and Export versions have separate totals for built and shipped cars.

548 'Cuda Convertibles

The Chrysler-Plymouth factory documentation that has been found and researched indicates an estimated number of cars built. These documents were used by the Chrysler Corporation to determine what models and options sold for a specific model year. This way they continued or discontinued a certain model or option for the next year. The factory reported 17,258 'Cudas (BS) built for the United States.

Of all the 'Cudas built, 3.175 percent were convertibles. It is accepted that 548 'Cuda convertibles were built and shipped to dealers in the United States. A true 'Cuda convertible, BS prefix model, is a rare car. A true Hemicuda convertible is an extremely rare fish.

The Hemicuda model (BS27R0B) is estimated at 2.6 percent of the 548 cars. That comes out to 14.248 cars. I can accept that 14 Hemicudas were convertibles built in 1970 with U.S. specifications (Y05). Nine had automatic transmissions, which is about 1.6 percent; five had 4-speed transmissions, which is about 0.9 percent of the 548 units built.

Probable Find

To the collector of rare muscle cars, a 1970 Hemicuda convertible is, indeed, a prized catch. To date, 13 of the 14 cars have been found and accounted for. Colors, options, data plate codes, broadcast sheets, history, and more have been documented for each of those cars. Eight of those with automatic transmissions and all five 4-speed transmissions are known.

That leaves one 1970 Hemicuda convertible with automatic transmission that is unaccounted for. It is believed to be the first Hemicuda convertible ever built. I have found a probable VIN: BS27R0B100012. The factory hand-built this pre–model year release car for various reasons. It was built at the same time as another Hemicuda hardtop, and these cars were tested and photographed during the same time

Notice anything unusual about the hockey stripe on the pilot car? The blade reaches down to the side-marker light, which is certainly not the norm for production cars. (Photo Courtesy The Revs Institute)

frame. A car such as this is sometimes referred to as a pilot car. A pilot car served many functions for the Chrysler-Plymouth factory. It was a pre–model year panel test-fitting car, test-driving car, press photo car, parts manual car, executive hands-on car, and any other factory requests. This car was photographed at the Chrysler Corporation Proving Grounds just outside Detroit, Michigan. Most likely it was in the early summer of 1969. A 15 x 7-inch bare steel wheel was standard unless you ordered the one optional wheel available. The 15-inch full wheel covers are not standard issue for the Plymouth E-Body line. A small dog-dish-type hubcap was the norm.

Perhaps these full wheel covers had been intended to be used during the model year, or just put on for the photo shoots; no one knows for sure. They were actually used on a different Plymouth car model during the production year. They were also used on the early test Rallye Red Hemicuda hardtop with VIN BS23R0B100010.

This unique convertible was also photographed with the more appropriate 15x7-inch rallye wheels with polished trim rings. They are the extra-cost optional wheels available for a Hemicuda.

Specs and Options

Very few facts are known about this particular car. It has an automatic transmission, Ivy Green Metallic exterior paint code EF8, and green interior coded H6F8. Studying the photos and magazine articles from 1969, I can determine options on the car. Some of them are A21 Front Elastomeric Bumper Group, B51 Power Disc Brakes,

C16 Center Console, C55 Bucket Seats (standard for the convertible), M26 Wheelwell Moldings, M31 Body Belt Moldings, P31 Power Windows, P37 Power Convertible Top, R11 AM Radio, V6X Sport Stripe Longitudinal Tape (black), Y91 Show Car Finish, and 26 Radiator.

I know for a fact that these early cars did not reflect all of the options that were installed during the assembly process. I have also studied some of the very early E-Body cars and their data plates that were installed on the inner fender during the "body in white" assembly phase. The data plate, or as some people call it, the "fender tag," contains some very interesting information, items that are slightly different from the conventional data plate for later-built cars. One of the items that is unique to this missing Hemicuda convertible is a "job number." That information denotes a very early-build car for factory use.

Several odd options that may be due to the pre-production status are a standard flat hood instead of the Shaker hood, the absence of a Shaker cold-air cable under the dash frame, the absence of the M25 Wide Sill Moldings (rocker fish gills), rear-seat shoulder-harness seat belts, a standard three-spoke steering wheel with semi-circle horn ring, and a standard instrument dash. A rallye instrument cluster was an extra-cost option throughout the model year.

The early sport stripe, coded V6X, is distinguished by the stripe end hanging much lower, almost to the side-marker light, than a standard sport stripe during the production year. This feature is accepted as extremely early and pre-production. The early Hemicuda hardtop also has this unique sport stripe. The normal sport "hockey stripe" tip did not hang down as low.

Rumors Abound

Some of the history that is rumored about this missing Hemicuda convertible is the following: The car lost the hemi engine and was replaced by a slant-6 in the mid-1970s. This car might be in Ohio or Texas. Someone once talked to a guy who owned this car in the 1980s. The last report is that this car was rusty.

I have been collecting information on these cars since 1984 and started the 1970–1971 Plymouth and Dodge E-Body Convertible Registry in 1997. It has taken many years of effort and dedication to collect all the information that I have on these exceptional convertibles.

If you have any information about this car or have heard any rumors, please contact me at cudaized@cudaized.com.

By Wes Eisenschenk

It doesn't make much sense to put a 429 Super Cobra Jet with 3.91 gears into a Ranchero. Of course, if you have to get 100 gallons of ice cream home and into the freezer for your child's birthday party super fast, then there might not be a better option. However, the concept of slamming Ford's most powerful engine into the bay of a pickup really isn't sensible when you have other more capable offerings to transfer that amount of power to the ground. So, why were these animals created? It's simple: because Ford could.

The 429 SCJ Ranchero is just one in a long line of interesting muscle cars and trucks created by auto manufacturers in the 1960s and 1970s. Four-door Hemi Coronets? Check. 440-6 Plymouth Furys? Yes. LS6 El Caminos? Oh, what the heck, sure. So why not stuff Ford's most potent engine into its truck? Makes sense, right?

It's estimated that as few as around 60 of these trucks ultimately were created with this combination across GT and 500 trim levels. The fact that Rancheros and El Caminos are half-car half-truck has created an odd spot in the hobby. Their counterparts, the Torino and Chevelle, typically sell for double in the exact same condition. This unique aspect has allowed collectors the opportunity to own an extremely rare car/truck without breaking the bank. Even so, among Ranchero GT counterparts, the separation between the 429 cars when optioned out isn't much. So what does it take to separate a 429 SCJ Ranchero from the rest? How about if it were one of two 1970 Ranchero Twister Specials?

A Little Background

If you're unfamiliar with the story of the Twister cars, they owe their creation to American Raceways International (ARI). That company created a handful of pace car Mustangs for use at a pair of its local circle tracks. ARI liked the pace cars so it placed an order for 100 specially prepped Mustangs to use for promotional purposes. But before it could finish placing the order, ARI filed for bankruptcy. Ford's Special Promotions Division was tasked with placing these Mustang Mach1s and succeeded through the Kansas City Sales District (DSO 53).

A sales promotion called the Twister Special was created to find outlets for these vehicles. It was determined that Ford and DSO 53 would expand the program and add a fleet of Torinos and some specially prepped Rancheros to the order.

In all, 96 Mustang Mach 1s, 90 Torinos, and an alleged 4 Rancheros were produced. Various websites and respected magazines state that the 4 Rancheros received the Twister Special package with 351C, automatic transmissions, and 3.50 Traction-Lok rear ends. However, like many unsubstantiated stories populating the Internet, these outlets keep perpetuating the story without fact checking. In truth, just 2 Rancheros received the Twister Special package. But here comes the kicker: Both cars were fitted with the 429 SCJ. Accompanying the potent big-block was an automatic transmission and a 3.91 Traction-Lok rear gear for some stump-pulling action. That changes things, doesn't it?

Options

The cars were painted Vermillion and featured a black vinyl Torino bench seat and the GT package. Other options included power front disc brakes, color-keyed racing mirrors, F70X14 belted raised-white-letter tires, tinted glass, and an AM radio. Both cars were identically prepped and are sequential in their VIN designations, yet the completion of their builds was one day apart according to their Marti Reports.

It's hard to say just exactly how the Twister Special graphics package was applied to these Rancheros because no image has ever surfaced of either car. You have to imagine that the side striping featured Ford's Blue Oval on the front fenders, much like the Mach 1s and Torinos, but what was on the door stripe is anyone's guess.

The Mach 1s had "Mach 1" lettering on the door and the Torino had "Cobra" lettering. Does that mean the Ranchero shared that same moniker as its Torino cousin? Who knows? It probably should have just said, "Rare"!

New Homes

One of these Rancheros was delivered to Noller Motors in Topeka, Kansas, and the other was delivered to Southtown Motors in Kansas City, Missouri. Noller Motors survives to this day, but no one

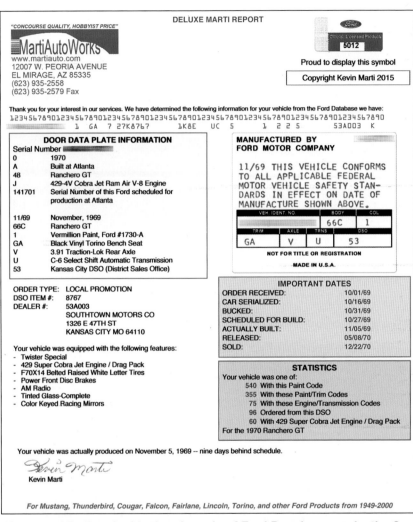

Thank you for your interest in our services. We have determined the following information for your vehicle from the Ford Database we have:

123456789012345678901234567890123456789012345678901234567890123456789 0

1 GA 7 27K8767   1K8E   UC 5   1 2 2 5   53A003   K

DOOR DATA PLATE INFORMATION

Serial Number

0	1970
A	Built at Atlanta
48	Ranchero GT
J	429-4V Cobra Jet Ram Air V-8 Engine
141701	Serial Number of this Ford scheduled for production at Atlanta
11/69	November, 1969
66C	Ranchero GT
1	Vermillion Paint, Ford #1730-A
GA	Black Vinyl Torino Bench Seat
V	3.91 Traction-Lok Rear Axle
U	C-6 Select Shift Automatic Transmission
53	Kansas City DSO (District Sales Office)

MANUFACTURED BY FORD MOTOR COMPANY

11/69 THIS VEHICLE CONFORMS TO ALL APPLICABLE FEDERAL MOTOR VEHICLE SAFETY STAN-DARDS IN EFFECT ON DATE OF MANUFACTURE SHOWN ABOVE.

VEH. IDENT. NO.	BODY	COL
	66C	1

TRIM	AXLE	TRNS	DSO
GA	V	U	53

NOT FOR TITLE OR REGISTRATION

MADE IN U.S.A.

ORDER TYPE: LOCAL PROMOTION
DSO ITEM #: 8767
DEALER #: 53A003
SOUTHTOWN MOTORS CO
1326 E 47TH ST
KANSAS CITY MO 64110

Your vehicle was equipped with the following features:
- Twister Special
- 429 Super Cobra Jet Engine / Drag Pack
- F70X14 Belted Raised White Letter Tires
- Power Front Disc Brakes
- AM Radio
- Tinted Glass-Complete
- Color Keyed Racing Mirrors

IMPORTANT DATES

ORDER RECEIVED:	10/01/69
CAR SERIALIZED:	10/16/69
BUCKED:	10/31/69
SCHEDULED FOR BUILD:	10/27/69
ACTUALLY BUILT:	11/05/69
RELEASED:	05/08/70
SOLD:	12/22/70

STATISTICS

Your vehicle was one of:
- 540 With this Paint Code
- 355 With these Paint/Trim Codes
- 75 With these Engine/Transmission Codes
- 96 Ordered from this DSO
- 60 With 429 Super Cobra Jet Engine / Drag Pack

For the 1970 Ranchero GT

Your vehicle was actually produced on November 5, 1969 -- nine days behind schedule.

Kevin Marti
Kevin Marti

For Mustang, Thunderbird, Cougar, Falcon, Fairlane, Lincoln, Torino, and other Ford Products from 1949-2000

Above and Facing: Is this the pinnacle of Ford Ranchero production? Perhaps. The only differences between these two Twister Rancheros are the build dates and the receiving dealerships. Otherwise they were identically prepped. (Copyright Ford Motor Company and Marti Auto Works)

currently with the company recalls the Ranchero. Southtown Motors, which was located at 1326 East 47th Street in Kansas City, has been out of business for decades. Attempts to find anyone who worked at those two dealerships in 1970 have been futile.

It's unknown what the original purpose was for these two Twister Rancheros, so all we can do is speculate.

DELUXE MARTI REPORT

MartiAutoWorks
www.martiauto.com
12007 W. PEORIA AVENUE
EL MIRAGE, AZ 85335
(623) 935-2558
(623) 935-2579 Fax

Proud to display this symbol

Copyright Kevin Marti 2015

Thank you for your interest in our services. We have determined the following information for your vehicle from the Ford Database we have:

```
1234567890123456789012345678901234567890123456789012345678901234567890
              1 GA  2 27K497S    1KTM  UC  5    1 2 2 5    53H517   K
```

DOOR DATA PLATE INFORMATION	
Serial Number	
0	1970
A	Built at Atlanta
48	Ranchero GT
J	429-4V Cobra Jet Ram Air V-8 Engine
141700	Serial Number of this Ford scheduled for production at Atlanta
11/69	November, 1969
66C	Ranchero GT
1	Vermillion Paint, Ford #1730-A
GA	Black Vinyl Torino Bench Seat
V	3.91 Traction-Lok Rear Axle
U	C-6 Select Shift Automatic Transmission
53	Kansas City DSO (District Sales Office)

MANUFACTURED BY
FORD MOTOR COMPANY

11/69 THIS VEHICLE CONFORMS
TO ALL APPLICABLE FEDERAL
MOTOR VEHICLE SAFETY STAN-
DARDS IN EFFECT ON DATE OF
MANUFACTURE SHOWN ABOVE.

VEH. IDENT. NO.	BODY	COL
	66C	1

TRIM	AXLE	TRNS	DSO
GA	V	U	53

NOT FOR TITLE OR REGISTRATION

MADE IN U.S.A.

ORDER TYPE: STOCK
DSO ITEM #: 497S
DEALER #: 53H517
NOLLER MOTORS INC.
TOPEKA AVE AT 23RD
TOPEKA KS 66603

Your vehicle was equipped with the following features:
- Twister Special
- 429 Super Cobra Jet Engine / Drag Pack
- F70X14 Belted Raised White Letter Tires
- Power Front Disc Brakes
- AM Radio
- Tinted Glass-Complete
- Color Keyed Racing Mirrors

IMPORTANT DATES	
ORDER RECEIVED:	10/01/69
CAR SERIALIZED:	10/16/69
BUCKED:	10/31/69
SCHEDULED FOR BUILD:	10/27/69
ACTUALLY BUILT:	11/04/69
RELEASED:	12/29/69
SOLD:	11/30/70

STATISTICS
Your vehicle was one of:
540 With this Paint Code
355 With these Paint/Trim Codes
75 With these Engine/Transmission Codes
96 Ordered from this DSO
60 With 429 Super Cobra Jet Engine / Drag Pack
For the 1970 Ranchero GT

Your vehicle was actually produced on November 4, 1969 -- eight days behind schedule.

Kevin Marti
Kevin Marti

For Mustang, Thunderbird, Cougar, Falcon, Fairlane, Lincoln, Torino, and other Ford Products from 1949-2000

I hope that with this disclosure some information will be unveiled on these two very special Rancheros, created through DSO 53 in the fall of 1969.

By Andrew Hack

A s has been reported, Ford was likely planning both a Boss 302 and a Boss 351 for 1971. However, a 1970 SCCA rule change allowed the use of larger displacement engines, eliminating the need for a small-block Boss. Moreover, with all that was happening with auto insurance, prices on muscle cars, the creation of the new-for-1971 EPA engine certification rules, the slowing of muscle car sales in general, and the fact that Ford was about to announce the cessation of its corporate sponsorship of all racing, the future of muscle Mustangs was in serious turmoil.

VIN Changes

In fact, this 1971 Boss 302 was probably built just hours before the corporate decision to cancel Boss 302 production for 1971. Kevin Marti has previously reported that eight 1971 Boss 302 Mustangs were scheduled to be built at Dearborn and Metuchen. Two were actually "bucked" at Metuchen, but canceled before they were built, making 1F02G100053 the last regular production Boss 302 Mustang built, and the only one ever built for the 1971 model year.

Dressed as a plain fastback 1971 Mustang, I figured I would take a chance on purchasing this car with its very early VIN sequence. And my hunch paid off. (Photo Courtesy Andy Hack)

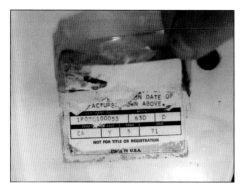

Viewing the tag underneath the tag reveals the all-important "G" in the fifth spot on the door tag. This "G" confirms that this car at one time was set to have a Boss 302 block between the fenders. (Photo Courtesy Andy Hack)

According to the official Ford documentation obtained from Kevin Marti, at some point following the Las Vegas Car Show, the vehicle was transported to the Los Angeles Ford assembly plant. Ford issued several revised billing invoices and the VIN changed over that series of documents. Initially, the car was invoiced as "1F05R," making it a Mach I/Boss 351. The final VIN appearing on the vehicle was 1F02H100053, after an official Ford communication memo in February 1971 from Dearborn Assembly to Los Angeles Assembly instructed the removal of Boss-specific markings, and replacement of the G-coded dash VIN tab and door sticker (patent plate), among other items. It is uncertain as to the specific time and place of removal of the Boss 302 "G"-code engine.

Trim Differences

The VIN change on this car may explain the unusual listing of the total for 1971 Boss 351 production as 1805/06. That dual number has been often published, but to my knowledge never explained.

Subsequently, the car was likely used for the introduction of the Boss 351 later that year. All of the identical "non-regular production" oddities are found on both cars. The unique combination of Boss and Mach I trims appear on this car as well as the Ford Boss 351 publicity car, as photographed in the desert with the mountains in the background.

In those photos, you can see where the 02 decal had been removed and replaced with an irregular 51 on the decklid and fenders. The two cars have a few other differences, such as replacing the Magnum 500s with the Shelby Magstar wheels. Also, a non-standard black stripe appears along the top edge of the decklid.

The decklid on my car still has a faint OSS 3 under the paint, almost completely obliterated, except for the effect left by the vinyl adhesive from the original decals. It seems as though you can never get rid of that stuff completely, especially when Ford was only reimbursing $75 for the removal of all Boss-specific markings, as stated in Ford's official communication memo. The actual decals are gone. However, a Boss 351 stripe is still on the lower decklid, which has been painted over. It is quite prominent under the Grabber Yellow paint.

The stripe that ran along the top rear edge of the decklid is not apparent at all and may have simply been added to the photos.

Similarly, the 1F02G door tag was only partially peeled from the top down, then broken off jaggedly, just above the pertinent data, before someone stopped and slapped the new tag over the old one. These are security tags that are not easily removed without deteriorating into a series of "VOID VOID VOID" markings, which explains the lack of persistence in removing the old tag. I certainly had difficulty lifting the new tag to reveal the old one, without ruining the top tag.

With the Boss 302 engine replaced, and the car's exterior markings "de-Bossed," the car was then displayed on the showroom floor of Wilson Ford, in Huntington Beach, California. The original purchaser was a young woman who was originally told that Ford had not released the car for sale. She was also told the vehicle was a 1970½ Mustang with non-standard equipment. This actually proved to be correct. Eventually, the dealer received the green light for the sale, and the woman bought the car. Astonishingly, she kept and drove the vehicle until 1999. During that time, the car was basically maintained and driven, with one partial repaint.

Sight Unseen

The next owner had the car from late 1999 until I purchased it in late 2004, when I came across an online auction of this Grabber Yellow Sportsroof. The VIN was listed as 1F02H100053. A few photos of the vehicle existed, and one shot in particular was almost identical to the old photo of the 1971 prototype. I told my wife, "This car could pass for the 1971 Boss prototype." I also laughed at that whole idea. After all, that old photo of the Grabber Yellow 1971 Boss 351 prototype had become such an icon, it certainly seemed unlikely to still exist, let alone that I would be the one to find it.

However, the low 100053 sequence number captivated me. The auction ended with no sale, so I decided to pursue the car. Regardless of any actual rarity, it was exactly what I was looking for and it would be a great reference for reassembling my other basket-case Boss 351 project car, which was disassembled when I bought it.

I wanted a fastback 351C 4-speed with Traction-Loc and this one even had the staggered-shock competition suspension. Although it was not a Mach 1, it had all of the Mach 1 markings, equipment, and interior. I assumed it was probably a "made-up car," but the lack of a NASA Ram-Air hood just didn't make any sense. That was usually the first item on the cloning agenda. I guess I was still secretly hoping that I had found an urban legend, the 1971 Boss 302 that everyone agreed never actually existed.

Although the intake, carb, and exhaust had been changed, the owner told me he kept the original parts. The car even had a tilt column from the factory. He did not know the car's history but had been told that only one woman owned it before him. It already had all of the Mach 1 trim when he bought it, and he stated he had not changed anything about the car's appearance. This car was just sounding too good to pass up.

The seller seemed straightforward and honest, so against sound better judgment I bought the car, sight unseen and without an inspection. With nothing in my hands, and a hole in my bank account, I waited about two weeks for the hauler to arrive. I instructed him to include all of the original parts, which he did.

Delivery and Inspection

When the car was loaded in San Francisco, the seller tried to call me, but I was not home. He left a message and raised his telephone in the air, so I could hear the engine revving through the Flowmasters, as the Mustang was driven up the ramps. He said, "Hear that, Andy? That's your Mustang going up the ramps. It's on its way to you." That was a really cool and memorable moment. In hindsight, I wish I had kept that taped message.

The car was shipped from San Francisco in December 2004. It was 15 degrees in Wisconsin when it arrived. Fortunately, I had instructed the seller to drain the "straight water" out of the radiator and put in an antifreeze mixture, and luckily, he did so. When the car arrived, it looked very good and was generally as described. At this point, I was relieved and happy with the results of my gamble.

With the car now in hand, I began to examine the trim inconsistencies. I put the car on a lift and was amazed at the cleanliness of the undercarriage. The ID tags on the 4-speed and differential were intact and were "numbers correct." In fact, everything seemed very original to this car. Even the underside of the front fenders was rust-free, and I was able to confirm the VIN stamped into the top of the shock towers.

I found two small rusty areas on the bottom of the rear quarters just behind the wheel housings. The car had typical rust-through from within the trunk drop areas and also the typical rust around the taillight assemblies. It did not appear this Mustang had ever been disassembled. All of the sealants still looked factory applied.

Further Research

Was this the 1971 Boss 302 Mustang that Ford never built?

If this had been a Wisconsin car, I would have guessed it to be only about five years old. It was, in fact, 34 years old. I still wondered about the car's low serial number and unusual conglomeration of options and trim. I then sent an email inquiry to Marti Autoworks requesting an Eminger invoice for the car. I was informed that Marti had not located any information for that VIN, but would let me know if it was later located. I was disappointed but even more curious.

Meanwhile, I called Ford Motor Company Historical Services for a report on the car. Ford sent a short letter that listed the date of production and the options ordered. I learned the car was invoiced with the 351-2V and Toploader 4-speed, even though several people told me this combination was not available in 1971; the 1971 Ford Dealer's Book also confirmed this fact. Ford's letter report made no mention of anything special about this car and certainly made no mention of a Boss 302, nor the Mach 1 trim package. Still, I was unconvinced there was nothing special about this car, number 53.

During the next 12 months, I did some minor maintenance, but did not undertake any modifications to the vehicle. In the summer of 2006 I received an email from Marti Autoworks stating that Kevin Marti had been trying to telephone me. He had some important information about my Mustang's history.

It was at that point I started to suspect what I had previously laughed at. Did I find and purchase either a 1971 Boss 302 or the 1971 Boss 351 prototype seen in the Ford promotional ads in 1970?

Changing History

It took a very long week and a couple of phone calls before I was able to reach Kevin Marti. When I finally spoke with him, he stated that he wanted to make sure that I knew what an important piece of Ford automotive history this Mustang represented. This car was indeed the only 1971 Boss 302 to be built before the program had been canceled.

We discussed the question of whether it had either a Boss 302 or Boss 351 engine when Wilson Ford eventually sold it. The last invoice revision showed a 351C-2V, or H-code, engine. It was unclear as to when the Boss 302 G-code engine had been removed. Kevin gave me a quick tutorial on what I should do to try to find out more about the car's history. He asked about the Mustang's current condition and where I found it. I took notes as he gave me pointers in rapid succession.

One of the last things we discussed was the existence of any physical markings on the car that Ford might have missed when removing the Boss markings. That's when I mentioned the thicker door tag that appeared to be placed on top of another tag. He asked me to let him know what I find, if I later lifted the tag.

After that exhilarating conversation with Kevin, I just sat in my chair and tried to absorb what I had just been told. I had actually found and acquired the only regular production 1971 Boss 302 ever built by Ford Motor Company. The car that never existed, or so we all believed.

A few weeks later I successfully peeled off the top sticker and found most of the original tag underneath. This was the "smoking gun." It clearly showed VIN 1F02G100053. This car was definitely a G-code Boss 302 build. The 1971 Boss 302 Mustang was a reality, and at least one rolled off the line in Dearborn on the first day of regular production for 1971. The history of the Boss 302 Mustang had just changed.

The irony here is that I own two rare cars in one. Being an H-code 4-speed Toploader car also puts this machine in one-of-one company. (Photo Courtesy Andy Hack)

This was also the last Boss 302 Mustang ever built, period. It was then the first 1971 Boss 351 R code for 1971, and the only 1F05R Mach1/Boss ever built. And finally, after the engine change, it was the only 1971 H-code/4-speed Toploader combination built.

Researching Previous Owner History

To anyone who grew up in the late 1960s and early 1970s, the songs "Surf City" and "Surfin' USA" usually bring back fond memories. I'm no different, and when I learned this Mustang was originally purchased in Huntington Beach, California, the real Surf City USA, I was even more entranced.

I found out that Wilson Ford was long gone, but several different Ford dealerships existed at that location in the past 35 years, and one was still doing business there. I called, but understandably no one could provide me with any information. This car had been built, displayed, and sold more than 35 years ago, and everyone connected with its history has probably already received a gold retirement watch or had "gone to the big R&D department in the sky." I started searching the Internet for information but kept finding the same few facts: "Ford canceled the Boss 302 in 1971, replacing it with the Boss 351" or "Ford pulled out of racing in 1970." Sometimes I could find photos. I often found the same few pictures of the Grabber Yellow publicity car from mid-1970, with the same man and woman posing with the car and mountains in the background.

Eventually, I learned the names of the only two previous owners of the vehicle. The first owner kept the vehicle until 1999. The second owner sold the car to me. I was able to locate and exchange pleasant emails with the original owner, who confirmed some of what I already knew about the car, such as date and place of purchase, and the car's original appearance and equipment. It was just plain luck that this car was kept fairly original by both owners for so many years. It was extremely lucky that I was able to determine its hidden secret identity, which Ford must have never expected nor intended to be unearthed, especially 34 years later.

When the car was first discovered, the Internet message boards "lit up" with both nay-sayers and praisers. Most have just been awed by the historical aspect of the find, and if they are Mustang people, they know how long this car has been thought to be just an urban legend of Ford Mustang history. Personally, I feel as though this car is a real, tangible connection to a moment in time when the names Henry Ford II, Bunkie Knudsen, and Larry Shinoda defined Ford Motor Company and their famous muscle cars.

The Specs

The car was built on the Dearborn assembly line on August 3, 1970, a Monday and the first day of regular production for the 1971 models.

It was built as VIN 1F02G100053 and is the only regular production 1971 Boss 302 built, as confirmed by Kevin Marti's official database.

The Gate Release invoice on August 4, 1970, states: "Ship To Convention Center, Las Vegas, NV." The invoice also states: "Sold To: Ford Marketing Corporation, Los Angeles District."

It was shipped to Las Vegas for display at an introductory 1971 model car show. After the Las Vegas show, the vehicle was likely the one used for the Boss 351 prototype photo car, shown in the Ford promotional materials with Magstar wheels and modified decklid striping.

Wilson Ford of Huntington Beach, California, eventually sold the vehicle to the first private owner in March 1971, with VIN changed to 1F02H100053. The Boss 302 "G-code" engine had been replaced with a 351C-2V H-code engine at Ford's direction.

Consistent with the original 1969 and 1970 Boss 302 cars, the following items are still present:

- Original 1F02G100053 door tag, under the later 1F02H100053 replacement tag
- Wide-ratio Toploader 4-speed manual transmission, tagged "RUG AV1," the same code used on the 1970 Boss 302. It was not even an available option in 1971 on H-code 351C-2V cars. According to Kevin Marti's book, *Mustang by the Numbers*, only one H-code 4-speed was built in 1971, making this a "one-of-one" vehicle on that basis also
- 31-spline "N" case 3.50 locking rear axle with Daytona pinion support, the heaviest-duty differential available that year and standard on all earlier 1970 Boss 302 cars. Interestingly, the later released 1971 Boss 351 cars used a 3.91 as the standard gear ratio
- The differential metal tag is still present and reads "WFD-F2 0GC 3L50," which is the correct tag for a 1971 Boss 302 specification car

- Hurst 4-speed performance shifter and linkage
- Competition suspension with staggered rear shocks, including front and rear anti-sway bars
- Tachometer and full instrumentation
- The original Magnum 500 "small center hole" wheels, as were also used on the prior 1970 year Boss 302 cars
- Color-keyed dual side-view racing mirrors
- Boss 302–style blackout hood, without hood locks or NASA Ram-Air, however. Yet, the special NASA "flat coil" hood springs are still present, and the earlier invoices for this car do list the NASA Ram-Air hood. It may have been removed for the "non-Ram-Air" publicity photos in the desert. This definitely gave the car that 1969 Boss 302 look, which may have been the intent
- Grille sportlamps
- Three telltale holes in the right shock tower where the rev limiter may have once resided
- Color-keyed lower front spoiler
- The power steering pump bracket is drilled for the placement of the power steering fluid cooler used only on high-performance engines, as in Boss cars

Additionally, and uniquely, all of the 1971 Mach I trims were also applied when built, including the following:

- Honeycomb tail panel
- Flip-down gas cap
- Urethane color-coded front bumper (the 1971 Boss 351 came with a chrome front bumper standard equipment)
- Exhaust extensions through the rear valance
- Mach I Sports Interior Group (black with gray inserts, upholstery)
- Side lower-body decor strips (aluminum strips along the top edge of the lower body blackout). These aluminum strips were factory painted black, unlike the Mach I, but consistent with the official Ford publicity photos of the "new" 1971 Boss 351. This also makes it likely to be the car in the official publicity photos

To my knowledge, no other regular production Mustang of any model year has ever been built as both a Boss and a Mach I, except the vehicle depicted in the Ford publicity photos, and this car.

In addition, this Boss was ordered with the following options:

- Full-length console with clock
- Tinted glass
- Power front disc brakes (rear drum)
- Power steering, with Saginaw gearbox used on Boss and Mach I cars
- Sport-deck fold-down rear seat
- AM radio
- Tilt steering wheel
- F60 x 15-inch wide-oval belted tires with raised white letters
- Exterior paint code "D" Grabber Yellow with black contrasting stripes

VIN and Code Details

It should be noted for those unfamiliar with Mustang VINs and body styles that a standard fastback or sportsroof Mustang body style is an 02 body code, hence the 1F02 preface in the VIN. The Mach 1 body style is the same fastback body, but has Mach 1 trims and so 05 is in the VIN, and a 1F05 prefix is in the VIN.

The Boss 302 cars, not being Mach 1s, were designated as 02 sportsroofs and carried a G code for the Boss 302 engine in the VIN, hence 1F02G. The later-released Boss 351 cars used an R engine code, so a 1F02R is in the VIN.

Because no Mustang could be both a Mach 1 and a Boss, there could be no 1F05R or 1F05G VIN, as both G and R engine codes were reserved for Boss-only builds.

And yet, a Mach1/Boss is exactly how this car was produced, documented, and displayed at the Las Vegas Convention Center in late 1970, and in the official 1971 Ford publicity photos.

Against the Odds

Promotional photos of a Medium Metallic Blue/Argent Silver Boss 302 are shown in *Super Stock* magazine during the fall of 1970. In an email I received from a fairly well-known engineer who worked for Ford in Dearborn in 1970, he stated that he had an opportunity to drive the blue car on Ford's test track. He believes that car was probably crushed because it lacked safety and other specifications necessary for sale to the public. However, enthusiasts should still keep an eye out for that blue car. Afterall, my lost Boss was thought not to exist too.

By Mark Meekins with Jeff Helms
of the National Chevelle Owner's Association

You have probably heard of the limited-production 1965 Malibu SS 396 Chevelle, commonly known by its regular-production option (RPO) code of Z16. And you may know that the reported production total of Z16s was 201 cars. What you may not know is that, as legend has it, that total consisted of 200 coupes and just *one* convertible.

A great deal has been researched and published about the Z16 option, including extensive treatment in a series of articles I wrote that were published during the 1990s in *The Chevelle Report* (the official publication of the National Chevelle Owner's Association, NCOA). Therefore, the details of development and marketing of the Z16 need not be detailed further here. (If you are interested in reading more about the Z16 Chevelle, please visit any of these websites: national-chevelle-owners-association.com, chevellereport.com, z16chevelle.com.)

But at least a little background is in order to set the stage.

Z16 Debut

In early 1965, Chevrolet Motor Division released a limited-production run of some very unusual Chevelles. Their primary purpose was to serve as the premier showcase for the brand-new Mark IV 396 engine. The program included an extensive marketing campaign, with road test information in numerous contemporary automotive publications, and high-profile racers and celebrities were given use of many of the cars for marketing purposes.

Z16 production was initially slated for 200 coupes. All were to be gussied up with a fabulous array of creature comforts, special ornamentation, and performance and handling equipment, in addition to the new mid-year Mark IV 396 engine. Chevrolet wanted the Z16 to not only draw attention to the new 396, but also to be distinct and more pleasurable than the typical Chevelle.

The Z16 option included the following:

- RPO "L37" 396 engine (rated at 375 hp with hydraulic lifters)
- M20 4-speed
- Special 3.31:1 12-bolt rear axle
- Special boxed convertible-style frame
- Power-assisted 11-inch drum brakes (adapted from the full-size Chevy passenger car)
- Large-diameter front sway bar
- Rear sway bar with boxed lower control arms
- Special radiator with fan shroud
- Power steering with a special-ratio gearbox
- 160-mph speedometer
- High-redline tachometer with top-of-dash clock
- Padded dash
- AM-FM radio with the new Chevrolet four-speaker Multiplex stereo adapter
- Deluxe front and rear seat belts
- Remote-control outside rearview mirror
- Simulated mag-wheel hubcaps mounted on special 14x6-inch riveted rims with gold stripe
- Firestone or Goodyear tires along with a very special trim package on the rear of the car, making it distinct from all other 1965 Chevelles

Coupes, Sedans and Convertibles

Two so-called prototype coupes were assembled at the Baltimore assembly plant originally as 327 cars and then sent to Chevrolet Engineering in Warren, Michigan, to be transformed into Z16s in approximately December 1964. These "prototype" Z16s had all manner of handmade and sample Z16 components and served to test fit and tweak all the special Z16 parts before regular production began. One of those cars is still in existence, the other reportedly having been destroyed.

All regular-production Z16 coupes were constructed at the Kansas City assembly plant from mid-February 1965 through the second week of April 1965, an eight- to nine-week production period. They were not built in a sequential format, but intermingled with regular Chevelle model production.

In addition, two other special 1965 396 Chevelles were also built at the Kansas City plant near or after the end of Z16 coupe production.

One was a 300-series two-door post sedan with the L78 396/425HP solid-lifter engine, hooked up to a rare 1965 M22 4-speed. It was not considered a Z16, but was a COPO car (and the very first performance COPO Chevelle). This car still exists and is verified by the original window sticker.

The other car, the subject of this article, is the legendary Z16 convertible. This is the missing link of Z16 production, the "1" in the "201."

The Hunt Is On

Although I had already become very interested in Z16s and completed a lot of research by that time, I had not heard of a Z16 convertible existing until the mid-1980s. I was contacted by a Z16 owner from the Midwest who shared information about his own Crocus Yellow car and gave details about how he had obtained original Z16 paperwork from the son of a Chevrolet dealer in Florida.

The dealer was fairly prominent and had ordered a Z16. A factory rep visited shortly after the car arrived and left copies of all the paperwork he had on these special cars. Thankfully, the documents were never discarded and are now the basis for many reported Z16 facts and figures.

Then the caller dropped another bombshell. He confided that Chevrolet had built one Z16 convertible and that he knew the first owner and the man's place of employment. This would explain why statistics showed 201 cars instead of the 200 mentioned in early publicity materials. So I was on the hunt!

I called the gentleman's workplace and managed to speak with him. He had been a Pontiac engineer and worked at the GM Tech Center when he had the chance to buy the Z16 convertible through a Warren, Michigan, Chevy dealer. (All fleet cars had to be processed through a local dealer for employee purchase.)

It was not painted one of the standard Z16 exterior color choices (Regal Red, Crocus Yellow, or Tuxedo Black) and did not have any of the standard Z16 interior colors either (black, red, or white). Instead, the Z16 convertible was painted Sierra Tan, with a Fawn interior and a beige convertible top.

Two NCOA members, who were also employed at the GM Tech Center in 1965, confirmed the existence of the car and its unusual color combination. They each independently saw the Z16 convertible on the GM campus and being tested in the dyno shop.

Also, a post on a Chevy forum more than a decade ago by a gentleman who was a teenager in 1965 and was friends with the original owner of the car reported that he received many hot rides in the Z16 convertible. He also reported the same information regarding the original color combo of the car.

The first owner reported that he kept the car for only about a year before selling it to a persistent young man who wanted to own a car with the new 396 engine. Shortly afterward, the car and its new owner disappeared from the area, so the original owner had no leads to pursue from there. However, he had heard that the car had been involved in a serious accident and was destroyed.

But the car did turn up later in 1969 as the subject of inquiry in a letter to the editor of a car hobbyist magazine. The writer had questions about his 1965 Chevelle convertible with a 396 engine and referenced other features consistent with Z16 options. The letter was signed with an unusual surname and listed the city and state of his residence. After another NCOA member sent a copy of this article to me in 1989, I was on the hunt again.

The Mysterious Mr. Smith

After nearly a week of searches of city and county records and many phone calls, I was able to determine from the gentleman's parents that (for possibly suspicious reasons) the man had changed his name some years earlier. But the parents were kind (or perhaps foolish) enough to provide his new name and home phone number to a stranger. For the rest of this story, I'll just refer to him as "Mr. Smith."

I called the number provided by Mr. Smith's parents, and his wife answered the call. After I explained my mission, she said Mr. Smith had gotten into some trouble and changed his name years earlier, and she was surprised I had found him. She reported that she had never seen the Z16 convertible, but that she had heard her husband talk about it from time to time. She thought he had sold or parked the car around 1972.

To add to the cloak and dagger, she reported that she was packing her bags and leaving Mr. Smith the next day because of his shady past. A call 24 hours later would have missed her altogether!

The wife reluctantly confided that Mr. Smith ran a garage and gave me the number, but only after I assured her that I wouldn't tell Mr. Smith how I found it.

A call to Mr. Smith with an introduction initially received a cordial response. I explained that I liked and worked on Chevelles, and a pleasant chat ensued. But Mr. Smith's next response was quite a surprise when I asked him about the Z16 convertible. Mr. Smith angrily asked how I had found his number and name, proclaimed that he didn't own such a car and had never owned one, and shouted that he was through talking and demanded that I never call him again. I don't know what his name change was meant to hide that upset him so much, but that was the end of that particular lead.

Owner Number Two

Fast forward to 2010, when I fielded a call from a gentleman searching for parts for the restoration of a 1965 Chevelle convertible with a 396 engine. After a lengthy conversation, and after asking all the right questions about the car, and getting all the "right" answers (including the special trim, speedometer, colors, engine stamp code, and numerous other details), I left the conversation convinced that the real Z16 convertible had been found.

This gentleman shared the following story about how he acquired the car and about its components. More than three decades ago he was traveling some side roads as he returned from a long-distance trip. He stumbled upon a 1957 Chevy parked in a yard. It was for sale, and he was a big fan of this model so he stopped. The owner said he would only sell the 1957 on the condition that the wrecked 1965 Chevelle convertible in the back yard be hauled away as well. The man didn't want the "newer" car, but he agreed to the condition in order to get the 1957.

Both cars were then trailered out-of-state to the new owner's business property, which included some cavernous warehouses. The 1965 convertible was parked in a back corner of one of them and was largely forgotten as other cars and business occupied the man's time. He did use it a couple of times to test fit an engine and headers, but that was about it. However, about six years ago, he started to focus on the car.

The convertible had been wrecked in the front and had some rear damage too. He referred to it as a "tan" car with remnants of a "tan" bucket-seat interior. It had the special Z16 moldings on the decklid, the 160 speedo assembly, and all the heavy-duty drivetrain and suspension components.

Because of the front-end damage, the 396 engine had been removed, but thankfully it wasn't discarded. It was stored in the trunk, with various pieces stashed in the interior. It was a true IX-stamped engine (the special suffix code for the Z16 L37 engine) and had the partial serial number of the convertible stamped on the pad.

So he had a mostly complete car that was just beaten up a bit. Fortunately, the 30-plus years in dry storage had helped preserve the remains. However, it has yet to return to the asphalt. A slow restoration of the car is in progress.

If this last piece of the puzzle pans out, it will show that at least two owners had the car off the road for decades, which would explain why the 1965 Z16 convertible hadn't been seen in nearly 40 years.

Confirming Documentation

In any event, the Z16 convertible is not a fairy tale as some doubters have claimed. I have, based on my research, believed the truth of the Z16 convertible's existence since the 1980s. Even if the real car had been destroyed, an owner in 1965, and multiple independent witness accounts, verified the car's existence, plus factory documentation supports the car's existence.

For those who doubt that a Z16 convertible ever could have existed, the first question is, "Why not?" We've all heard the verified stories of the one-of-one pink 1964 Corvette, which was retrofitted with a 396 in 1965, and the one-of-one 1968 Z28 convertible, both built at the behest of top-level GM executives. If those special orders were possible, then why not a Z16 convertible?

Given the facts reported from 1965 (that the Z16 convertible had special colors, spent time at the GM Tech Center, and was eventually sold through the same Detroit dealership that prepped and delivered executives' cars), it is not a stretch to believe that someone high up at Chevrolet commissioned the car's construction, but then lost interest in it in favor of another toy, resulting in the car being made available for sale to a Tech Center employee.

And even if you ignore the latest report about the possible survival of the car, substantial factory documentation supports the contention that at least one Z16 convertible did exist. I have amassed a sizeable library of Chevelle facts and figures documentation from a variety of sources, including numerous factory documents that state that the Z16 option was available as both a hardtop model (13837) and convertible model (13867).

The earliest paperwork is a Mark IV engine unit parts list, with an original date of November 27, 1964, and a revision date of January 12, 1965. This sheet comes from the Engineering Parts List of Chevrolet Motor Division, Engineering Center in Warren, Michigan. The data shows the part name as: "Engine Assembly as shipped, part number 3872715, RPO L37 (Z16 engine only) on 13837 (SS sport coupe) - 13867 (SS convertible) used only with RPO Z16."

This engineering list has two other sheets with Z16 convertible production data. Both are from April 1965. One is a new engineering unit parts list with a description of the RPO numbers. It has an original date of February 17, 1965, and a revision date of April 1, 1965, with a list of items, including "RPO Z16 Special Sport Coupe & Convertible."

The other sheet is from Chevrolet Tonawanda Product Engineering Department reissued on April 26, 1965. It is a 1965 M4 engine identification (built at Tonawanda) list for all models, including the RPO codes and the suffix ID codes. At the center of this sheet appears: "A Body (13800) Special Sport/Convertible Trans. LD and Holley carburetor" with "engine number 3872715 assigned to RPO L37" and suffix code "IX," which is the Z16 engine code.

I also have a 26-page bulletin containing all technical data supplied by the manufacturer, Chevrolet Motor Division: AMA [Automobile Manufacturers Association] Specifications - Passenger Car - Chevelle RPO Z16. It is dated February 22, 1965. Many sections in this data list model "13867" (which is the model code for a Super Sport convertible), alongside the coupe model number of "13837."

The final document in my collection is the Chevrolet Accumulative Production Report - 1965 Models through August 31, 1965, Final 1965 Model Year Report, which details totals for all models. Under the RPO section for Chevelles is "Z16 Special Sport Coupe and Convertible Equipment* options - 201."

The asterisk note at the bottom of the page stated, "Z16 Entered Production February, 1965. Production limited to 201."

In Conclusion

So, more than enough factory documents state that the Z16 option was available as both a hardtop and convertible model. However, no one has yet to see any documentation (or any other form of proof) produced by any of the naysayers to establish that one was not built or could not have been built.

By Wes Eisenschenk

Mike Dolence, like many of his contemporaries, was a budding muscle car fan and owner in the 1960s. One day in 1965, his brother picked him up in his all-new Impala Super Sport, which had the freshly produced 396 with 325 ponies on tap. According to Mike, his brother took the Chevy to the track, where, with just a few modifications, they were able to dip the car into the high 13s. Mike told his brother that if Chevy ever offered the 396 in a Nova he would be first in line to scoop one up.

That day came in August 1968. Pressure from Dodge and its 383-equipped Darts made dropping a big-block into a compact a viable option for big performance. Chevrolet relented and began offering the 396 in its freshly designed Nova. Of the 901 big-block Novas built, 667 carried L78 power.

Mike drove to the nearest dealership, Merit Chevrolet in St. Paul, Minnesota, and began to study three such equipped Novas parked on the lot. Mike noted that all three of these cars were L78 equipped; two had bucket seat cars and one had a bench seat.

Seafrost Green is a rare color for any Chevy muscle car, let alone an L78 1968 Nova SS. With just 667 L78 copies made, it's safe to say that Seafrost Green makes this car even more unique. (Photo Courtesy Mike Dolence)

As if it weren't enough to have the most potent engine under the hood in stock configuration, why not throw a Corvette Tri-Power into the mix? (Photo Courtesy Mike Dolence)

Chevrolet didn't offer an automatic in the L78 Nova until a special batch of 50 cars was created for Dick Harrell, which made the 4-speed the only option at the time.

Mike had asked to test drive the cars and was abruptly declined by the sales manager. The manager's rationale was that these were too potent to allow test drives. So, with little more than just sitting behind all three of the cars' steering wheels and pretending to drive, Mike settled on the bench-seat car. He felt that the buckets were too tight and restricted movement too much.

Mike chose the 4.56-geared, 4-speed SS Nova in a very rare color, Seafrost Green. Mike's car came equipped with a black vinyl top, power disc brakes, AM radio, tinted glass, exterior décor package, heavy-duty battery, and the L78 powerplant. After financing and insurance through Merit, Mike paid the bill of $4,624.80 and drove his Nova home for the first time.

The Sale

I've never driven a 4.56-geared L78, but from all accounts, it's something akin to strapping yourself onto a rhino that has the speed of a cheetah. To say Mike was glad the car had power disc brakes is an understatement. One day at work in the Sears service department, Mike's co-worker made him an offer that he couldn't refuse. The co-worker was looking to replace the Tri-Power setup on his 1967 Corvette with a 4-barrel version. Mike made the deal happily and swapped the setup, straight up.

Looking back on things, the car's salesman must have put the fear of God into him; Mike never took the car to the track. He was

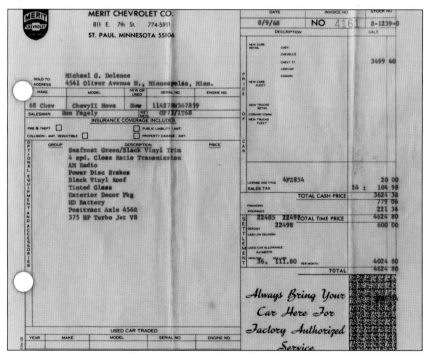

Paperwork is one of the key components that drive up prices on muscle cars. It's a good thing and lucky for this Nova that Mike kept his original bill of sale when he purchased this car. It was the VIN on the receipt that helped track down the current owner in June 2015. (Photo Courtesy Mike Dolence)

afraid that he would hurt the engine if he did, even though he often wonders how the Nova would have performed with that setup. Mike put 16,000 miles on the odometer, and in late 1971 he sold the car. He regrets it to this day.

The lucky buyer was Don Johnson of Anoka, Minnesota. Don had already had a consistent lineup of Chevrolet performance vehicles. The first had been an L79 1965 Chevelle and then came a brand-new 1967 Camaro SS. After having a midsize and a pony car, Don felt it was time to see what it was like to sit behind the wheel of a big-block compact.

His recollections are similar to Mike's. When the car wasn't digging for traction, it was blazing through the gears, laying waste to everything on the streets from 427 Corvettes to Shelby Mustangs.

Don enjoyed the Nova so much that he purchased a 1969 Nova SS L78 as a companion. The second one was black with bucket seats. Don eventually sold the Novas and purchased a new 1971 Camaro Z/28, which he still has.

With the original powertrain missing the current owner opted for a 502 crate Chevy and some other performance modifications. The new color on the Nova is Black Cherry. (John Wilcher Photo)

Another Sale

Don sold the car to a kid who was attending Elk River High School in Minnesota around 1973. We can all speculate what a kid would be doing with an L78, 4.56-geared Tri-Power Nova. Most of it bad. However, many of these cars made it through the muscle car era parked with a hurt engine or something else that made the car undriveable. Some other guys actually had the forethought to park their cars and take good care of them. Weird, huh?

One thing is for sure: A 1968 Seafrost Nova SS with this driveline is certainly a rare beast. And with a Corvette Tri-power adorning the intake, you can rest assured that you will never see another car like it.

Final Owner

As this book went to press, the Nova has been located and accounted for. In the mid-2000s, a woman in Faribault, Minnesota, discovered it. Her father in Savannah, Georgia, was looking for a 1968 car, so she contacted him. He purchased the Nova for $8,000 and modified the car because it was missing the original L78.

CHAPTER THREE

Race Cars

A n old saying from Henry Ford is, "Auto racing began 5 minutes after the second car was built." Maybe the greatest era from a racing standpoint was the 1960s. Sure General Motors had its racing ban, but that didn't stop folks from racing them. Many of these cars have become iconic staples in the history of the muscle car.

Based on sheer volume, factory race cars are viewed as rare. At one time the Big Three and AMC all competed in the three separate disciplines that were the top of their series in the country: NASCAR, NHRA, and Trans-Am. The cars separated into two categories: those that competed and those that were built for homologation so the manufacturers could participate in those series.

For example, the championship-winning 1970 Boss 302 driven by Parnelli Jones would be worth at least 10 to 20 times more than the homologation version built for public consumption, and those homologation versions are worth triple a standard Mustang fastback. The 1970 Boss Mustangs are valuable but not rare.

In contrast, the 1970 Trans-Am Boss Mustangs are extremely valuable and extremely rare. The reason 1970 Boss Mustangs are valuable is a reflection of success of their Trans-Am counterparts. Oh yeah, they're pretty nice looking cars too.

Race cars received alterations to go faster. Although these cars didn't typically see the use and abuse of their street counterparts, they were subjected to severe modifications causing massive changes to chassis and body parts.

Much like celebrity-owned iron, these cars had the allure of being driven by racing personalities, including Bill "Grumpy" Jenkins, Hubert Platt, Parnelli Jones, and Richard Petty. When these cars have been discovered the drivers often assisted in verifying the authenticity, or to the chagrin of the owner, denying the car's lineage.

Race cars found with odometers still in the dash usually have low mileage, a tribute to their owners keeping them off the streets after their lives on the dragstrips and racetracks. Thankfully, many magazines chronicled racing and sometimes made mention of a car's history.

The 1970 Boss Trans-Am cars were carried over into the 1971 racing season. The number 15 car driven by Parnelli Jones started on the outside pole for the rain-soaked Trans-Am race at Lime Rock. The car's last campaign finished with a DNF. (Photo Courtesy Rick Kopec)

By Wes Eisenschenk

On October 20, 1964, Chrysler sent out a notice through its news bureau announcing the revised and updated Plymouth Super Stock 426 Stage III program. In all, 155 cars were built across the Savoy, Belvedere, Fury, and Sport Fury lines, creating an all-out assault against the remaining participants still engaging in Super Stock. Plymouth's lineup of drivers was formidable, including Hayden Proffitt (Yeakel Plymouth), Joe Smith (Fenner Tubbs), Lee Brown (Glenwood Motors), and Al Eckstrand (Lawman) battling Ford's Thunderbolt and Mercury's Comet anywhere two paved lanes of blacktop were chalked off. Dodge was viewed as a competitor rather than an ally and a fierce rivalry developed between the brands for supremacy. Many weekend finals came down to Dodge's Dick Landy squaring off against Plymouth's Tom Grove; the winner sat atop the Mopar heap until the next week.

In Texas, the Super Stock wars were as alive as anywhere in the country. A bevy of existing and new tracks populated the Lone Star State, and you could find a dragstrip in less than an hour's travel from virtually any point. The most popular dragstrips were Houston International Dragway (Houston), Double Eagle Dragway/San

This is how Aggravation *appeared prior to a partial disassembly. Blue pinstriping adorned the roof, C-pillars, and decklid, along with a multi-color application of the name of the car. So far, no luck tracking down the phone number or company advertised on the rear quarter panel. (Mike and Sharon Craig Photo)*

Antonio Drag Raceway (San Antonio), and Green Valley Raceway (Dallas/Fort Worth). However, records indicate that as many as 40 dragstrips populated Texas in 1964.

All of this action inspired an individual to order the most potent of all Super Stock Plymouths at the time, the Stage III aluminum-nose 4-speed. The story of this lost Plymouth doesn't involve trying to locate its whereabouts or its demise. The car is safely tucked away in a good friend's garage and is well cared for and treasured. What this Stage III lacks is the ability to explain just where it's been and with whom. The car's history is lost, stricken with a case of muscle car amnesia. Researching this old Plymouth has included decades of research with as many highs and lows as the Millennium Force roller-coaster at Cedar Point Amusement Park.

Pedigree

Aggravation was one of seven Super Stock Plymouth Savoys ordered in Ebony (BB1) with a red (L1R) interior. Delivered to Jack Rieger Chrysler Plymouth in San Antonio, Texas, on January 15, 1964, this car came with a 4-speed and 4.56 gears. *Aggravation* came minus radio and heater; this helped it shed useless weight. Of its sister cars, just one other was built with identical attire, options (or lack thereof), and performance. Speaking of sister cars, among the Stage III and Hemi cars, a mere 13 units were built in the aforementioned color combination. Total production on Stage III Savoy sedans for 1964 was 64 units, including a nine-passenger wagon.

The history of this Super Stock Plymouth doesn't begin on January 16, 1964, as you'd expect. Instead, its earliest known history traces back to the late 1980s, when it was found residing in an Oklahoma field with another well-known race car. Ever heard of the 1968 Hemi campaigned by Herb McCandless known as the *Mr. 4 Speed* Dart? Yep, these two Mopars were rescued as a pair. You have to wonder what those two warhorses chatted about while grazing away in that Oklahoma field.

Misinformation Abounds

Gathering information on an unregistered car is difficult. Gathering information on a race car that's never been registered is even harder. In the 1980s, *Aggravation* went through a series of owners, making research muddied and difficult.

Along the way some incorrect information was attributed to the car, which may have significantly hindered authenticating its history. It's really no one's fault because these cars were just beginning to become collectible commodities; cars were seemingly discovered daily. Through an attempt to authenticate the car, one of the owners reached out to famed drag racer and former Plymouth standout Hayden Proffitt. Of all the lightweight Plymouths that were black with a red interior, Hayden's Yeakel-sponsored Mopar was one of the most well known. With a number of letters and a couple of phone calls, Hayden was convinced that his old Plymouth had been rescued from an Oklahoma cornfield.

Years went by with ownership changing hands and the car remaining an old beat-up race car. No one really dug into authenticating the car; the assumption was that the car was Hayden's old Savoy sedan.

In the early 1990s, a Central Minnesota Mopar collector purchased the Savoy. Years passed and the story of it being Hayden's old Savoy still clung to the old Plymouth. Over a few years, this owner began opening up about the Plymouth. He is a very private individual; talking about his car was a bit like trying to pry the lid off a pickle jar with wet hands. But with more face time came more stories.

Eventually, I asked him if I could research the history of his car for him. At this time he still firmly believed that his car was Hayden Proffitt's 1964 Hemi racer. Sure, the serial number indicated it was a Stage III car, but in the early days of Hemi Plymouths, many, many things were happening under the table, and Hayden was a factory-backed Plymouth driver.

Evidence of early-conversion Plymouth Hemi cars existed with the 2-percent cars of *Melrose Missile VI* and Al Eckstrand's car. Photos

Lending credence to its Division 4 NHRA racing heritage, Aggravation *was assigned car number 4945. NHRA and Division 4 records are absent during this era and this car and number are not on file together. (Photo Courtesy Mike and Sharon Craig)*

taken of these cars show them running Max Wedge hood scoops with Hemi grilles, lending credence to the notion that not all was buttoned up during the early years of Hemi Plymouth creation.

Delivery Date

With the owner's permission, I began to dig a bit into the car. First I couldn't quite get past the supposed delivery date of this Plymouth when it came to authenticating it as the Proffitt Hemi car. January, the car's delivery date, was a full month before the Plymouths went 1-2-3 at Daytona, and it wasn't until May that Chrysler was able to place Hemi-equipped cars into the hands of its race teams. Yes, it's true that Eckstrand had tested the Hemi at Lions in early spring of 1964, but no documented proof can be found that the cars saw competition until much later than that.

Communication with Proffitt revealed he took delivery of his cars at Yeakel Plymouth in Downey, California, whereas this car was delivered to Jack Rieger Chrysler Plymouth in San Antonio. Proffitt was a Texan, but by this time he was a transplanted Californian; he had campaigned Plymouths in the Golden State since 1963. So I began to track the car forward from the dealership in San Antonio.

It didn't take long to figure out that this was going to be a non-starter. The dealership folded in the mid-1970s and the few names found from dealership advertisements were dead ends, literally. Jack Rieger, the dealership owner, had passed on in 2000, which meant all tracking of this car had to go from the current owner on

In its last known configuration, Aggravation ran a high-riser intake with a multi-carb setup. (Mike and Sharon Craig Photo)

back. It took a couple of years to successfully trace the history to the further point back that the current owner had reached. But, like any determined researcher, I kept at it. I was able to find the last owner in Texas, Mike, who could provide visual documentation. This brought me to the late 1980s, just before the flipping process began.

The Name Game

What I know from Mike is that this car campaigned under the name *Aggravation*; also, the name is on the side of the car. How long was it called *Aggravation*? Who knows?

Mike also recalled that he purchased the car from a fellow named Roland from Pasadena, Texas, in the mid-1980s. Roland was on his way out West and needed to move the car. When Mike purchased it, the car was running a 440 with a tunnel ram setup.

The car also had a roll cage and it had been lightened via removal of the interior components. A leaded trunk lid was still attached; this was an old trick to add weight on the tail of the car. Telltale painted remains included red and blue pinstripe art on the decklid, door, roof, and sail panel, as well as the sponsor's name, H&H Roofing.

Because of my research, I've concluded that this car spent the majority of its life in Texas and it ran a 426 wedge, Hemi, and 440 engine configurations. The odometer currently reads just past 1,500 miles.

If you have info about a Stage III 1964 Plymouth Savoy named *Aggravation* campaigning throughout Texas in the 1960s, 1970s, and 1980s, please contact me.

Just like most race cars, weight savings were gained with the removal of door panels and factory dash clusters. Who needs a speedometer when the window attendant hands you your ETA anyway? (Mike and Sharon Craig Photo)

By Doug Boyce

Bill "Grumpy" Jenkins purchased *Grumpy's Toy IV*, a 1968 Camaro, through the dealership of longtime sponsor Ammon R. Smith, who ran a dealership in York, Pennsylvania. Between 1961 and 1963, he sponsored the *Old Reliable* Chevys of Dave Strickler. Strickler and his Chevys became nationally known, thanks, in large part, to the tuning abilities of Jenkins.

A Few Changes

Jenkins' Camaro was the second *Grumpy's Toy* purchased through Ammon R. Smith and it arrived sporting an aluminum head L89 396-ci engine, producing an underrated 375 horses. The NHRA saw through the GM-fabricated rating and factored the engine to 425 horses. The potent semi-Hemi was an $868 option for most buyers, but not for the Grump. Chevrolet covered his costs because of the close tie he enjoyed with Vince Piggins, Chevrolet's man in charge of performance.

Although Jenkins seemed hung up on ermine white cars going back to his second *Toy*, a 1966 Chevy II, his 1968 Camaro was ordered with the optional butternut yellow paint. Jenkins had considered

Over time, Grumpy's Toy IV ran SS/C, SS/D, B/Gas, match race, and Pro Stock under Jenkins. Later, it ran Modified Production with its new owner, Brooklyn Heavy. Regardless of where the Camaro ran, it was always a winner. (Doug Boyce Photo)

getting away from his standard white because photographers continuously complained of the cars "burning up" the photos. For whatever reason, Bill had a change of mind and covered the butternut with his familiar white, which was blasted on by paint and body man Dan Carlucci. Although Dan did a supreme job on the outside, he never did paint the underside of the trunk lid and it remained butternut yellow even after Grumpy sold the car.

A basic big-block Camaro, if such a thing exists, *Grumpy's Toy IV* sported a common black interior that was cleared of frills, including the radio, heater, and insulation. Eventually, the rear seat was pulled and the original bucket seats gave way to lightweight fiberglass units.

1968 Summer Racing

Grumpy's Toy IV made its debut in April 1968 at Englishtown, New Jersey, during a heads-up Super Stock event. Still working the bugs out of the car, Jenkins turned the reigns over to hired gun Ed Hedrick, who fell victim in the first round to Bill Blanding's SS/EA Camaro.

Not used to the slick-shift transmission, Ed recalled letting off the gas pedal during gear changes. "I bent the accelerator pump lever on the Holley from whacking on and off the gas pedal," he said. After settling in, Ed went on to win the Super Stock Eliminator with 11.0 times.

On a dollars-earned versus dollars-invested basis, Grumpy's Toy IV was Jenkins' most profitable car. During the three years that he ran the Camaro, Jenkins earned approximately $150,000 on his $8,000 investment. Of Jenkins' 17 Toys, this one is the most desirable, and the one everyone wants to find. (Doug Boyce Photo)

Jenkins or Hedrick ran the Camaro through the summer of 1968, making appearances at the fourth annual Super Stock Nationals at Cecil County. Running heads-up Experimental Super Stock, Grumpy and the Camaro were hitting their stride in low-10-second times.

Into the Fall

Bill prepared three cars to do battle at the NHRA Nationals in September. Ed Hedrick qualified *Grumpy's Toy III* in SS/C with a 10.98, which the Chrysler fraternity immediately protested. The L78-powered car proved to be legal, and with Jenkins taking over the wheel, it won class but fell in eliminations to Arlen Vanke's Mopar.

Dave Strickler drove *Grumpy's Toy IV* in A/MP, powered by an L88, and Ed Hedrick drove the L78-powered 1968 Nova in SS/D. Apart from the fact that he had three cars at the race, it was a forgettable weekend for Jenkins, with both Hedrick and Strickler each eliminated early.

As a side note to that Nationals weekend, Jenkins won the *Car Craft* magazine All Star Awards for Super Stock Driver and Stock Engine Builder. Although impossible to verify now, it has previously been reported that between 1965 and 1968, cars prepared by Jenkins were responsible for an average of 20 class records per year.

In October, Jenkins Competition made a grand entrance at the NHRA World Finals at Tulsa, Oklahoma, arriving with four cars in tow, three of Bill's own cars, and Dave Strickler's Super Stock/F Z28 Camaro. In addition to Dave's car was Bill's SS/D Nova, and in a reversal of the Nationals, *Grumpy's Toy III* ran A/MP and *Grumpy's Toy IV* ran SS/C with the L78 engine.

Bill drove the Nova throughout the event while Ed Hedrick hopped back and forth between the two Camaros. In the Super Stock final, Dave Strickler's Z28 defeated the Nova with an 11.80 at 116.20 to a losing 11.48 at 120.64. Either way, it was a win-win situation for Jenkins Competition. *Grumpy's Toy IV* was match raced on and off through 1968 and into 1969, making use of a Chaparral 427 aluminum block that Bill had received from Chevrolet late in 1968. Chevrolet had developed the special aluminum 427 late in 1966 in conjunction with Jim Hall for use in his Chaparral race cars. These aluminum blocks were available to select racers through Chevrolet's Performance Group and it's believed that Bill was the only one in drag racing to use the engine. At the time, Bill found that, except for the weight savings compared to a cast-iron engine, there was no advantage in using the Chaparral.

1969 Testing and Racing

In mid-1969, Bill headed to Detroit Dragway where Chevrolet "plugged" *Grumpy's Toy IV* into its mobile instrumentation van. Bill recalls the interior of the Camaro being packed with instrumentation, data recording equipment, and telemetry stuff that was required to broadcast the data so that it could be picked up by the van.

In his book *Chevrolet Racing: Fourteen Years of Raucous Silence!* Paul Van Valkenburgh stated, "A typical recording might include engine speed, speed of both rear wheels, engine torque, and axle torque." Although it's a given that horsepower is lost through the drivetrain, Paul says that it was an unexpected amount of horsepower being lost. This led to further investigation into geartrain efficiency.

They also discovered that the engine over-revved quite a bit more than expected in wide-open-throttle speed shifting. Regardless of the quickness of the driver, declutching at a 7,200-rpm shift point allowed the engine to spike to almost 9,000 rpm.

Overall, each felt that not a lot was learned from the test session, although Bill said that at the time there was no data to base results on. Experience was gained regarding what you could and couldn't get away with, how things had to be done, and how different designs affected a road-race or circle-track car. It was a good learning experience for everyone, and to say that no initial performance was gained is not true.

At the fifth annual Super Stock Nationals held at York, Bill won Experimental Super Stock with *Grumpy's Toy IV*, recording the fastest time of the event while downing the Barracuda of Sox & Martin with a 9.94 at 141.93 to a 10.13 at 135. This was the first sub-10-second time recorded by a Super Stock car.

At the NHRA Nationals in September 1969, Bill ran *Grumpy's Toy IV* in B/Gas, something he had done on and off through the season for no reason other than that it was another class to run. The aluminum 427 Chaparral, sporting a Weiand tunnel ram and a pair of 850 Holleys, propelled the car to low-10-second times. Dave Strickler did him one better while running the Camaro at Maple Grove, where he made a 10-flat pass.

By the year's end, Jenkins shocked Don Nicholson, Ronnie Sox, and company by turning match race times in the 9.70 range with the Camaro using the same aluminum engine.

1970 and a Sale

The final incarnation of *Grumpy's Toy IV* was as a Pro Stocker. The new-for-1970 NHRA category first ran at the season-opening Winternationals. Powering the Camaro was a 430-inch aluminum Can-Am engine, a few of which Bill had received courtesy of Chevrolet in mid-1969. As qualifying began during this inaugural event, Ronnie Sox, in the all-new Sox & Martin Hemi 'Cuda, nailed down the number-one qualifying position with a 10-flat elapsed time. Jenkins grabbed the second spot with a 10.08 at 139.31 mph. Less than a half second covered the 16-car field with Sam Auxier Jr. in his Boss-powered Maverick grabbing the final spot with a 10.49 elapsed time.

On his march to a final-round appearance, Jenkins eliminated Bill "Mr. Bardahl" Hielscher, Mike Fons, and a red-lighting Dick Landy in his 16-plug Hemi-powered Dodge Challenger. In four out of the five elimination runs, Jenkins' Camaro produced 9-second times. The reported crowd of 90,000 watched Bill strap a 9.99 final-round defeat on Ronnie Sox, who came up short with a 10.12. Bill's 139.55 on the final run proved to be the top speed of the meet.

This was proving to be a costly trip for the Californians. A week later at Orange County, for the United States Pro Stock Championship, Bill propelled the Camaro through a 16-car field. He defeated

At the inaugural NHRA Pro Stock race at the 1970 Winternationals, the Grump and his two-year-old Camaro laid a strapping on the best that Chrysler had to offer. After defeating the Dodge Challenger of Dick Landy, the Grump took on and defeated the new Plymouth 'Cuda of Sox & Martin in the final. (Les Welch Photo)

Don Nicholson in his SOHC 427-powered Maverick in the final go with a 9.87 to a red-light 9.93. A best of 139.96 mph saw that Bill went home with both ends of the Orange County International Raceway track record. Total two-week earnings for the not-so-grumpy one approached $20,000.

The next stop was Florida, where the first annual NHRA Gatornationals was held in mid-February. Once again, Grumpy's Camaro held down the number-two qualifying position behind the 'Cuda of Sox & Martin with a 9.81 to Sox's 9.79; the pair met again in the final round. To reach the finals, Jenkins waded through Hubert Platt, Billy Stepp, and Dick Landy; on the other side of the fence, Sox defeated Dick Loehr, Herb McCandless, and Don Carlton. Leaving Sox on the line, Jenkins captured his second national event victory, beating Ronnie on a holeshot with a 9.90 to a losing 9.86.

Jenkins capped off the month with a trip to Detroit Raceway, where he match raced the SOHC Maverick of Sam Auxier Jr. He defeated Sam three-straight to close out the month; he earned close to $30,000.

Bill had stated that, for obvious financial reasons, the 1968 car was always one of his favorites and at one time he considered buying the car back after tracking it down in New Jersey in the early 2000s. The car required an extensive rebuild because, over time, it had reportedly been heavily modified as a Pro Street car.

In mid-1970, Jenkins sold the complete Camaro to Rufus "Brooklyn Heavy" Boyd, minus the killer 430 engine. Heavy, with Carmen Rotonda at the wheel, ran the Camaro briefly as a Pro Stocker; in 1971 he ran it as an A/MP car.

In mid-1970, Jenkins sold the Camaro to Rufus "Brooklyn Heavy" Boyd, minus the killer 430 engine but with a steel 427 and Chrysler transmission. Rufus, with Carmen Rotunda at the wheel, ran the Camaro briefly as a Pro Stocker and in 1971 as an A/MP car. My information has Rufus selling the Camaro in 1973 to Frank Carnisacola from F&J Speed Shop (formerly Rotonda Speed Shop) in Bloomfield, New Jersey. Bob Veniero bought the Camaro in 1974 and sold it to Joe Algieri in 1979. Bob, reaffirming what Jenkins states in the book Grumpys Toys: The Authorized History of Grumpy Jenkins Cars, "Joe back-halved the car to fit 14 x 32s under it and run the car in Super Gas. It really looked great but nobody knew we &$@#-up a Picasso." Joe sold the Camaro to someone in Georgia and there the trail goes cold. Joe has hired a private detective in hopes of finding the car but to date, the holy grail of drag cars remains lost.

Grumpy's Toy V: 1968 Chevy II Nova

By Doug Boyce

Grumpy Jenkins' 1968 Chevy II Nova made its drag racing debut in March 1968 and competed in NHRA's SS/D with an L78 396-inch 375-hp engine. The Nova joined a growing line of feared *Grumpy's Toys* cars and was named *Grumpy's Toy V*. Before Jenkins retired as car owner in 1983, the number of *Toys* reached 17.

Jenkins' Nova was manufactured by Chevrolet with an L79 327 engine and was pulled off the assembly line and used by Chevrolet's engineering group as a test mule at its Warren, Michigan, facility. Instead of scrapping the Nova when they were finished with it, which was usual for such vehicles, the Nova was offered to Jenkins with the hope that he could do something with it. Jenkins, who first formed ties with Chevrolet's Vince Piggins in 1966, was getting used to these kinds of perks. Although the factory gave little financial support, it was pretty generous with handing out cars and parts to its most successful drivers. The muscular Nova was a new body style for 1968. Chevrolet wanted it to be seen in action by the youth who they hoped would buy it, and Jenkins made the trek to Michigan to take delivery of the Nova. He later stated that the car never raced with the

Ed Hedrick warms the hides on the killer Nova at Island Dragway in New Jersey. Ed, having proven his prowess the previous season behind the wheel of his own car, was hired by Jenkins in 1968 and did the majority of his driving behind the wheel of the Nova. (Photo Courtesy J. S. Elliot/Doug Boyce Collection)

original L79 engine. What became of that engine once Jenkins pulled it in favor of the 396 is unknown, but those potent L79 engines are very hot commodities.

The Nova was not a Super Sport model; it featured a Muncie 4-speed transmission, a 12-bolt rear end, and a black bucket-seat interior. It was a no-frills car, but that's the way most muscle cars were assembled in the 1960s.

Racing Exploits

Having made the decision to run multiple cars in 1968, Jenkins hired Ed Hedrick to assist with the driving chores. Ed, who was coming off a championship year driving his Sport Production–winning Shelby Cobra, was looking for a ride in 1968 because the new NHRA rules had made his Cobra more or less uncompetitive. Bill and Ed became acquainted at the track and shared a mutual friendship with Jere Stahl. Jere suggested that Ed talk to Bill about driving for him. Ed made his first pass for the Grump in February 1968 driving *Grumpy's Toy III* at a divisional meet at Aquasco Raceway in Maryland.

More often than not, Ed was seen driving the Nova or match racing Jenkins' older Camaro, while Bill took control of his newest pony car. Even though the Nova competed in the Division 1 Super Stock circuit, it was never match raced as were Jenkins' two Camaros, and comparatively speaking, it saw little abuse.

In 1968, Chevrolet advertised the L78-powered Nova as the "Toughest Block on the Block." Jenkins and Hedrick proved it by running record-setting mid-11-second times. (Photo Courtesy Doug Boyce Collection)

Ed Hedrick takes a breather behind the wheel of Grumpy's Toy V. *The Nova didn't see a lot of action because Jenkins concentrated most of his efforts on his two Camaros. (Photo Courtesy Doug Boyce Collection)*

In one of the Nova's memorable moments, Hedrick took the SS/D class at the NHRA Springnationals in 1968. Ed shifted the 4-speed Chevy II to an 11.30 at 123.28 mph over the broken Chevy of Jim Brougham before falling to the fabled Road Runner of Ronnie Sox in eliminations.

Prior to the NHRA World Finals at Tulsa in October, the Nova set the class record with an 11.45 elapsed time. Ed recalled that the quickest time turned for the Nova was an 11.17 qualifying time at the NHRA Indy Nationals in September.

At the World Finals in Tulsa, the Jenkins-prepared Z/28 Camaro of Dave Strickler defeated Bill and the Nova in the final round. Jenkins often found himself squaring off against cars he had prepped. Ed Hedrick noted that history just might have recorded different results if the Nova's rear end hadn't slipped off the leaf-spring centering pin, which caused the wheel to make contact with the body on the final run.

New Owner

Finding that racing and maintaining multiple cars while running a successful business was too much to handle, Jenkins sold the Nova at the end of the 1968 season to local racer Paul Seisler. Paul, who had been running a 1966 GTO dubbed *Sir Tiger*, wanted to get more serious about his racing and felt that the GTO was just too nice to cut up, so he approached Jenkins about buying one of his cars.

Says longtime friend Carl Ruth, "Paul and Jenkins agreed on a price for the Nova and Paul made plans to pick the car up midweek. I suggested he surprise Jenkins at the track and pick the car up there. I was worried that Jenkins would take all the good parts off the car."

So Paul and Carl headed out to Maple Grove, Pennsylvania, one weekend where Ed Hedrick was driving the Nova and had just defeated Bill Stiles' Barracuda. Money was exchanged on the spot, and as the car had no title (having come from Chevrolet proving grounds), a bill of sale was written.

New Name

When the car was finally home, the guys picked up on a number of modifications that had been made to the Nova but were undetectable to the naked eye. Starting at the rear, Jenkins added lead to the trunk lid as a way to improve traction.

Carl mentioned, "You needed two hands to open and prop up the lid." The wheelbase of the Nova had been altered slightly; one front wheel was 1½ inches farther forward than the other. The firewall appeared to have been moved, as were the mounting points for the seats. All of the nuts and bolts securing front-end parts and panels were replaced with aluminum pieces.

Sir Tiger *initially ran as a Super Stocker, then in Pro Stock, and finally as a Modified Production car in 1973, before disappearing. To my knowledge, this is how the Nova last appeared on the track. (Photo Courtesy Carl Ruprecht)*

Paul chose to change the color and repainted the Nova orange and rechristened it *Sir Tiger*. He and Carl ran the Nova with the same 375-hp 396 engine through 1969 in the NHRA, SS/E class. In 1970, with Paul doing most of the driving, the pair went Pro Stock racing. A glass front clip was installed, and with the same Grumpy-prepared single 4-barrel 396, the Nova hit 10-second times. After scorching a few bearings, the engine was rebuilt and eventually the Nova touched the 9s.

Recalled Carl, "We retained the single 4-barrel Jenkins engine and were still knocking off tunnel ram, twin 4-barrel Pro Stocks." They ran the Nova as a Modified Production car into 1971 and 1972, but by 1973, Paul was losing interest in drag racing. It was while they were out at Maple Grove that a pair of "young guys" from Philadelphia approached them; they wanted to buy the Nova as it was and offered Paul good money. On the spot, he accepted the cash.

Final Owners, Final Mystery

Paul never finished the race that day; instead, he loaded the Nova onto his enclosed trailer and had the new owners install their own lock until they could pick it up a couple days later. Any spare parts that Paul had for the Nova, including the original front clip, were sold with the car. It's believed the new owners planned to return the Nova to stock and run it in either NHRA Stock or Super Stock.

Whether or not their plans ever came to fruition is unknown. The Nova and its new owners seemed to have disappeared. Many rumors regarding the car's whereabouts have endured through the years. Who these new owners were, as well as their names, is unknown.

By Jon Mello

Just out of high school in the mid-1970s, I was looking to get my first car. A friend had a 1966 Pontiac GTO with a 455 in it, but my dad looked it over and was unimpressed. "Why don't you get something neat like a Z28?" he asked.

Trying to maintain my cool, I muttered something along the lines of, "Okay, sounds good." After looking far and wide, I finally found a good candidate right in my own town. The car I bought was a Fathom Green 1969 Z28. My folks cosigned on the loan, but I made all the payments at $69 a month. I enjoyed that car so much that I have pretty much always owned one or two first-gen Camaros since then.

The Dealerships

Because of my enthusiasm for the car, I remember being very excited when I saw a book around Christmas in 1978, *The Great Camaro* by Michael Lamm. I really enjoyed the book and I guess you

The Heishman Camaro sits on pit road during a practice session prior to the 1968 Daytona 24-hour race. Johnny Moore is seated in the car and his co-driver Jim Murphy is standing alongside. (Photo Courtesy Michael Booth Archive)

could say that it left a lasting impression on me. I especially enjoyed the chapters that dealt with the early Z28 and the Camaro racing activities because I spent many years at the Trans-Am races in the early 1970s (my parents were SCCA tech inspectors at that time). One thing I remember reading about was the first 25 Z28s built and how they went primarily to people who were going to race them.

The book mentioned lots of famous dealerships, including Nickey, Yenko, Alan Green, Ron Tonkin, and Roger Penske. Interestingly, the very first Z28 went to some dealership I had never heard of: Aero Chevrolet in Alexandria, Virginia. According to Mr. Lamm, all of this information came from the files of Vince Piggins, who was one of many GM people interviewed for the book.

Most Chevy enthusiasts recognize Piggins' name; he was the person who headed Chevrolet's "back-door" racing efforts and considered to be "the father of the Z28." Well, I was really intrigued with this list of cars. But for somebody living in Southern California and with all of these dealerships not even remotely close, I didn't think too much more about it.

I mean, what were the chances that any of the cars were still around anyway? Probably about zero. The cars were already 10 years old at this point. That was *forever* for a race car. At least it seemed like that to me at the time.

A Project Car

Fast forward to the late 1990s when I was the proud owner of a very nice Mountain Green 1967 Z28, which I had only owned for about a year or two. By this time I had come to realize that the 1967 model year was my favorite. I thought that it would be nice to have a second 1967 Camaro as a project because the green car was an unrestored original. I went to look at a car for a friend who needed some engine pieces for his restoration. The seller wanted to get rid of some stock parts so he could make his car more of a hot rod.

I looked his car over and could tell it had some racing history behind it. It had signs of a roll bar, side-exit exhaust, patched-over hood pinholes, etc. This could have been any sort of race car or just something a kid had hopped up in the past, but I liked its potential plus the fact that it was originally a gold car with few options. Granada Gold is one of my favorite colors and I prefer 4-speed cars with no console.

The car was a daily driver until its history was discovered. It was repainted on three different occasions, first Rally Green in 1968, then red, and finally blue. A Keystone mag with a white-stripe bias-ply tire was still in the trunk. (Photo Courtesy Jon Mello Collection)

I made him an offer for the car and he said he'd think about it. A month or so later, he called and accepted my offer.

After getting the car home, I was able to spend more time looking things over. From the build date of the car, I knew it was around the time when the first Z28s were built. The cowl tag didn't offer much help; it showed the 4P code. This worked for a very early Z28 but could also indicate an SS350 or 327 4-barrel with a 4-speed.

I scratched around on the paint job and saw some evidence of Z28 striping so I spent some time looking at pictures of old Z28 race cars. If this was a Z28, it would be a very early car and could have been raced in the Trans-Am series like those cars I remembered reading about so long ago.

Could It Be?

In my research, I came across a photo of a Z28 that had broken an axle at a race. The view of the car was of the back end. You could just make out the flip-top gas filler cap where the roof sail panel met the quarter panel on the driver's side of the car. In the same area on the passenger's side was a smaller hole for what seemed to be a vent line. My car had patched-over holes in what appeared to be the same exact places.

The car in the photo that broke its axle was driven by Johnny Moore from the Alexandria, Virginia, area. I thought I should try to track him down and ask some questions about his old car. I used an online service and was able to locate about 30 John Moores in Virginia, but was totally lucky and made contact with his wife on the very first call. She gave me the phone number at his shop. When I connected with John, we spent a half hour talking about the car he used to race.

John came to the conclusion that it sounded like a possible match but confided that he was only the driver and mechanic of the car back then, not the owner. He said it belonged to Hugh Heishman and knowing what Mr. Heishman was like, he probably still had the original paperwork for the car. I gave Heishman a call and had to wait about a week or two for him to return from a vacation. Then, we had a very nice conversation and it turns out that he did indeed buy a 1967 Z28 when they very first became available.

And he said that he did in fact still have the original sales invoice from Aero Chevrolet where he ordered and purchased the car. He asked me for the VIN of my car. Lo and behold, it was a *match!* You can imagine my feelings at this point.

Racer to Daily Driver

So, how in the world did this old race car end up on the street as a daily driver in California, 3,000 miles from where it was sold new? Heishman told me that the car was only raced for a year and then they replaced it with a 1968 Camaro. This was due to some uncertainty as to whether or not the Trans-Am series was going to allow the new cross-ram intake manifold and four-wheel disc brakes to be used on 1967 models.

The last race for the car was at the 1968 Daytona 24-hour endurance race. After that, Heishman switched drivetrains and brakes between the 1967 and 1968 and sold the 1967 to his postal service letter carrier.

Johnny Moore in the gold Z28 runs alongside Jerry Titus' Mustang at the Daytona 24-hour race in early February 1968. This was the last race for the Camaro before being converted back into a street car. (Photo Courtesy Michael Booth Archive)

The new owner wanted all traces of being a race car to be removed and a repaint to the new Camaro color Rally Green. Sure enough, it was easy to see the remnants of Rally Green over the top of the original gold. Recollections were that the letter carrier moved to California with the car only a year or two after buying it. The car still has its black California license plates from late 1969.

Heishman sent me the car's original sales invoice as well as a notarized Certificate of Authenticity for the car, stating it was the one he bought new. I also contacted Michael Lamm to request a copy of the document that Vince Piggins gave to him in the 1970s when he interviewed Vince for his book. You could clearly see that the car listed as Z28 number 1 was delivered to Aero Chevrolet and was purchased by a local VW dealer (Heishman) and that it was to be driven by Johnny Moore at Daytona.

Everything checked out. The National Corvette Restorers Society (NCRS) Muscle Docs service has verified the VIN as being sold new through Aero Chevrolet.

Back to Racer

I am truly honored to own this piece of Chevrolet history and my intent has been to restore the car to its as-raced condition. I'm sure some would like to see it restored to the way it looked when it rolled off the assembly line and I can understand that. However, I feel that the real history of the car was made on the racetrack and I want it to reflect that proud heritage.

My 1967 Z/28 Camaro re-debuted at the Monterey Historic Races in August 2015. (Jon Mello Photo)

By Wes Eisenschenk

Yenko. In the collector car hobby, this name generates excitement and exudes prestige. Sitting near the top of the Chevrolet muscle car food chain are the 198 COPO Camaros ordered through Yenko Chevrolet in 1969. And at the summit sits the Holy Grail of lost muscle cars, Ed Hedrick's 1969 Yenko Camaro.

Few cars have captured the imagination of automotive researchers and historians as Ed Hedrick's vehicle has. It seems that every online forum dedicated to classic muscle cars or drag racing has a thread dedicated to this missing machine. Of all the lost muscle cars still waiting to be discovered, this Yenko Super Car (sYc) is Amelia Earhart, Jimmy Hoffa, and the *Titanic* all rolled into one.

Jenkins then Stahl

The story of Ed Hedrick's foray into the world of campaigning Chevrolets began in 1968 when he teamed with Bill "Grumpy" Jenkins to race Da Grump's 1968 Camaro SS/C and 1968 Nova SS/D

Running under the Grump's Group banner, the Jenkins Competition Yenko Camaro was a tough customer at any event or race. (Photo Courtesy Ed Hedrick Collection)

(both highlighted in this book) known as *Grumpy's Toy IV* and *Grumpy's Toy V*, respectively. If running those two cars weren't enough, Ed also piloted the Grump's 1967 Camaro (*Grumpy's Toy III*) at various match race events that kept him on the circuit almost every day.

Ed had a successful year, having taken *Grumpy's Toy III* to Super Stock Eliminator honors at Aquasco Raceway in February 1968 and class honors in *Grumpy's Toy V* at the NHRA Springnationals. Unfortunately for Ed, Grumpy decided to thin the herd to one car in 1969, which left him without a machine to campaign. Ed was left with finding a ride if he wanted to continue to race and found one with Jere Stahl.

The Yenko Connection

Around the same time, famed super car creator Don Yenko was looking to market his 1969 Yenko Camaros in the world of drag racing. Hedrick, at that time, was going to campaign a Super Stock 1969 Z/28 that Jere Stahl had set him up with through another dealership. However, when Yenko noted to Stahl that he was looking for someone to drive his Camaro, Jere was quick to mention Ed's availability. Word got back to Ed that Don was interested in having him pilot his Yenko Camaro and Ed jumped at the opportunity. Ed made his way to Cannonsburg and took delivery of the car.

"The rear quarter panel on the Camaro was caved in from a towing accident so Don sold me the car at cost. He also gave me a 1969 Chevrolet station wagon, which is what I used to tow the Camaro to the drag races throughout the entire season," Ed said in *Yenko: The Man, The Machines, The Legend*. Other than Dave Strickler's alliance with Jenkins, Ed's Yenko was the only car associated with Grumpy's Group and ran out of his shop.

To get Hedrick up and running, the factory L72 block was pulled and Jenkins fitted the Yenko with one of his dyno engines. When the bugs were worked out of the car, the original mill warmed over by Grump was plunked back down between the fenders of the COPO. "That year I was not only the Division 1 NHRA Super Stock Eliminator champion, I was also the top points–scoring Chevrolet in the nation," Ed said. Hedrick's driving and Jenkins' tuning sent the COPO to a top ETA of 10.71 at 131 mph, running consistently under the NHRA SS/E national record.

The crowning achievement for Hedrick was at the 1970 Gatornationals, held in Gainesville, Florida, competing in SS/DA. Ed qualified the Camaro with an 11.28 pass that was also under the class record of 11.43, showing his competitors that the Yenko was going to be tough in Florida. Through the subsequent rounds, he beat the Hugger Camaro and the Hemi Barracudas of Ronnie Sox and John Tedder on his way to taking the SS/EA title and giving Yenko his only NHRA national win. Capturing such a prestigious event surely didn't hurt the legacy and future value of Don Yenko and the sYc.

The Fate of Pusher Man

Like all great combinations though, Ed's time in the Camaro came to an end. He noted, "Since the SS/E national record was too low for the Yenko to be competitive at all tracks and on all days, I sold the Camaro to Charles Wright in Pittsburgh, Pennsylvania, and teamed up with Bill Stiles to run a 1970 Plymouth Duster in NHRA Pro Stock." Charles "Chuck" Wright campaigned the car in Pennsylvania until about 1973, running the car in a variety of paint schemes.

The car was repainted blue and campaigned under the name *Pusher Man*. Later, it was painted pearl white with maroon on the lower rear fenders, doors, and quarters, along with the decklid. This was the last known configuration of the Hedrick Yenko Camaro.

After that the stories sound like someone telling you what happened to Jimmy Hoffa. Everything from the car being stolen to mob affiliations to alien abductions (well, maybe not that) surrounds the fate of the car. In truth, it still may exist as a race car, showing no evidence of its former life.

Many online forums have a thread attempting to locate this car. Among the "tricks" people use include asking for information on the car as it was campaigned *after* Hedrick owned it. "Looking for Chuck Wright's old Camaro" and "Searching for the *Pusher Man* Camaro" are common on the Internet. You gotta hand it to them for trying, but around the third posting, someone blurts out that it's Ed Hedrick's lost Yenko Camaro. The next thing you know the finders' fees triple and quadruple, as everyone wants to be the guy who uncovers one of the most prized missing muscle cars of all.

Whatever may be the case with Hedrick's lost Yenko, it remains one of the most searched-for American muscle cars of all time. And, if one day it does surface, it will be featured in every magazine and another car will climb to the top of the lost muscle car pile.

Ed Hedrick, the North Carolina native, blasts his Yenko Camaro off the line at the famed New Jersey dragstrip called Old Bridge Township Raceway Park in Englishtown. (Photo Courtesy Doug Boyce Collection)

This lost 1969 Yenko Camaro is most likely the most sought-after missing muscle car of all time. Here Ed launches the car at the 1970 NHRA Gatornationals; he later took the crown running in SS/DA. (Photo Courtesy Ed Hedrick Collection)

By Geoff Bradley

Darrell Droke, owner of Autodynamics in Downey, California, had been a successful competitor in the Mobil 1 Economy races held annually in Los Angeles, California. These races, separated into different classes, challenged drivers to achieve the greatest MPG averages driving from Los Angeles to destinations such as Detroit, Minneapolis, and New York. During the 1960 campaign, Darrell teamed with speed legend Mickey Thompson.

Although they didn't take the crown in their class, he had established a racing relationship with Mickey and had been asked to help with the *Challenger 1* Bonneville Salt Flats car. That machine set the land speed record with a one-way top-speed pass of 406.60 mph, and that introduced Darrell to the world of high-speed racing.

In 1962, he campaigned a 1962 Ford in A/FX and Super Stock. Darrell and his brother Larry also prepped the banned NASCAR star Curtis Turner's 1962 Ford that won the Pikes Peak International Hill Climb. With still not enough on his plate, Darrell took second in his class in the Mobil 1 Economy Race.

Here's a rare shot of the missing T-Bolt launching hard at the Big Go West in Pomona, California, circa 1965. Production on 1965 Thunderbolts was just a pair of cars; this one was the only car to feature the high-riser 427. (Photo Courtesy Lynn Wineland Archive via quartermilestones.com)

Factory Involvement

By late 1964, Ford racing chief John Cowley was aware of Droke's accomplishments while campaigning Fords. In the fall, Charlie Gray Jr. of the Ford Motor Company contacted Darrell with a proposition.

As we all know, Ford made 100 1964 Thunderbolts. Their success in drag racing is the stuff of legend, and their battles with Mopar and Ford's sister company Mercury made Ronnie Sox, Hubert Platt, and Gas Rhonda household names. After the NHRA changed its mandate from 50 production cars to 500 for S/S competition, Ford pulled the plug on the Thunderbolt program and began concentrating its efforts in the Experimental classes, mainly with its new Mustang.

For the upcoming year, Ford still wanted a Fairlane presence on America's dragstrips. On September 23, 1964, Ford asked Dearborn Steel Tubing (the creators of the 1964 Thunderbolts) to construct a 1965 Fairlane in a fashion similar to the previous cars, although with a budget not to exceed $5,000.

This Thunderbolt was delivered new with a 427 high-riser engine and the car was painted Poppy Red (the same as Gas Ronda's Mustang) and sent to California. There, "Autodynamics" was scrolled on the fenders, and "Thunderbolt" was lettered in script on the leading edge of the rear quarter panels, leaving no doubt that it was built in 1965. The Thunderbolt was tabbed with the moniker *Wonder Colt*.

Droke's Racing Accomplishments

Initially Dick Brannan made some passes with the car, but he kept tearing out rear ends. Dick ended up in an A/FX Mustang for 1965, so a short time later the car was given to Darrell to sort out. The brothers wrenched on it at Autodynamics. Droke installed a truck rear end and hardened axles in an effort to amend the rear-end failures. He was instructed to *never* touch the front end that Dearborn Steel Tubing made and he respected Ford's wishes. The car's weight was increased to 3,800 pounds, making it legal in NHRA's B/Factory Experimental class, and Droke was officially tapped to drive the car as a new member of Ford's Drag Council.

Around that time, the 427 SOHC engine was making its way into the hands of Ford racers and Darrell wanted one. So, a 427 SOHC with Doug's Headers was installed, replacing the high-riser in the

1965 Thunderbolt. With no real seat time in the car, Darrell entered it into the 1965 NHRA Nationals. Downey Ford sponsored the car and gave him a station wagon for towing duties.

The awards began to mount up for Droke and his B/FX terror. Among the notable wins was capturing the B/FX trophy at the 1965 NHRA Nationals, Junior Stock Eliminators champion at Carlsbad, setting the MPH record in B/FX with a 126.05-mph pass at Half Moon Bay, and a Sportsman Eliminator title at the AHRA championships.

The car also match raced around the country, going up against "Dyno" Don Nicolson and others. Some competitors were not too happy to see that B/FX Thunderbolt line up against them. At one point the car ran on fuel, in the 10.50 range. It was some sight to see no front hood and eight huge velocity stacks sticking out of this little box of horror.

Destroyed in Detroit?

After the 1965 season, the car was given to Jerry Harvey, who ran it under Paul Harvey Ford sponsorship. Jerry changed the color to a deeper red with gold-leaf lettering.

In 1966, it was clear that Ford wanted the Mustang to be out front in its drag efforts, courting the youth crowd as Fairlanes and Galaxies began disappearing from the dragstrip. Droke himself had a long-nose 1966 Funny Car Mustang.

After Harvey's turn at the wheel, the Thunderbolt was to go to Ed Schmidt of Michigan. Ed was the son of Harry Schmidt, owner of Ubly Dragway. It's unclear how the plans fell through, but Ed ended up getting a Holman-Moody–prepped 1967 Ford Fairlane 427 car.

It's here where the history of the 1965 Thunderbolt becomes muddy. It was rumored that the car was returned to Ford in Detroit and destroyed, even though no one within Ford has ever confirmed this.

In truth, this was a remarkable one-of-one car in the very capable hands of Darrell Droke, and their legacies are as intertwined as cake and ice cream. Search his name on the Internet and pictures of his 1965 Thunderbolt populate the results. If it's ever found, there's no question that *Wonder Colt* would go straight to the top of the Thunderbolt mountain as one of the most coveted cars ever built in Detroit.

By Bobby Schlegel

Performance wasn't often the first thing that came to mind when hearing someone talk about American Motors in the mid-1960s. Ignoring the whole muscle car movement, the Kenosha auto manufacturer plugged away with its line of economy-based cars while the debuts of Pontiac's GTO and Ford's Mustang captured the imagination of America's youth. Toward the end of the 1960s, AMC knew that if it were to remain in business it would have to create offerings that were going to help reshape the company's image among the buying public.

For the fall of 1967, a pair of performance-oriented offerings debuted: the Javelin and the AMX. With those two entrants, AMC was ready to enter the muscle car wars.

My brother Skip and I are a perfect example of the intended target of AMC's advertising campaign. From Lake Carmel, New York, we had been fond of the new AMXs, even though we hadn't committed to making the transformation to AMC ownership. That was all about to change with the debut of the performance package offered on the midsize Rebel body called The Machine.

Lettered up and ready for the dragstrip, Lil Miss Carnivorous *and I are ready to devour the competition. Just 2,326 Rebel Machines were produced by AMC. (Photo Courtesy Skip Schlegel Archive)*

Geis Motors formally announces its partnership with the Schlegel brothers through this ad in the local newspaper. Both of us worked for Geis at the time. (Photo Courtesy Putnam County Courier)

Dealer Sponsorship

Geis Motors, an American Motors dealership located in Shrub Oak, New York, was also looking to bolster its image when it came to selling AMC muscle. We were mechanics for the Geis family dealership group (I worked at the AMC dealership, Skip worked for the Geis Buick dealership) and realized there may be an opportunity to get a sponsorship if we bought and possibly campaigned a Rebel Machine.

We had been involved in drag racing for a few years already, racing our personal cars and paying for the "performance" parts out of our own pockets. A pairing with their employers seemed a natural fit for a partnership. Geis Motors obliged with sponsorship funds when we approached them about campaigning the new Rebel Machine, and we set a date of April 11, 1970, to debut *Lil Miss Carnivorous* at nearby Dover Dragstrip in Wingdale, New York.

Media Encouragement

The *Putnam County Courier* took note of our aspirations: "Tenaciously holding on for their big opportunity in auto and drag racing circles, the Schlegel brothers plan to open the 1970 season at Dover Dragstrip with their stock Rebel Machine named *Lil Miss Carnivorous*. Successful drivers of Rebels have been few on the East Coast circuit thus far, but it is in this class that Bob and Skip hope to make their mark.

"We figure if you win with a Chevrolet, Ford, or Plymouth, it's everyday news, but if we can take the honors in a Rebel, we'll be noticed. That's what we want," said Bob.

"The Rebel Machine has the optional high-performance engine and, although highly decorated with red, white, and blue reflective strips, is no different than any other car purchased from a dealer. It has a 390-ci engine that has 335 advertised hp, but the S&B team firmly stated, 'Anybody can do what we're doing with our car. Everything is legal by the rule book.'

"If everything worked out for the Schlegels on the racing beat, then the next goal on their agenda, driving for a salary or having their own garage for stock class cars and dragsters, would be a big step closer."

Ready to Race

I remember being in the tech inspection line at one of the dragstrips in their division when a new 1970 SS Chevelle with low options pulled up next to him. It was a new car, never on the street, set up for racing, and it had the new 402-ci big-block engine with an "advertised" horsepower rating of 350. Because the Chevelle was a midsize car, it was going to run in the same class as their Rebel. Back then, all the engines were under-rated for insurance costs and we knew the Rebel had its work cut out for it to be competitive.

Even so, the Rebel was dressed for battle, sporting its BorgWarner 4-speed, transplanted 4:11 gears, Hooker Headers, Schaeffer clutch assembly, Lakewood safety shield, and wearing a set of M&H 7-inch racing slicks on Cragar S/S wheels. Per the class rules, we had to run their stock heads and intake.

We won a few races and trophies with *Lil Miss Carnivorous*, campaigning the car throughout the 1970 season.

Disappointment Times 10

For 1971, we were in the preliminary talking stages as to whether or not the dealership would spring for sponsorship money again and were waiting to see what happened.

One day at the AMC dealership, with the Rebel parked in the lot, a man asked about the car and was told it belonged to the Schlegel brothers. He really dug the old AMC and wanted the car. I told him that we were waiting to see what the dealership was going to do for the next racing season. When we received the answer that there would be no help from Geis Motors, I contacted the man, and within a week the car was sold.

We never saw *Lil Miss Carnivorous* again.

After the sale of the car, Skip took a large amount of film down to the local store to have it developed. When he went to pick it up, he received the terrible news that the store lost 10 rolls of pictures that featured shots of the car being built and dyno tuned at S&K in Long Island, New York. He was told that the order was lost and that he could have 10 new rolls for replacement. Anyone who has ever lost a singular picture knows how disappointing it is to lose that history, let alone *10 rolls!*

With that, the Rebel Machine drifted off into oblivion.

By Scott A. Hollenbeck, Mustang 428 Cobra Jet Registry

At the start of the 1968 model year, Ford Motor Company's Mustang pony car was in serious need of a performance boost to keep pace with its big-block competition. The 1968 Camaro offered four 396-ci engine options with 325 hp or more. The Mustang's S-code 390 FE was rated at 335 hp and 427 ft-lbs of torque, but the general public didn't think of it as a performance engine. Ford's answer came in the form of the 428 Cobra Jet, or 428 CJ.

Ford developed a plan to introduce the 428 CJ to the performance world where it mattered most: on the dragstrip. On January 28, 1968, Hubert Platt introduced the 428 Cobra Jet Mustang to the racing world during the AHRA Winter Nationals held at Lions Dragstrip near Los Angeles. He drove a specially prepared 1968 Mustang in C/Stock and red-lighted a 12.62 run in the first round of Top Stock.

One week later the 428 CJ made its drag racing debut at the eighth annual National Hot Rod Association (NHRA) Winternationals, held from February 2 to 4, 1968, at the Los Angeles County Fairgrounds in Pomona, California. Ford sponsored five drivers (Gas Ronda, Jerry Harvey, Hubert Platt, Don Nicholson, and Al Joniec) to race six 428 CJ-equipped Mustangs.

Ford sponsored five Cobra Jets at the 1968 Winternationals in Pomona. Among them was number 985, campaigned by Hubert Platt with Paul Harvey Ford sponsorship. Of the five cars that campaigned that weekend, this is the only one unaccounted for. (Steve Reyes Photo)

The Mustangs raced in the C Stock Automatic (C/SA, 9.00 to 9.49 pounds per advertised horsepower), Super Stock E, and Super Stock E Automatic (SS/E manual transmission, SS/EA automatic transmission, 8.70 to 9.49 pounds per advertised horsepower) classes.

The engine lived up to expectations as four of the cars made it to their respective class finals. Al Joniec won both his class (defeating Hubert Platt in an all-CJ final) and the overall Super Stock Eliminator title (defeating Dave Wren). Hubert Platt drove two cars, number 984 (C/SA, sponsored by Tasca Ford) and number 985 (SS/E, sponsored by Paul Harvey Ford).

The Mystery of 985

As time went on, these six cars were modified, sold, raced by others, and generally became used race cars. Amazingly, five of the six are known to have beaten the odds and have survived. The cars that are known to exist today are the ones that were driven by Jerry Harvey (983, SS/E), Hubert Platt (984, C/SA), Al Joniec (986, SS/E), "Dyno" Don Nicholson (987, SS/EA), and Gas Ronda (992, SS/EA). What about Hubert Platt's 985 car?

Research using period magazine and newspaper articles has helped me document some of the race results for 985. Here's what I've been able to learn:

On July 4, 1968, Hubert Platt lost control of the Cobra Jet Mustang and crashed at the top end at Southeastern International Dragway in Dallas, Georgia. Platt was unhurt, but the Mustang needed repairs. (Photo Courtesy Marvin T. Smith)

- Lost (red light) to Al Joniec (12.12 109.48) in SS/E class final.
- Defeated Arlen Vanke in eliminator round one.
- Defeated (11.09) Ronnie Sox (11.74) in eliminator round two.
- Lost (red light) to Al Joniec in eliminator quarterfinal.

Ford documentation describes the car as "Sold to Hubert Platt under $1.00 contract," and Hubert continued to race the car after the Winternationals. Sponsored by Foulger Ford, the Georgia Shaker eventually found himself in Dallas at Southeastern International Dragway on July 4, 1968.

During a race against Harold Dutton's Barracuda, Hubert lost control of the car at the three-quarter mark. The car flipped and landed on its wheels; Hubert later reported that the loss of control was due to the car's rear end coming unlocked. He escaped without a scratch, but the car was considered a total loss. Such cars often end up in the crusher. Did this one? How could I learn more?

A Registry Is Born

Race cars are often repainted or have body panels changed, so current appearance isn't always helpful when it comes to identifying a particular car. Vehicle history research is made much easier if you have the VIN. With that in mind, the first goal in my attempt to find the car was to identify the VIN. Thankfully, a number of resources are available to make that possible.

This is where the wonder of the Internet plays a role. I bought a 1970 428-CJ Mustang in 1996 and spent several years learning everything I could about the car and the bits I needed to restore it. Very little accurate published information was available at the time, so I thought it made sense to document everything I learned on a website.

My research was focused primarily on 1969 and 1970 Mustangs, so I partnered with 1968 expert Chris Teeling to start a registry project in 1998 after it became clear that an earlier registry project had gone dormant. That website has grown into a community of like-minded enthusiasts who have been invaluable research partners. Chris and I were "crowdsourcing" long before the concept became mainstream. Armed with some basic information, I started tapping the network.

One member shared documentation that described the disposition of vehicles produced by Ford for drag racing. The list of vehicles includes VINs, racing classes, and driver names. The document listed five of the six Winternationals drivers (it didn't mention Al Joniec), so it was an excellent start. I've seen differences between documentation and reality, so the next step in the research was to confirm the listed VINs and identify the one that was missing.

Kevin Marti of Marti Auto Works negotiated an incredible deal with Ford several years ago. He has licensed access to original production records starting with the 1967 model year, and his company produces reports and does record research for very modest fees. I called Kevin, explained what I was trying to do, and asked if he could confirm the information I had and also fill in the missing pieces. He gave me a price for his service, I agreed, and he promised to get back to me shortly.

My phone rang a few days later. Kevin told me that my information was accurate and he was able to identify the VIN for the Joniec car. Reports for each car were mailed to me. I soon had factory production information that could be used to cross-check the information from the network of registry people.

Rusty Gillis and 985

The website allowed Chris and me to reach people who we never would have found otherwise. I've been able to talk to Hubert Platt and Jerry Harvey, but neither was able to recall specific information about these old cars from that long-ago event. I was also able to talk to Bill Barr and Arlen Whittington, but again, these were just a small number of cars that they worked with a long time ago.

Our network of enthusiasts helped us locate and confirm the identities of five of the six cars, leaving only Hubert's 985 car (with partial VIN 8R02S117XXX; yes, it was serialized as an S-code 390) unaccounted for. And then we heard from veteran drag racer Rusty Gillis. Rusty is the owner of Gillis Performance Restorations of Port Richey, Florida.

I was amazed to learn that Rusty had once owned Hubert's car. He told me that the wrecked car was rebuilt and raced by Randy Payne. Hubert confirmed that Randy did indeed campaign the car when I had a chance to interview him in 2008. I recently asked Rusty if he could tell me anything more.

Rusty said, "Hubert had two cars. One Super Stocker and I've seen pictures of an automatic that I think was a stocker. Randy Payne told

Hubert Platt (near lane) squares off against Randy Payne (far lane) in a matchup of the Georgia Shaker's old Cobra Jet versus his new Cobra Jet. Confused yet? (Photo Courtesy Rusty Gilles)

me that the one I had was the one that Hubert wrecked. He fixed it and Randy raced it for a while.

"The only 1968 Mustang that I know Hubert wrecked was the silver and black Foulger Ford car. When I got it, there was an automatic in it, but it had a stick brake pedal. Hubert had loaned it to Patty Young after she wrecked her car. He offered it to me while riding in the Ford Drag Team truck on the way to Detroit. He said he was getting the car back from Patty and wanted $3,500 for it, so I borrowed the money from my uncle."

This was big news! I now had a more complete trail of ownership information that led into the early 1970s. What happened

Randy Payne took Platt's battered 985 car and had it rebuilt, renaming it Bullet Proof. By the fall of 1968, Randy campaigned Hubert's 1969 Torino as part of the Ford Drag Team. Number 985 was sold to racer Rusty Gillis. (Photo Courtesy Marvin T. Smith)

Rusty Gillis, the 985's third owner, was extremely successful campaigning the Cobra Jet after Hubert Platt. Here, Rusty poses with his trophy after taking down the class at the 1971 Winternationals in SS/FA. (Photo Courtesy Rusty Gillis Collection)

next? Here's what Rusty had to say: "Hubert Platt called yesterday to ask me what I did with my 1968 Super Stock Mustang that he raced at Pomona and I bought from him in 1969. I had to give him the bad news that in 1975 we started to update it to current NHRA rules by tubbing it. The gas crunch was putting my dad's used car lot out of business and I left the shell behind the body shop that I was renting when I left; I had nowhere to take it. Someone smashed the acid-dipped fender and we never finished tubbing it. About 30 years ago I heard that it was in a junkyard in Bradenton."

An Update

While writing this piece, I took the opportunity to exchange emails with Rusty again to secure his permission to quote him and to share the pictures that he generously shared with me. He offered these final bits of information: "I don't know if I told you this before, but that car had 16 miles on it. I still have the key. I get so upset every time I think about leaving that car behind my shop in Bradenton. I almost forgot that we stripped all the paint off. It was painted pearl white and raced SS/FA at Pomona in 1973; we were runner-up in class."

This is where the trail has gone cold. I've had no reports of recent sightings. It's entirely possible that the car met its end in that Florida junkyard, but who knows? I can only hope that someone recognized it and saved it from the crusher.

By Daryl Klassen

During the mid-1960s, American car manufacturers were battling over who had the fastest production car, particularly in NASCAR and the quarter-mile drag races. They all had the mindset of "Win on Sunday, Sell on Monday," and they were doing whatever it took to stay one step ahead of the competition.

For the 1968 model year, Chrysler attempted the knock-out punch by putting its most dominant engine into the lightest production-based body available. The result turned out to be the 426 Hemi, specially installed by Hurst Manufacturing into 70 Barracudas and 80 Dart models. Hemis had now arrived in the A-Bodies.

Bodies and Engines

Just 150 bare bodies were pulled off the assembly line and delivered to Hurst for modifications and final assembly. These cars were in primer only with no paint, drivetrain, or interior. So naked were these Mopars that they were shipped to Hurst sans undercoating and seam sealer on the joints.

Chrysler separately sent out the cross-rammed race-prepared 426 Hemis, transmissions (both automatic and 4-speed), and specially

Factory race cars really don't come any more imposing than this 1968 Hemi Dart. With its Hemi scoop and cross-ram intake, these quarter-mile warriors are still a force to be reckoned with at the dragstrip. (Photo Courtesy Geoff Stunkard)

geared 4.88 Dana 60s and 4.86 8¾-inch differentials. On the production-based cars, the wheel-bolt pattern was 4 inches. These cars were prepped with special Kelsey Hayes four-piston front calipers and rotors that had a 4½-inch bolt circle. The differentials were stock-length B-Body versions (Road Runner, Coronet, etc.) that had the 4½-inch bolt circle. Because of the width difference of these cars, a special offset rear wheel was required with the Darts and Barracudas, substantially opening the rear wheelwells for tire clearance (more so on the Darts).

The bodies received fiberglass front fenders and hoods adorned with a large hood scoop for carb clearance. The doors were stamped from thinner gauge sheet metal and weighed 18 pounds each for weight reduction. The front bumper was stamped from thinner gauge metal and weighed 13 pounds.

The side glass in the doors and quarters was replaced with lightweight glass from Corning Glass Works. Door glass was operated using a strap made from seat belts and the normal hardware was scrapped. Either the window was all the way up, or it was completely down. Nothing was done with the windshield and back glass and they kept their original thickness. Cosmetically, the final detail was placing a delete plate where the outside driver-side mirror was normally located.

Fitting the Hemi into these small cars was no easy feat. The passenger-side shock tower received clearance via a cutting torch and sledgehammer. The K member was dropped 1/2 inch using spacers, again to gain some hood clearance. The master cylinder interfered with the driver-side valvecover so it had to be relocated. Valvecover removal for valve adjustment was still not possible without removing the master cylinder, so it was given flexible brake hoses so that it could be laid over on the inner fender well. The battery, a large commercial version, was relocated to the right rear of the trunk to aid in weight transfer.

The interior had no heater or radio; a delete plate covered each vacancy. The car had no rear seat or carpet, with only a cardboard divider used to separate that space from the trunk. Its front seats were from the A100 truck/van line; they were lighter than production car seats and were mounted on non-adjustable aluminum seat tracks that were Swiss-cheese drilled to lighten them.

The cars left Hurst in gray primer with black gel-coat front fiberglass and were sold with no warranty whatsoever. A sticker applied to the driver-side front door pillar stated, "This vehicle was not manufactured for use on the road, streets, or highways, and does not conform to motor vehicle safety standards." The exhaust consisted of two glass-pack mufflers with straight pipes bolted to the headers. Welcome to the world of factory-backed drag cars.

My Search Is On

I got into the Mopar brand many years ago. My first affiliation with the brand was an original 1970 Plum Crazy 4-speed Hemi 'Cuda that I purchased when I was 18 years old in 1976. Even in the post–muscle car era, this car drew crowds wherever I went.

In 1987 I took the 'Cuda to the Mopar Nationals. It was here that I had my first live sighting of a car that I had only read about in magazines and other publications, such as *National Dragster*: a Hemi Dart. I watched as the owner unloaded it from a box right across the lane where I was parked. I couldn't believe it. I drooled over this car all weekend, I told myself that I had to own one of these iconic cars one day. It was a truly awe-inspiring moment to see one of the meanest cars ever built right there in front of me. I *had* to have one!

I started looking in different publications for one of these machines. Finally in the fall of 1996, I saw an ad in *National Dragster* that caught my attention. It was a project car that had a restoration started but not completed. I flew down to inspect the car to verify that it was in fact an original LO23 Hemi Dart. I was hooked and the deal was made; I had it shipped home.

Most of these cars had a unique paint scheme throughout their racetrack history, so I figured I'd spend some time carefully sanding it down to see what I would find. It was last painted in the early 1970s so there weren't many layers of paint to cut through to find its original colors. I found a base coat of silver, with an orange inlay along its sides, with blue stripes across the top. These were the colors of Dick Landy; the color scheme matched. What I had there in my shop was the king of all Hemi Darts. All others fell into place behind this one!

Deal of a Lifetime

I spoke with Dick Landy and sent pictures and videos of my discovery of his old warhorse. I had enough evidence to convince him to come to my place and inspect and document this car as being his 1968 4-speed Hemi Dart.

Word started getting around like wildfire of my trophy. Soon after, the phone started ringing with people wanting to purchase the car; it was not for sale. After all, owning a Landy Hemi Dart is a once-in-a-lifetime experience. However, one very persistent individual didn't give up, and after several attempts at outright purchase, and failing to do so, he asked what it would take for me to let this car go.

When I thought about the huge amount of money and time that I was going to spend on this car, I told him that I might consider a trade. But not just any trade. It would have to be turnkey, needing nothing. I told him that I was interested in only two cars. Both were original LO23 Darts. The first one was Bill Bagshaw's *Red Light Bandit* and the other was Tim Hennessey's restored Hemi Dart.

Long story short, he found both of these cars. After a couple of weeks, he called again, telling me the *Bandit* was not for sale, but he now had in his possession the Tim Hennessey Hemi Dart. "Want to trade now?" he asked.

A persistent man is a persistent man. So, a deal was made and the Hemi Darts were traded in 2001. The Landy Dart was heading south again to the United States and the Hennessey Dart was coming north to Canada.

That very same red Hemi Dart that I first laid eyes on in 1987 at the Mopar Nationals is the car that now resides in my garage. And, that very same Plum Crazy 1970 Hemi 'Cuda is sitting beside it. I met my wife in that car. It was our wedding car, and both our kids rode in the back seat of that car from their baby carriers until the day they couldn't fit comfortably back there anymore.

Charlie Castaldo's Car

Now, why is this red LO23 Hemi Dart in this book? At the time I acquired this car, I thought I knew its complete history. After owning it and showing it at a few shows, including the All Chrysler Nationals in Carlisle, Pennsylvania, I started questioning its origins after speaking with a couple of people. I was under the impression that it was campaigned by Charlie Castaldo, but some folks said it was not. I had to know this car's origin so I found the names of some of the crewmembers from Castaldo's team and made some calls.

In discussing this with one of Castaldo's crew, Charlie Licata, he told me that Castaldo had passed away, which was unfortunate. But he could tell me some of the mods that were done to his car to compare with what had been done to mine. Nothing matched. It seems that Castaldo made a lot of modifications to his Dart to keep it competitive in different classes, including Modified Production.

Charlie has put a 4-speed in it and cut out the trunk pan for a fuel cell. My car has never had a clutch pedal in it, and the trunk floor had never been removed or modified. In fact, very few changes were made to my car, with the exception of being mini-tubbed many years ago. So, my car is not Charlie Castaldo's.

Nailing Down History

My search on this car's real history began almost 10 years ago as of this writing. I started a thread on an online racing forum, class-racer.com, to see what information I could gather. This forum is full of experts, and sourcing the history couldn't be that hard, right? After all, they only built two batches of these cars. The first batch had 50 sequential serial-numbered Darts and the second batch of 30 came a short time later to fulfill the customer demand. To top it off, my current Dart is a very early build car, one of the first 10 in the first batch of 50. In fact, this car is only two serial numbers away from my old Dick Landy Dart, so it was an early car and most likely was well known. Wrong again.

During the time that I have been on this "gotta know" quest, I have talked with dozens of people. Most have given me names of more people to speak with. Recently, the information was slowly drying up and I was beginning to run out of "experts." It felt as though I had spoken with half the population of New York State.

The Internet, though, has a wealth of information. Forums continually feature new pictures from personal collections. Over the years, I've looked at thousands of pictures of Hemi Darts, thinking

Cast your gaze beyond Dick Landy's Coronet and feast your eyes on the evidence that confirmed the history of my Dart. This shot shows the damaged rear quarter panel on the Manhattan Speed Parts Hemi, which I have identified on my car. (Photo Courtesy Bob Snyder)

that one day a picture of my car might be posted. That day finally came in 2014. A picture posted of Dick Landy's 1968 Coronet shows, in the background, a silver 1968 Hemi Dart with a black hood.

How do I know it's my car? The right rear quarter panel has a weird dent. It looks like something, such as a heavy post, fell on it from the topside and continued down. By the wheelwell opening, there's no damage to suggest that someone drove into the side of it. Inside the trunk of my car is evidence of a repair made in the exact same place of the topside damage, ending before the wheel opening.

The other thing is that the early Darts (first 10 or so) were delivered without hoods, probably because of a supply issue. They were later shipped to the new owners in black gel-coat. Because this car was a very early example, it can be identified by its black hood. My car was known as the Manhattan Speed Shop Dart and this picture was taken at the 1968 Super Stock Nationals held at New York National Speedway. Its previous history or current location was unknown to this point.

1968 to 1980 Mystery

Most of the Hemi Darts' whereabouts are accounted for, but this is one that eluded many very knowledgeable people, including Mark Janaky and Dell Jones. These guys are rightfully credited as the best Hemi Super Stock historians in the business.

After several years of searching, and with the help of many contributors to that online thread (including Paul Ceasrine), I believe I've locked down the history of my car's early days, at least the first year, anyway.

Paul also started a thread on classracer.com a short time ago named Manhattan Speed Parts 1968 Hemi Dart. He has done a lot of research through this thread and has found some very interesting information on my car, but you'll have to visit the thread to read about it.

Currently, I don't have any info on this car from late 1968 to approximately 1980, when then-owner Lou Vignona brought it back into the limelight. I can account for every person from Lou's ownership to mine, but prior to Lou it just falls off the planet. I've followed many leads, but so far, nothing.

If you have any information on the Manhattan Speed Parts Hemi Dart, please don't hesitate to seek me out on the forum. Thanks to Paul Ceasrine and other guys, I have information on the early history of this car, and maybe one of you holds the keys to the final part of this Hemi's story.

By J. D. Feigelson

I had just come home from work. The phone was ringing. I grabbed it. It was an urgent call from my dad. "What's up, Pop?" I asked.

"It's here."

"What is?"

"The car."

"*The* car?"

"*The* car!"

"Holy cow! You're kidding."

"No. They just called me. I'll meet you at Sutton's."

I was gone like a shot, easing through stop signs and pushing yellow lights. In 10 minutes, which seemed like 10 hours, I was there: Sutton Motor Company, the Beaumont, Texas, Chrysler Plymouth dealer. My pop's car was already there. I hurried in through the front door. Pop was waiting in the showroom talking to Jerry Hanna, a racing buddy who had joined us. The sales manager, Ed Grosse, came out grinning and said, "Okay, guys, let's go have a look."

Among the most feared rearview mirror sightings anyone in racing can experience is seeing a single-headlight Hemi-scooped Savoy. Plugging your ears is a good idea when this elephant lets out its roar. (Photo Courtesy J. D. Feigelson)

We headed back from the showroom through a small corridor to the shop. It was a big, high, tin building. Ed stopped and pointed. At the far end of it sat "the car." We had ordered a hardtop Sport Fury Stage III 426 Wedge. There sat a black, plane Jane, Savoy two-door business sedan. We were stunned. What happened? My heart dropped.

Two Chevys

Here's how it all started: I had a friend whose dad owned a filling station. In 1957, he bought new a Chevy Bel Air hardtop. It was washed and wiped every day. In the early 1960s, I asked him if he would sell it. He said he was getting married and needed something more practical. We made a deal and I left with the car. Well, don't you know, I had plans for it: conversion to stick shift and rework the engine to a 245. The interior was black and turquoise so I planned to paint the top black to match. It ran great. Terrific low-end torque. So, with night falling I headed to the streets of Beaumont, Texas.

One Sunday I took the Chev to the Golden Triangle Dragstrip and entered it in "F" stock. And what do you know? I won.

Now I really had the bug. However, on my way home one evening, I was sitting at a light. It changed and I was off, right into another car. It had turned in front of me from the other side of the light. Neither of us were hurt, but my sweetie was dead, a total loss. Well, maybe not!

Pop had become interested in the racing thing, and seeing how I was moping about the Chev, he suggested we build a car just for racing. We found a cheap Chevy two-door post with a 6-cylinder so we bought it. Out came the engine and in went a blueprinted 270 with a 4-speed. Pop had calculated that this car was perfect for the sweet end of class "E" stock.

One side note here that's kind of amusing: In building the engine, Pop went down to the Chevy dealer, Beaumont Motor Company, to buy a new set of rods. They let him go through the inventory. There he was, on the floor in the parts department, mic'ing every rod they had in stock for eight "heroes." Long story short, the car was a stormer: 13.5 in the quarter-mile when most were struggling to get out of the 14s. Pop even bettered Traction Master by building a push-pull traction bar system.

One day, when we were really running on the national record, a group of guys had gathered around the car. Pop was tweaking. They were all asking him his secrets and he was telling them. I pulled him aside and asked him what the hell he was doing giving all our secrets away. He just smiled and said, "I'm not worried; they won't do them."

He was always tweaking a little more. One day I came in and he was on the phone deep in conversation. A couple of times I heard him call the other person Zora. When he was done, I asked him what that was all about. He said he'd been on the phone with General Motors, consulting on cam timing with, you guessed it, Zora Arkus-Duntov, "the father of the Corvette." Seems they had a lot in common. Both of Russian extraction, both engineers, and born the same year. They talked often after that.

We campaigned the car all over Texas and Louisiana. Then, as usually happens, we started thinking of moving up in class. But to what? 409s, Pontiacs, Thunderbolts, what? The Plymouths were now at Stage 3. Impressive. So we decided that was our baby. It was ordered, a Stage 3 Plymouth SS/A Fury 440 Wedge. And what did we get? A *Savoy!*

Savoy Mystery Solved

So there we were in the dealership with our jaws on the ground. What happened? The sales manager Ed Grosse had the sales agreement in his hand. "Yep, you ordered a Stage 3 Fury. I don't understand."

Then I noticed it: Something was way out of place on the business coupe. American Mag wheels on the front. We went closer. A big air scoop was built into the hood. *What?* We looked inside. Push-button shifter, no stick. Only a minimal bucket seat and no back seat. The carpet wasn't much more than a bath towel. I opened the door. It was light. Real light! Aluminum. And the window was Plexiglas. And the fenders, the hood were all aluminum too. The whole car from the doors to the front bumper was aluminum.

We went to the hood. No hinges. A lift-off. It exposed the whole engine compartment. What is *that?* Of course we all know now. A 426 cross-rammed Hemi. At the time it seemed as big as the car. What had we stepped into? No one had an answer except that this was a monster.

I got in. The keys were in the ignition. Pop said, "Go on. Fire it up." So I did. Well, it sounded like Judgment Day. Exhaust exploded through the open pipes. It was deafening in that metal building.

People came running from the showroom, including the owner, Billy Sutton. "Cut it off! Cut it off!" He was screaming and barely audible. I killed it. Billy agonized, "You'll knock all the windows out!"

Once everything cooled down, we sorted out what we had. We had been selected by Chrysler (unknown to us) to get one of the 50 SS/A Plymouth Hemis. It seems Chrysler had decided to really get into the racing game big time. The company had secretly planned and designed the Hemi to compete with the best Chevy, Pontiac, and Fords. It was, of course, a sales strategy aimed at the youth buyers.

Dragstrip Debut

Pop had built a trailer for the Chevy, and that weekend we loaded the Hemi and headed for Golden Triangle. It was in vogue to find a gutsy name for your car, especially one at the high end. I remembered that President Roosevelt had made a speech after the bombing of Pearl Harbor. He referred to it as "a day which will live in infamy." So, "Infamy" was painted on the doors. Lots of heads turned as we trailered her into the pits. No one knew what we had. Chrysler had planned it as a surprise to the public. But everyone suddenly had an idea about it when we fired her up and the ground shook.

I killed the engine. Onlookers came running over as we pulled the hood. Pop inspected everything and did a few tweaks and we were ready. With approval of the dragstrip officials, Pop had me make a few easy passes up and down the strip. I could feel the tremendous power of this monster just waiting.

I pulled back into the pits and Pop removed the hood. He checked everything again then said, "Okay, let's see what it'll do." I fired her up again and eased out to the strip. They announced that I was going for a time trial. That brought everyone to the fence.

Pop put some detergent down on the strip and I eased into it, and then drilled across. The tires spun through the soap, headed up, and caught. I backed up and Pop lined me up. I stood on the brake, punched up first gear, and revved to stall speed. I nodded to Pop and he to me. Then looking down the 1320, I let go of the brake and stabbed it.

Oh, my god! The thing thundered, lurching forward and I saw only sky as I hung a huge wheelie. Startled, I let off the gas. Down she came. Wham! Down onto the track.

Hey, come on guys; cut me some slack. Nobody had even driven one of these creatures before. It turned out that was it for the day. The front end was out of alignment big time. Pop rigged the car with the rear-end traction control system similar to the 1957 Chevy. It worked.

Now you could give it everything you had; the car rose slightly and shot down the 1320. Pop told me that wheelies looked cool, but in fact I was losing time as the pinion rose on the ring gear. It was running great now.

Then something strange happened. Over a period of about 25 runs, it began to slow. Why? Everything checked out. Then out of frustration Pop did an engine rebuild and we went back to the track where it stormed. Even lower ETs than before. After several conversations with Plymouth Racing Division, Pop figured it out. Rings. Yep. They were super soft, intended to seat immediately with no break-in. But they also wore out really fast, as we found out after 25 runs.

Now this car really was "infamy," lowering dragstrip SS/A ETs all over our region. Ed Iskenderian ground a cam for Pop that spread the torque range a little better. Doug Thorley built us a special set of headers. It ate all the Thunderbolts, Catalinas, and 409s around, only getting a good run out of other Hemis, which brings me to an interesting story.

First Match Race

I received a call from the local dragstrip that a famous West Coast Hemi Dodge was coming to town. Those at the dragstrip wanted to know if I would grudge match race him; no one else would. Pop and I talked about it and decided to go for it. That weekend, while we were prepping in the pits, the big Dodge trailered in. The group that had gathered around our car quickly abandoned us and went to the Californian. Truck and trailer were gloss and chrome. The car was a rainbow of colors with the driver's name emblazoned on the doors. He stepped from the truck and walked aloofly among his admirers. He didn't even glance over at us.

Prepped and ready, his car thundered out onto the strip for a time trial. He cleaned his tires and reset. Then he wheeled off the starting line and roared down the quarter. Amazing! It was 132 mph and just breaking the 11-second barrier. Confidently, he returned to the pits and his admirers.

Our turn. I pulled onto the strip, cleaned my tires, and reset. Then stabbed it. No wheelie, just a slight rise and straight down the strip. I turned 120-plus mph, but at a 10.52. Our best time ever. We weren't as fast, but we made it to the end a lot sooner.

Well, how 'bout that? I returned to the pits and Pop was all smiles. We pulled the hood and Pop began checking everything for the actual race. Then we heard through the PA system that there wouldn't be a Plymouth versus Dodge grudge match. Pop and I looked at each other in surprise as we glanced across the pits and the Californian was loading onto the trailer. Pop didn't say anything; he just smiled. And so went the racing season of 1964.

Quick Sale

On one particular stop we headed to Tyler, Texas. Because the strip was an old airfield, it was concrete and I cut our best times ever during time trials. Then, the hand of fate descended. We were back in the pits finessing the engine when a well-dressed fellow came over and watched. Finally he said to Pop, "You've really got her cranking today."

Pop smiled and thanked him, after which the fellow asked, "Want to sell her?"

This stunned us both. His expression was serious. Pop and I looked at each other, then we huddled. Our discussion concluded with the fact that in the next racing season we would be illegal in SS/A. And we were tired. We had worked on the car six days a week to race one. Pop walked back and introduced himself.

The fellow said he had come down from Dallas looking for this car. Pop confided to him about the NHRA rules change for next year and the fellow said, "Doesn't matter. This is what I want."

Well, in a few minutes they had made a deal: trailer, car, everything. Then unbelievably (at least to me), the guy opened his wallet and shelled out *cash!* Pop would send the title later. Before leaving the car with him, Pop gave the guy many instructions and, most of all, cautioned him to be damned sure to turn on the electric water pump before and after running the car.

We didn't wait around to see her hauled off. I was hit with a mix of emotions as we drove away. Glad to be free of the long hours of work, but pained at having to part ways with my sweetie. I never saw her again, but Pop heard through the grapevine that the new owner had forgotten his admonition about the water pump, had gone out on the track, and had blown the engine. Well, that was that.

All that's left of *Infamy* is this picture. She gave us a great deal of pleasure and brought a father and son even closer together. Now that Pop is gone, I sometimes wonder if, in the end, bringing us together was her real purpose.

By Wes Eisenschenk

When the name Hubert Platt is mentioned in the world of drag racing, thoughts of Cobra Jet Mustangs and 427-powered Fairlanes come to mind. "Hube Baby" will be long remembered for two particular cars: the 1968½ Cobra Jet Mustang and the 1964 Thunderbolt. Of course, Platt campaigned nearly a dozen other Ford-powered muscle cars, including the 1968 Ford Torino shown here.

Two Mustangs and a Torino

Hubert was very busy in 1968. For starters, he still possessed his 1967 Fairlane that Ed Terry campaigned at the 1968 Winternationals. Hubert wouldn't be campaigning the car as he had two Cobra Jet Mustangs to race, the Tasca Ford car (number 984) and the Paul Harvey Ford machine (number 985).

After the Winternationals, Hubert had 985 repainted in a beautiful black and silver with yellow lettering. However, on July 4 in Dallas, Georgia, he crashed the car thanks to a locked rear gear. Ford, quick to react, had another Cobra Jet delivered to Platt so he didn't miss a beat. The smashed 985 car ended up with Randy Payne, who rebuilt the car and had it back on the track later that summer.

The Georgia Shaker *moniker has been long associated with Hubert Platt. A native of Georgia, Hubert campaigned often in the Southeastern United States. (Photo Courtesy Allen Platt)*

Dick Landy's Coronet squares off against Hubert Platt's 1968 Torino. Both Platt and Landy enjoyed lengthy, successful careers in drag racing. (Bob Snyder Photo)

The car Hubert received after 985 (the other Cobra Jet Mustang) was painted in a tri-color configuration with one-third of the car in black (driver's side) and one-third in white (passenger's side) with a thick gold stripe separating the two. Hubert campaigned this Cobra Jet for the rest of the summer.

This brings me to the car that Hubert took delivery of in August 1968: a 1968 Ford Torino Cobra Jet, courtesy of Foulger Ford. It was delivered to Hubert painted white and featuring a red interior and a 4-speed transmission. Chuck Foulger had a long and lasting relationship with Ford and Hubert Platt, so it was natural for them to campaign another car together.

Hubert was fond of the look of his second Cobra Jet Mustang so he had Max Thompson paint the Torino in the exact same color scheme.

Hubert and Foulger conducted several "clinics" when they gave educational seminars for youths at some of the Los Angeles County Juvenile Halls. Foulger noted, "Hubert and I feel that we both have the means and, more important, the obligation to help these kids return to mainstream society." This led to Ford's new idea for marketing drag racing to its fan base.

Hubert Platt and Randy Payne fronted the East Coast drag team division of Ford's overall drag racing program for 1969. You can see the West Coast drag team cars in the background. (Photo Courtesy Rusty Gilles)

East Coast Drag Team

Randy Payne had also just come off a successful season campaigning a 1968 Cobra Jet Mustang. Hubert had asked his fellow Georgian if he would drive him to Michigan because he had a deal in the works with Ford. As Randy joked in *Ford Drag Team*, "The reason he called me is that he didn't have a damn driver's license and he wanted me along as a chauffeur and for protection."

Once at Ford, Randy was introduced to Lee Iacocca, who was going to make him an offer also. Ford was creating East Coast and West Coast drag teams for 1969 and Hubert and Randy would be heading up the East Coast version of the program. They would also conduct performance seminars at dealerships and other various Ford-related events. Randy was Hubert's assistant at these seminars, and was paid $12,000 plus expenses, with race winnings kept by the driver.

Randy Payne further noted in *Ford Drag Team*, "We educated the public through seminars and demonstrations at Ford dealerships and competition races at major racetracks across America. The company's goal was to move drag racing from the streets to sanctioned tracks. Hubert Platt and I were the professional drivers who met with the public representing Ford Motor Company. I prepared the speeches for the seminars and demonstrations where Hubert and I discussed innovative techniques in engine performance."

Racing Campaigns

The two cars they piloted were a 428 Cobra Jet Mustang (Hubert) and a 428 Cobra Jet Torino (Randy). The Torino in this arrangement was none other than Hubert's former tri-colored car. The East Coast and West Coast drag team cars were shipped to Holman-Moody, where the East Coast cars received a new paint job in the familiar Ford blue with a white hood and decklid. The West Coast cars had the reverse treatment featuring white cars with blue accents. Ed Terry and his assistant Ed Wood handled driving duties on those cars.

Platt and Payne campaigned the two Cobra Jets in tandem and conducted seminars for most of 1969. Randy had a successful tenure campaigning the Torino. He says the car ran 11.22 on its first pass out. When asked what else could be done to make the car better, Randy said, "Wash it."

Randy won three of the four NHRA national events in 1969, running SS/J, and missed on the U.S. Nationals, although team orders from corporate may have been to help the newcomer.

Payne found himself in a Boss Maverick for the following season in the new Pro Stock class. Platt campaigned a pair of Mustangs before ultimately switching to Pro Stock in another Mustang and eventually a Boss Maverick as well.

After Payne stopped driving the Torino, Hubert returned the car to Chuck Foulger. Randy tried to track down the car years later and learned that it ended up on the street in north Alabama. It may have been sent to the crusher after being wrecked, but that hasn't been verified.

What is confirmed is that this Torino led a successful and colorful life with Platt and Payne. Randy noted that this was the "best" and "most successful" car he ever ran.

The Trans-Am Championship-Winning Boss Mustang

By Edward Ludtke

In June 1969, Ford had Kar Kraft order the last three Trans-Am Mustangs in preparation for the 1970 Trans-Am season; they were VIN 9F02M212775, -776, and -777. The 1970 team cars were built at Kar Kraft with a special three-link rear suspension designed by Ed Hull and Lee Dykstra (later of DeKon racing fame) and Mitch Marchi. These Mustangs were supposed to feature a high rear shelf and longer shocks that mounted vertically to an upper crossmember, clearly visible from the inside of the car.

The 1969 Trans-Am race at St. Jovite in July changed Ford's plans. One Sunday afternoon, three of the four Mustang team cars were involved in a big wreck that nearly wiped out the Ford Trans-Am effort. So, number 777 was not modified with the special rear, and it was completed quickly to replace the damaged Mustangs. Parnelli Jones raced it in the final two Trans-Am races of the 1969 season. Mustang lost the Trans-Am championship to Camaro, but valuable lessons were learned for the 1970 Trans-Am season.

1970 Ford Team Wins

Ford went with just one factory-backed team in 1970: the Bud Moore Engineering team. Bud received all of the Shelby team Mustangs and parts, as his team was the one contracted. The number 073 Shelby prototype was fitted with the 1970 sheet metal and tested in the Lockheed Aerospace wind tunnel. All the remaining 1969 Mustangs were converted to 1970 specs and painted the new "school-bus yellow" team color; they were to be used as backups.

Bud Moore took three Mustangs for the 1970 Trans-Am season opener to Laguna Seca. Parnelli Jones drove the number 777 Mustang; he qualified it on the pole and won that first race. He then followed with another victory at Lime Rock in the next Trans-Am race. George Follmer gave Mustang its third victory in number 776 at Bryar, New Hampshire. Parnelli ran 777 again at Mid-Ohio and gained his third victory.

After some disappointing finishes in the following Trans-Am races, it all came down to September 20, 1970, and the race at Kent,

Bud Moore footed the bill for a championship-winning chassis in 1970. Here, George Follmer paces the car at Road America in Elkhart Lake, Wisconsin. This is chassis 9F02M212775's final race; it finished a respectable second. (Photo Courtesy Edward Ludtke Collection)

Washington, to decide the championship. Parnelli had been working with Ford engineers and Bud Moore to dial in the new Mustang to his liking.

He won the race and the championship for Ford driving number 775. Parnelli followed that with leading the final event at Riverside, but a slow car pushed him off the track. When he restarted, he was in ninth, but not for long. His damaged Mustang charged back to the front and finally passed Follmer in the closing laps to take the win. Many famous photos of Parnelli jumping over the curbs to get the Mustang to turn have made that race part of his legend. The three Mustangs designated to be the team cars for 1970 did the job, winning six Trans-Am races and the Trans-Am Championship for Ford and the Boss 302 Mustang.

New Home, More Wins

On the day before Thanksgiving, November 1970, the Detroit papers read, "Ford Withdraws," and Ford pulled out of all forms of racing. The workers showed up at Kar Kraft in Dearborn and the doors were locked. It was a very sad day in Dearborn and for

Ford fans everywhere. Everything that was Trans-Am Mustang at Kar Kraft was packed up in semitrailers and shipped to Bud Moore Engineering in Spartanburg, South Carolina, where he also built NASCAR stock cars. This included the four 1970 body-in-white (BIW) shells, parts, fixtures, and even the surface plate used to construct the Mustangs.

Bud received all the team cars and promptly sold off number 776 to Warren Tope of Michigan. He sold two Mustangs to Troy Promotions race team, one being number 777. Bud sold off enough Mustangs to run the 1971 Trans-Am season. He kept the number 775 Championship Mustang and it was to be the number 15 primary team car again for 1971.

Bud also completed one of the BIW Mustangs for new team driver Peter Gregg. Yes, the same Peter Gregg of Porsche fame. Peter brought the SS Jacobs builder's sponsorship with him. In addition, he convinced Parnelli Jones to drive in the Lime Rock Trans-Am, the first race of the 1971 season.

Parnelli was brought in with additional money from the New York Ford dealers. The day ended after five laps.

George Follmer was hired to drive for Bud for the rest of the season; he promptly won both of the next Trans-Am races at Bryar and Mid-Ohio. In the next Trans-Am race at Edmonton, George finished second. The team did not enter Donnybrooke in Minnesota (now known as Brainerd International Raceway). George came back with another second at Road America in Wisconsin. It was the last race for Bud Moore and number 775.

It was reported to have been sold to a racer in Mexico in 1971, but other than some spare parts that have made their way back to the United States, not much else is known of the current state of the car. Parnelli Jones made one attempt to find and purchase this Mustang between 1989 and 1991. I was told he could not even get a sniff of the whereabouts of his famous car. Other attempts may have been made, but the car has never surfaced.

Final Home

The trail becomes cold on number 775 after that. Two known attempts to purchase the Mustang have been made and both failed. Other offers to purchase it have been made, but the owner is not interested in selling this famous Mustang. It is a shame that the

No other Boss Mustang can lay claim to being the car that clinched the 1970 Trans-Am Championship for Ford. Here, the championship car is at the picturesque Road America track in Elkhart Lake, Wisconsin. (Photo Courtesy Edward Ludtke Collection)

championship-winning 1970 Boss 302 Mustang is not back in the hands of Ford or even the Henry Ford Museum.

The race record for 9F02M212775 is:

1970 Trans-Am
- Pacific Raceway, Kent, Washington: Parnelli Jones 1st
- Mission Bell, Riverside, California: Parnelli Jones 1st

1971 Trans-Am
- Lime Rock Park, Connecticut: Parnelli Jones DNF
- Bryar, New Hampshire: George Follmer 1st
- Mid-Ohio: George Follmer 1st
- Edmonton, Canada: George Follmer 2nd
- Road America, Elkhart Lake, Wisconsin: George Follmer 2nd

By Wes Eisenschenk with Allen Platt

When chronicling Hubert Platt's illustrious career campaigning cars with the Blue Oval, things can be a little confusing. After all, as one of the factory-backed Ford drag racers of the 1960s, Hubert was in high demand and was frequently changing his ride as the manufacturer launched new models or was looking for exposure with a high-powered drag car. Among the cars slated for Platt to campaign in 1967 was a Ford Fairlane XL 500. This Fairlane left enthusiasts scratching their heads for nearly 50 years.

The Specs

In an early May test session in 1967, Hubert tested a new Ford Fairlane with a 427. The car featured the medium riser mill with 13.2:1 compression, L1-F1 camshaft, 2-inch inside-diameter headers, 4.86 Detroit Locker rear, and 10.5 x 15 slicks. He brought the new car to Bristol, Tennessee, and made 18 passes, coming up with a best time of 11.42 at 123.79, with his slowest pass of 11.76 at 120.64 mph.

He was testing the car for the NHRA Springnationals that were to be held on June 10 and 11, 1967, at Bristol. Ford wanted Hubert to run one of its fully dressed Fairlane 500 XLs for exposure, so Ford sold

In May 1967, Hubert Platt bought this Fairlane for the lofty price of $1. The car was brought to Bristol International Dragway straightaway for a test session to prepare for the NHRA Springnationals. (Allen Platt Photo)

him this all-black version for $1. That's right, a 427-powered Fairlane that ran mid-11s for a buck. According to Hubert, the car even came with power windows.

Identity Lettering

At this period in drag racing, drag racers typically ran cars that kind of looked like cars they had run in the past. It was a good way for fans to follow and recognize their favorite drivers. But the appearance of Platt's cars was constantly evolving.

The all-black Fairlane had "Hubert Platt" applied in white block lettering on the door and "Ford" painted in white lettering with a blue-accented outline. The sponsor name of "Paul Harvey" was laid down in a three-dimensional script lettering; a light shade of tan with a red shadow behind that. The car really had the look of a luxury racer with its molding and black vinyl roof. It appears that this car stayed in this visual configuration for roughly a month or so until changes were made before the Super Stock Nationals.

The first visual change to the car came with the removal of the tan and red lettering. In its place was silver script, calling out the names "Hubert Platt" and "Paul Harvey." The "Ford" white-and-blue script remained untouched. In addition, "Indianapolis" and "Indiana" were placed under the name "Paul Harvey" with "Georgia Shaker" added to the rear quarter panels.

At times, cars had subtle changes before national events. This car saw these changes before the Super Stock Nationals held June 23 to 25, although the quarter-window decals remained the same.

As on most drag cars, the graphics on the 1967 427 vinyl roof car were ever-changing. Here, the car is without its Georgia Shaker *moniker and sports orange and yellow lettering, not the familiar silver script. (Fermier Brothers Collection Courtesy Charlie Morris)*

During the summer months of 1967, Hubert Platt and Harold Dutton campaigned a pair of Paul Harvey Ford–sponsored Fairlanes. Visually, the differences were that Hubert's car had a vinyl roof and was named Georgia Shaker, *whereas Dutton's car was without vinyl and named* Drag Hag.

Hubert Platt was one of Ford's busiest factory-backed drivers. In 1967, he campaigned this Fairlane, which was delivered new to him with a vinyl roof. (Photo Courtesy Hubert Platt Collection)

Racing Results

Hubert campaigned the car in SS/B at the national event. Dick Aarons took home the Super Stock Eliminators trophy with an 11.63 over Ronnie Sox's even faster 11.02.

It's never going to be an easy day at the office when Hemi-powered Chryslers surround you in the staging lanes. This photo from October 1967 at Tulsa for the Nationals shows the car in its two-tone scheme. (Photo Courtesy Chuck Conway)

On July 2, Hubert set the national record at Houston County Drag-Way in Georgia with an 11.38 in the SS/B class. Platt had been giving the Mopars and Chevys all they could handle. Arlen Vanke told Hubert that 1967 would have been a great year for Mopar had it not been for that "pesky Fairlane."

That pesky Fairlane continued to be a thorn in everyone's side at the U.S. Nationals on Labor Day weekend. During qualifying, Platt tripped the lights with a blazing 11.10 at 125.17 mph, pacing the field in SS/B.

Just one week earlier, Platt's car had a vinyl roof, now absent at Indy. It might have been good for a tenth of a second! In eliminations, Platt ripped off a 10.96 for a new low elapsed time, showing the world that the Fairlanes were the cars to beat, with the Hemi-powered Mopars a tenth behind. However, in the world of handicap racing, the stellar ET didn't matter because Jenkins wore the crown as the first Super Stock champion at Indianapolis Raceway Park in his 1967 Camaro.

A Makeover

Before the World Finals in Tulsa over the last weekend of October, the car received a heavy makeover. It now sported a two-tone paint job featuring silver and black paint. The lettering on the door also changed: "Hubert Platt" was now yellow, "Paul Harvey" was yellow/green, and "Ford" was yellow with a red outline. Just as with the

Platt's Fairlane made a return trip to the Winternationals in 1968 with Ed Terry behind the wheel. (Photo Courtesy Steve Reyes Collection)

earlier black paint scheme, the words "Georgia Shaker" weren't seen on the car until after a few events had passed.

It's been often speculated that Hubert campaigned two different Fairlanes in 1967; however, he has said that it was just the one car. Visual evidence supports this; the rear quarter window decals stayed the same during the transition from the all-black paint job to the new two-tone rendition.

New Owners

The car campaigned under Hubert's name one more time under his ownership at the 1968 Winternationals with Ed Terry behind the wheel because Platt had double-duty campaigning a pair of 68.5 Cobra Jet Mustangs. Terry ran the car in SS/C but was bested by Grumpy Jenkins for class honors. On that trip, Max Smith accompanied Hubert and had arranged to buy the Fairlane after the Winternationals. Max took the car back to Phenix Dragstrip in Phenix City, Alabama, and ran it the next night, winning his class in SS/C. Max ran the car for the better part of a year locally, making passes at Phenix, Panama City, and other Southeastern dragstrips.

On Hubert Platt's recommendation, Max sold the car to a Missourian named Jim Morton, from Sappington, a suburb of St. Louis. Jim ran the car at the U.S. Nationals in 1969. This time the car wore Yates & Stevens Ford sponsorship and was campaigned under the name *Strange Stuff*. This is the last verified time that the former Platt Fairlane was campaigned at an NHRA event.

Hubert sold the car sometime after the 1968 Winternationals to Jim Morton of Missouri. Here are the remnants of the Paul Harvey sponsorship along with its new name, **Strange Stuff**. *(Photo Courtesy Carl and Char Hirst Collection)*

Rumors and speculation have the car going back to Alabama after Morton's tenure, where it was possibly campaigned briefly. It's thought that the powertrain was removed and dropped into a 1967 Fairlane sedan, and the body sold to a circle-track racer from Tallahassee. The body eventually succumbed to racing damage from the very taxing world of oval racing. However, none of this has been verified.

Jim Morton, the Fairlane's last confirmed owner, may actually know the truth. However, countless searches for Jim have come up empty.

It is known that this Ford Fairlane was in fact *one* car, not *two*. Moreover, this Fairlane 427 was a five-time NHRA national event competitor, along with a SS/B record holder, and was one of the most beautiful machines Hubert Platt ever campaigned.

If you have any information on Hubert Platt's old 1967 Fairlane, or information on Jim Morton, please contact Wes Eisenschenk.

By Bernard Durham

To understand the history of the very successful Chevelle my dad campaigned in the mid-1960s, a bit of the backstory is necessary to explain how it all came about.

My dad, Malcolm Durham, started dabbling in the world of drag racing in 1957 with his 1956 Chevrolet. In similar fashion to Ronnie Sox, Dad cut his teeth racing on obscure dragstrips in North Carolina in the late 1950s. After moving to Washington, D.C., Dad took an automotive course at a technical trade school and began to hone his craft with the 1956 Chev.

With his added knowledge, he began working at Hick's Chevrolet as a mechanic and campaigning a 1962 SS 409 Sports Coupe. At Hick's Chevrolet, one of the sales managers, an avid SCCA racer, introduced Dad to some of the folks at corporate General Motors. Through that connection, he took delivery of one of the ultra-rare and ferociously potent 1963 Z-11 Impalas.

After a year campaigning the Z-11, Chevrolet pulled out of factory-backed racing. Dad plucked the Z-11 out of the full-size Chevy and set his sights on using the rat in the all-new Chevelle. *Strip Blazer II*

My Strip Blazer II *Chevelle ran Z11 power under the hood (I am at the front of the car on the left). Later, as* Strip Blazer III, *this same car ran the potent Z16 engine. (Photo Courtesy Richard "Mac" McKinstry)*

was a very special car for my dad for several reasons. This car was critical to his early success because it had the uneasy chore of following the very successful *Strip Blazer I* 1963 Z-11.

Strip Blazer II

In 1964, Ford built the Thunderbolt. After looking at the Thunderbolt, my dad decided to use the 1964 Chevelle as a base to build a GM version of it. He modified the 409 from the 1963 Z11 with a stroker crank that produced 427 ci and inserted it into the petite 1964 Chevelle. He also set the engine back 8 inches from its stock location, improved the heads and the induction system, and added a few additional mods to balance the playing field against the T-bolts. The lighter 1964 Chevelle *Strip Blazer II* exceeded expectations.

With GM's exit from its racing programs, and drag racing in particular, many of the racers switched to Ford or to the lethal Hemi-packing Mopars. My father's decision was to stay with General Motors and the 1964 Chevelle during this period and that really increased his popularity within the GM fan base.

I recall my father talking about one of the highlights of this car after Ronnie Sox had won the 1964 NHRA Winternationals. At the time, Sox & Martin were competing in Mercury's version of the Thunderbolt, called the Comet.

Dad remembered, "When he [Ronnie Sox] came back East, we were ready for him. We raced him on three consecutive days: Friday evening at 75-80 Dragway in Monrovia, Maryland; Saturday at Cecil County, Maryland; and Sunday at Dover, New York; and beat him all three times. That Chevelle was a real winner."

The popularity of newly built *Strip Blazer II* soared. My father continued his association with the famed East Coast–based S&S racing team with *Strip Blazer II*.

Strip Blazer III

In 1965 Dad altered the wheelbase and added a straight axle, a new front clip, new taillights, and injectors to the Chevelle. The front and rear wheels were moved forward to compete with the other altered-wheelbase cars that were beginning to take over drag racing.

The Chevelle was painted blue and re-lettered with "Strip Blazer III" across the rear quarters. *Strip Blazer III* had two different lettering

Dressed in its Strip Blazer III *attire, I power the Z16-milled Chevelle down the quarter-mile dragstrip at Aquasco Speedway in 1966. (Photo Courtesy Ron Gusack)*

jobs with the initial letters on the door noting "Durham Bros" and "Washington D.C." and adding "Charles Durham" as the mechanic on the front fender.

In later configurations, you see "Malcolm Durham" listed on the front fender, along with "Race Car Engineering" and "Bladensburg, MD." The different lettering jobs were consistent with the move of Dad's race shop from Washington, D.C., to Bladensburg, Maryland.

Later, my dad switched to Chevrolet's new 396 "porcupine" engine and added nitromethane to the lineup. The car ran consistently in the mid-9s at more than 150 mph. *Strip Blazer III* was proclaimed the world's fastest Chevelle, a fitting title for such a radical machine.

Strip Blazer IV

The 1965 Chevelle and other altered-wheelbase, nitro-injected cars of this time are often credited with being at the forefront of the transformation from door car to modern Funny Car. These cars are known for their stretched bodies, altered wheelbase, and nitro-breathing engines. With the new Funny Car category, my dad was one of the first racers who match raced all across the country, often gone for weeks at a time.

In 1966, Dad sold the Chevelle to build a Corvair, his first blown tube-framed car called *Strip Blazer IV*. He continued his career in a Camaro and later a Vega. He stayed true to Chevy until he retired from drag racing to help me through college. He returned to the strip in 1984 with a Pro Stock Camaro, but a crash at Rockingham in 1985 put the car back on the trailer and out of professional competition permanently.

Chevelle Rediscovered?

In 1989 my father built a replica of his 1965 Chevelle to compete in the Legends of Drag Racing Series. This car was a modern version of his 1965 Chevelle but with all the latest safety equipment, a gasoline-powered big-block Chevy, and a Lenco. This car brought back memories for many fans and traversed the quarter-mile in the low-7s.

The last time I can recall anyone mentioning any details about the 1965 Chevelle was during NHRA's inaugural Winston Showdown at Bristol Dragway in 1999. I was racing Super Gas and a local gentleman was standing in the pit looking at my car for about 10 minutes.

Finally, he came over to my dad and me and said, "I know where your 1965 Chevelle is." He said that a friend of his was driving it on the street about 30 miles from the track. He added that the current owner had raced it for several years on the dragstrip and converted it back to a street car. My dad asked him several questions about the straight axle and the altered wheelbase, and the gentleman replied, "It still has everything in place."

My father had a difficult time believing that someone could be driving an altered-wheelbase car on the street and he wanted to see the car. The gentleman said he would come back after eliminations and take us to see it. He never returned and that is the last we heard about the potential whereabouts of the 1964/1965 Chevelle.

I spoke with my dad about it later that evening and he said, "I sold that car to some racers from another part of the country, not in the Tennessee area."

The One and Only

Strip Blazer II and its later configuration into *Strip Blazer III* is often confusing and some people think of them as being two different cars; the truth is they are one and the same. There's no doubt that match racing with this Chevelle helped propel my dad into drag racing history, further proven when he was named as one of the NHRA's 50 Greatest Drivers of all time.

If you know where *Strip Blazer II/III* is, I would love to hear about the Chevelle and its possible whereabouts.

By Ryan Brutt

Y ou never know what you are going to find out there anymore. I travel around the country documenting cool and unique cars and engines in barns, fields, junkyards, old churches, large oil drums, etc. My travels have allowed me to see some extremely rare cars that have been out of the public eye. Thankfully, I put all my money into *finding* more cool cars, so I don't have any money to *buy* those cool cars.

I always open the conversation with the owners by letting them know that I am no threat to the car. I don't want to buy it or part it out. I just want to hear the story, and then they usually open up and tell me their story.

Old Cars and Pepsi Bottles

I was following up on a lead from a friend of mine while I was traveling through North Carolina. He had told me that a yard full of Mopars was hidden in a wheat field out in the middle of the state. My friend was fortunate enough to have the phone number of the man who owned the cars and said that the guy was a real southern gentleman. So I gave him a ring to arrange a visit.

A woman answered; I introduced myself and asked to talk to the man whom I was told was the owner of the cars. She informed me that he was her husband and he had unfortunately passed away a few years earlier. I apologized and let her know that obviously my information was old and I didn't mean to bother her, but asked if any of

The Outlawed *Barracuda, piloted by none other than Richard Petty, takes flight at the AHRA Winter Nationals at Beeline Dragway circa 1965. (Photo Courtesy Paul Hutchins Collection)*

Yes, this is all that's left of Richard Petty's famed Outlawed Barracuda *drag car. The car was involved in a fatality and was ultimately scrapped by the Petty family. (Photo Courtesy Ryan Brutt)*

his old cars were still lying around. She said she had "one or two" and that I was welcome to come by and take a look.

With that, I was off like the wind that afternoon. As I approached the property, I found a small driveway with the right address, but no cars in sight. It just went up a hill to a little house. My heart sank, but I continued anyway. Once I made it over the hill, I was rewarded. Hidden behind the hill was a large yard full of classic Mopars.

The woman was there waiting for me. I introduced myself and thanked her for allowing me the opportunity to see the collection. She was more than happy to see someone excited about rusty old cars. The man's brother was there as well, and he showed me the majority of the collection.

We started by the main barn/office. The family had been deeply ingrained in NASCAR and particularly close to the Petty family. They had the largest collection of Richard Petty Pepsi-Cola bottles I have ever seen. I had no idea they existed before that. But there they were, case after case of them. But it wasn't just the Pepsi bottles that linked them to the Pettys. They had signage, engine parts, pictures, and a little bit of everything. But the largest piece was out back.

Making our way around the barn, I saw a wrecked first-gen Barracuda. I looked at it for a second and thought about it. It looked familiar, but I could not place it. Then the woman asked, "Do you know that special car?" So it *was* special, and I could make out some Petty Blue paint on the roof. That's when it all clicked. This was the first Richard Petty drag car!

Drag Racing

In 1964, NASCAR outlawed the 426 Hemi and the SOHC Ford engine from racing. For Ford, it was not an incredible loss because the engine was basically a special build for NASCAR. But for Chrysler, tons of money and time were invested in the Hemi and it could not be abandoned so easily. So the automaker sat out the 1965 NASCAR season and pushed the Hemis into drag racing more heavily. And with Richard Petty not doing anything, he went drag racing.

This was the first iteration, the famous 1964 Barracuda, that he had built at his shop. It was painted Petty Blue and had the trademark "43" on the rear quarters in front of the tire and a "Jr." marking as a joke. But right on the doors, the Pettys had painted "Outlawed" as a nudge at NASCAR. The car debuted in November 1964. A sign on the front of the car read, "NASCAR, If you can't outrun 'em, outlaw 'em."

Richard Petty did well with the car, running it all around the country match racing. Unfortunately February 28, 1965, changed everything. While piloting the Barracuda at a match race against Arnie Beswick's blown GTO at Southeastern Dragway in Dallas, Georgia, a suspension problem occurred that caused the Plymouth to hook into the stands, killing an eight-year-old boy and injuring at least eight spectators.

The whole incident seriously bothered Richard and he just about quit racing altogether. The car was brought home after the wreck and thrown into the Petty junkyard back behind the shop and left there to rot. Plymouth still wanted him drag racing and promoting the brand, so another Barracuda was built (*43 Jr*) with no reference to being "outlawed."

By the time it was ready, NASCAR had seen the error of its ways and let the 426 Hemi back into the fold. So when the 1966 NASCAR season started, Richard left drag racing for the oval tracks and never went back.

A Piece of History

So *Outlawed* was left to rot behind the Petty shop for decades too, getting run over by bulldozers and having parts cut off by fans. From what I was told, the Pettys eventually decided to expand the shop and everything in the junkyard was going to be crushed. Their friend didn't want a piece of history to be destroyed, so, with the Pettys' blessing, he took it home with him and put it out back behind his shop.

That's where I found it, languishing behind his shop just where he had left it, a footnote in the history of both NASCAR and drag racing.

By Thomas Benvie

For the longest time, American Motors used the slogan, "The only race we are interested in is the human race." Content to win the Mobil Economy runs, American Motors produced cars aimed squarely at the middle-class family man. In 1966, the company introduced a newly designed V-8 with 290 ci. A total of 625 cars were produced with this engine, which included a special run of 500 two-door Rogue hardtops in two-tone colors.

The 343 was introduced in a limited number of cars in 1967. Some of the dealerships took notice of the power in the small car and it started to show up at the tracks. Roberts Rambler, Rockford Rambler, and Richmond Rambler were a few of the more successful dealers.

American Motors clearly became interested in other types of races in the fall of 1967. The automaker entered the pony car field with the brand-new Javelin, a two-door long-hood/short-deck combination that could be ordered with the potent 343 4-barrel, dual exhaust, and a 4-speed transmission. It was an immediate hit with the dealers and they also began to show up at the tracks.

AMC sponsored a pair of Javelins in the Trans-Am series races and they were quite successful. AMC also sponsored a giveaway at the Javelin Speed Spectacular at Bonneville where three teams of three mechanics set up cars to be run by Craig Breedlove. At the

Mack Massey Motors, Inc. was an AMC dealership in El Paso, Texas, and sponsored Uncle Sam. *(Photo Courtesy Dennis Kincaid Collection)*

quarter-mile tracks, Ron Root, Corkey Booze, and Bonanza Rambler became competitive in a short time. AMC had a winner!

SC/Rambler and AMX

In February 1968, American Motors became a game changer with the introduction of a shortened version of the Javelin, a two-seat sports car called the AMX. Along with the car, a new engine size was also introduced, the AMX 390. Within a month, this engine became available in the Javelin and the big-body AMCs, Rebel, and Ambassador. At the track, Dave Kempton raced an automatic and Lou Downing of Nebraska raced a 4-speed called *Steakmaker*.

One of the weaker parts of the car was the sloppy 4-speed shifter. A meeting was held with Hurst Performance in October 1968 to rectify this and market the American Motors cars, particularly the Javelin and AMX, with the Hurst Super Stock Shifter. Two interesting proposals came out of the meeting.

The first was to create a 390-powered Rogue with 4-speed transmission, dual exhaust, Posi-Traction, and a wild hood scoop and paint job. It became known as the Rambler SC/Rambler, and 500 were planned. The orders quickly filled, and a total of 1,512 cars were produced.

The second proposal was for the development of a strip-ready AMX by Hurst, to be made available to American Motors dealers. It would be designed to qualify for the NHRA Super Stock class. Fifty cars would have to be documented and produced. A letter was sent to the dealers November 4, 1968, asking for an indication of their interest. At the same time a stock 1968 AMX was pulled from the line and sent to Hurst's Ferndale, Michigan, facility (the same facility that just created the Hemi 'Cuda and Hemi Darts).

Only 41 dealers signed up, so a second letter was sent out on December 2 as a reminder and had a little more information. The required orders came in and the project was a go. AMC also signed H. L. and Shirley Shahan to campaign one of the new cars.

Delivery to the Dealers

The first car was tested and was ready for the press by February 1969. AMC introduced the Shahans and the new Hurst Super Stock AMX at the Orange County International Raceway later that month. By March, the cars were ready for delivery to the dealers. Some of the

Joe Ortega (left) was the crew chief and Tom Shelton (right) was the first driver of Uncle Sam. *Dennis Kincaid later piloted the car. (Photo Courtesy Dennis Kincaid Collection)*

dealers' employees drove to Michigan to pick up their cars; others had them delivered via standard auto transporters with the usual new-car deliveries.

The cars were built without a heater system, carpet underlayment, sway bar, one horn, and some other miscellaneous parts. Added to the car was a metal hood scoop, hood pins, an Edelbrock STR-11 Street Tunnel Ram intake (or cross ram) for special Holley dual 4-barrel carbs, a Mallory Dual point distributor, special production heads modified by Crane Engineering, headers, axles, a special clutch assembly, and a blowshield.

Some of these cars became famous in their own right. Some of the more notable NHRA record-holding cars were *Drag-On Lady* (driven by Shirley Shahan), *Pete's Patriot* from Nebraska (driven by Lou Downing), the Beachy Brothers' entry from Indiana, *AMX-1* from Virginia, and an AHRA record holder campaigned by Stowe Engineering in New York.

Other well-known cars that weren't record holders included one from Mack Massey Rambler in El Paso, Texas. It was named *Uncle Sam* and wore red, white, and blue lettering painted on the door and front fender. A large portrait of Uncle Sam from the "I Want You" recruiting poster was painted on the white part of the door and rear quarter. Sporting Cragar chrome mags and the stock SS hood scoop, the car was a crowd-pleaser and stood out in the pits.

Uncle Sam on the Track

Tom Shelton and Dennis Kincaid shared driving duty for the car. One of the first outings was at the 1969 AHRA nationals in Tucson, Arizona, where the car promptly set the speed record. NHRA events during the next few years included the Springnationals, Summernationals, U.S. Nationals, and Winternationals. The car was probably best known around the Southwest as a match-race car. In this format, two or three cars raced for the best three out of five. *Uncle Sam* was a consistent winner, often taking three straight to win.

In 1970, AMC sent the owners of the cars a changeover kit that consisted of all the parts to update the car to the new 1970 AMX look. This included hood, grille, taillights, and interior parts. Although many cars were not converted, *Uncle Sam* was. Then, the NHRA immediately ruled that these cars had to be changed back if they wanted to race in class.

At the end of the 1970 season, Tom Shelton left to race an AMC-powered gas B/Dragster. Ray Griffin raced the AMX for the 1970 season and had the car repainted red, white, and blue. It was still called *Uncle Sam*, but the name was painted in smaller block letters on one line. A different version of the image of Uncle Sam was also painted on the middle white section. The car was primarily a Southwest track car and did not compete at any national AHRA or NHRA races.

In 1971, Griffin converted the car to run A/Gas. The only exterior change was a new hood and scoop, but the remainder of the paint

Uncle Sam *is one of just 53 S/S AMXs built by AMC in 1969. Many of the cars were painted with the patriotic red, white, and blue configuration. (Photo Courtesy Dennis Kincaid Collection)*

scheme was the same. Instead of the cross-ram dual quads, a tunnel ram was installed.

Ron Cappuccelli of Albuquerque, New Mexico, was the next owner, but I do not know when or for how long it was campaigned. He sold it to Randy "Sid" Siqueiros in El Paso. It sat there at a repair shop owned by Joe Duran, until about 1983 or 1984. At that point it was still painted a faded red, white, and blue and still ran.

The car was sold to the owner of a brown Jeep monster truck called *The Moose* and loaded onto an enclosed trailer with the Jeep painted on the side. From there the trail goes cold. No record of the owner or location of the car, or the Jeep monster truck. It is rumored to be in the San Francisco area.

The Final Six

Of the 53 total 1969 Hurst Super Stock AMXs built, eight are still missing. Two of those have been destroyed. Could the other six still be hiding in a long-forgotten corner of a garage?

By Wes Eisenschenk with Jay Sabol

When it comes to authenticating the history of collector cars, typically, nothing comes easy. Even more difficult is attempting to put the pieces back together on a retired old race car that's been thrashed, smashed, and stolen. That certainly is the case for the famed S/S AMX (VIN A9M397X213605) known as *Hicksville Rambler*. The story may be best suited for an episode of *Unsolved Mysteries*.

First Owner

In a never-ending attempt to catch up in the muscle car wars, in 1969 AMC created a batch of 53 AMX race cars slated for drag racing competition. Harry Provence, who owned an AMC dealership in Hicksville, New York, was the lucky recipient of one of these AMXs and fittingly named it *Hicksville Rambler*. The car was raced and campaigned by Gary Stowe of Stowe Engineering in Far Rockaway, New York.

One of just 53 Super Stock AMXs built by AMC, Hicksville Rambler *(later named* The 2nd Attempt *and then* The Go Package*), terrorized the East Coast until disappearing into a cloud of dust in the mid-1970s. (Photo Courtesy Tommy Erwin Archive)*

By all estimation, *Hicksville Rambler* was a very successful car. Luminous wins came at the AHRA's Grand American Championships at Rockingham International in Top Stock Eliminator, Top Stock at the IHRA Spring Nationals, and a win at the Grand Touring Eliminator Bracket at the AHRA's Grand American Championships at Detroit Dragway.

The Grand American Championships was a series of 10 races that accumulated points to crown a national champion. For the 1970 season, AMC sent out kits to update the 1969 cars to 1970 in order to keep them current for NHRA classifications. Before Stowe wrapped up his time in the car, he installed the rear taillights on the 1969 AMX from the kit. The updated 1970 VIN was also sent but never installed. The best ET that the car ran under Gary's tenure was a 10.79 at 127.34 at Rockingham International.

Second Owner

One day the AMX was missing from the dealership, General Motors reported to Gary. It would have been extremely difficult to remove the car from where it was located in the building because so many other cars were blocking it in, leading to speculation that someone inside the Hicksville dealership arranged for its removal.

Visual evidence seems to back up the theory that The 2nd Attempt *was in fact the repurposed* Hicksville Rambler.

Luckily, *Hicksville Rambler* was returned to Hurst, where it was possibly repackaged and sold to Roy Crandall of Homer, New York. Roy purchased his AMX from Plank Motors in Cortland, New York, and he had the car repainted with the moniker *The 2nd Attempt*.

With the car now in Roy's hands, a second 1970 conversion kit was sent out, including the VIN, but just as before, it was never applied. Roy campaigned the car locally at Bear Creek, Cicero, and Tri-Cities before retiring from drag racing in 1970 after 20 years on the tracks. Roy returned the car to Plank Motors and traded it in on a Wagoneer.

Third Owner

The third owners of this S/S AMX were Skeeter and Barbara Hernandez of Maryland, who happened upon the car sitting on the lot at Plank Motors in 1972. The duo owned a paint and body shop and had the car repainted and renamed, this time as *The Go Package*, with the car garnering a spread in the July 1974 issue of *Super Stock & Drag Illustrated*. Both Skeeter and Barbara took their turns behind the wheel of the AMX.

The Hernandez family took the AMX with them when they moved to the Florida panhandle in the late 1970s. John Sealock, a local resident, spotted the AMX and made an offer to buy it from the

After its tenure in New York, **The 2nd Attempt** *was sold to Skeeter and Barbara Hernandez of Maryland. The car found itself in Florida after the couple moved and was rebadged as* **The Go** *Package. (Photo Courtesy Barbara Hernandez)*

Hernandez family. They weren't interested in selling then, so John sourced another S/S AMX called *Pete's Patriot*.

With time, though, Skeeter and Barbara listed their AMX after purchasing a 1971 Hemi Challenger. The ad read:

FOR SALE

1969 AMX, original Hurst car. Super Tricks, 390" engine, Milodon, Crane & custom paint. All the best money can buy & more. 420" modified engine, Brooks pistons, rods, plus spare blocks, heads, cams, Pro Shift trans. & more, $4,500. Contact: Skeeter, (904) 785-XXXX

Fourth and Fifth Owners

Jack Thomas was next to own the car after trading cash plus a small motorhome for it. Jack had the car but never raced or titled it. Not long after Jack purchased the car, John Emmi came into the picture and purchased the AMX via a trade for his 1972 Corvette.

John painted the car pearl orange and silver and dropped a 343 4-speed and a Chrysler rear into it and put it on the street. Unfortunately, John had a bad accident with the car; he rolled it and it was totaled. State Farm paid the claim and John was allowed to keep the wrecked AMX.

John Emmi purchased the S/S AMX and converted it for street usage. The car featured a beautiful two-tone paint job and retained its S/S hood. (John Emmi Photo)

After State Farm paid the claim on the S/S AMX, John was able to keep the car. He was in the process of acquiring the necessary parts to put the car back together when it disappeared. (John Emmi Photo)

John had the car towed back to Jack's place. However, the tow truck operator forgot to put the transmission in neutral and wrecked the 4-speed. John purchased a 1968 AMX and began to switch the parts over to the car, and when he went to Jack's shop one day to work on it, the S/S was gone.

Jack told him he had the car crushed, much to John's dismay.

Crushed? Stolen?

You think that the story should probably stop there? Well, not quite. Like any good old car story, the rumors have continued with this car. One story has the car not going to the crusher but being sold to a collector in Nebraska. Of course, all of this could be verified if the surviving wrecked car still retains its serial number, but of course the alleged current owner is unwilling to acknowledge if he or she owns the car. It may sound far fetched, but with the State Farm claim noting that John Emmi could keep the car, it could be considered stolen.

What I can confirm is that this car was stolen/removed twice from a current owner or competitor, and that alone makes for a compelling tale. Surely the saga of the *Hicksville Rambler* has to be one of the strangest stories surrounding any of the 53 S/S AMXs.

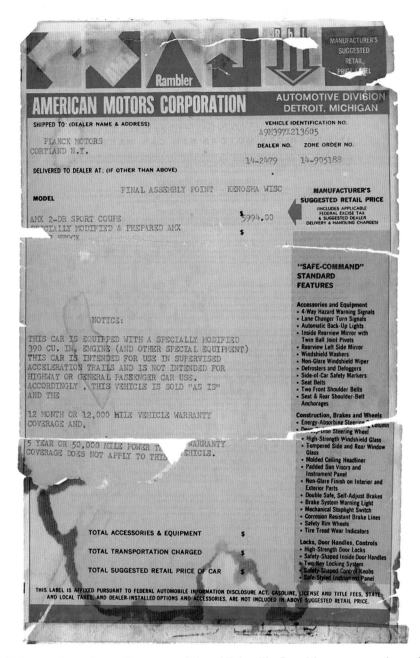

AMERICAN MOTORS CORPORATION

Rambler

AUTOMOTIVE DIVISION
DETROIT, MICHIGAN

MANUFACTURER'S
SUGGESTED
RETAIL
PRICE LABEL

SHIPPED TO: (DEALER NAME & ADDRESS)

PLANCK MOTORS
CORTLAND N.Y.

VEHICLE IDENTIFICATION NO.
A9M397X213605

DEALER NO.   ZONE ORDER NO.
14-2479   14-905188

DELIVERED TO DEALER AT: (IF OTHER THAN ABOVE)

FINAL ASSEMBLY POINT   KENOSHA WISC

MODEL

AMX 2-DR SPORT COUPE $5994.00
SPECIALLY MODIFIED & PREPARED AMX $
STOCK

**MANUFACTURER'S
SUGGESTED RETAIL PRICE**
(INCLUDES APPLICABLE
FEDERAL EXCISE TAX
& SUGGESTED DEALER
DELIVERY & HANDLING CHARGES)

**"SAFE-COMMAND"
STANDARD
FEATURES**

NOTICE:

THIS CAR IS EQUIPPED WITH A SPECIALLY MODIFIED
390 CU. IN. ENGINE (AND OTHER SPECIAL EQUIPMENT)
THIS CAR IS INTENDED FOR USE IN SUPERVISED
ACCELERATION TRAILS AND IS NOT INTENDED FOR
HIGHWAY OR GENERAL PASSENGER CAR USE.
ACCORDINGLY, THIS VEHICLE IS SOLD "AS IS"
AND THE

12 MONTH OR 12,000 MILE VEHICLE WARRANTY
COVERAGE AND,

5 YEAR OR 50,000 MILE POWER T   WARRANTY
COVERAGE DOES NOT APPLY TO THIS   EHICLE.

Accessories and Equipment
• 4-Way Hazard Warning Signals
• Lane Changer Turn Signals
• Automatic Back-Up Lights
• Inside Rearview Mirror with
  Twin Ball Joint Pivots
• Rearview Left Side Mirror
• Windshield Washers
• Non-Glare Windshield Wiper
• Defrosters and Defoggers
• Side-of-Car Safety Markers
• Seat Belts
• Two Front Shoulder Belts
• Seat & Rear Shoulder-Belt
  Anchorages

Construction, Brakes and Wheels
• Energy-Absorbing Steering Column
• Deep-Dish Steering Wheel
• High-Strength Windshield Glass
• Tempered Side and Rear Window
  Glass
• Molded Ceiling Headliner
• Padded Sun Visors and
  Instrument Panel
• Non-Glare Finish on Interior and
  Exterior Parts
• Double Safe, Self-Adjust Brakes
• Brake System Warning Light
• Mechanical Stoplight Switch
• Corrosion Resistant Brake Lines
• Safety Rim Wheels
• Tire Tread Wear Indicators

Locks, Door Handles, Controls
• High-Strength Door Locks
• Safety-Shaped Inside Door Handles
• Two Key Locking System
• Safety-Shaped Control Knobs
• Safe-Styled Instrument Panel

TOTAL ACCESSORIES & EQUIPMENT $

TOTAL TRANSPORTATION CHARGED $

TOTAL SUGGESTED RETAIL PRICE OF CAR $

THIS LABEL IS AFFIXED PURSUANT TO FEDERAL AUTOMOBILE INFORMATION DISCLOSURE ACT. GASOLINE, LICENSE AND TITLE FEES, STATE
AND LOCAL TAXES, AND DEALER-INSTALLED OPTIONS AND ACCESSORIES, ARE NOT INCLUDED IN ABOVE SUGGESTED RETAIL PRICE.

This may have been the second time Hicksville Rambler was purchased "new." Interestingly enough, both the Hicksville dealership and Roy Crandell were listed as recipients of the updated 1970 packaging for the car. (John Emmi Photo)

CHAPTER FOUR

Celebrity-Owned Muscle Cars

For decades manufacturers compensating professional athletes and Hollywood stars automobiles for "achievements" was commonplace. Manufacturers loaned and gave stars vehicles as marketing tools to sell cars.

Not your typical attire for drag racing, but Alan Page wasn't your typical drag racer. Here Page casually poses with his Superbee while spectators check out his B-Body Mopar. (Photo Courtesy John Foster Jr. Collection)

Celebrities being seen driving cars was no different than seeing Audrey Hepburn wearing designer sunglasses or Sean Connery wearing a Rolex watch while on screen or promoting a movie. Ford gave Babe Ruth a 1948 Lincoln Continental as a gift of gratitude for his devotion to little league ball players. Sure it was a token for his humanitarian work, but it was also a visible tool used to show that Babe Ruth liked Ford products.

By the time the muscle car era rolled around a different type of celebrity was seen endorsing transportation products. Steve McQueen, James Garner, and Paul Newman all became closely associated with the automobile not only by their acting credentials but with real-life interest in cars. All three competed in various forms of auto racing with Garner having the closest association with muscle cars through his L-88 Corvettes and Baja SC/Ramblers.

Hollywood action films such as *Bullit, Vanishing Point,* and *Dirty Mary, Crazy Larry* featured muscle cars as virtual co-stars. Actors Patrick Dempsey, Vin Diesel, and Paul Walker continued these traditions carrying the torch of "car guy" into the 21st century.

It wasn't only Hollywood endorsing the American muscle car, musicians such as Jim Morrison (1967 Shelby 500) and Alice Cooper (1966 Fairlane GT) piloted their own factory hot rods, furthering the *cool* factor of owning or leasing these machines. They didn't need them to verify their status, they simply loved the cars.

Then muscle cars ad celebrities were thrust into a different spotlight when *Playboy* founder Hugh Hefner began to give away a car to the Playmate of the Year. Connie Kreski received a Shelby GT 500 and Angela Dorian received an AMX. Both pink cars oozed sexuality while also offering the masculinity of factory muscle.

After the faze ended, leased cars were given back to the dealership and resold off the used car lot, which meant that many of these cars drifted into oblivion. Cars given to celebrities typically stayed with the person until he or she needed money or simply couldn't accommodate the extra vehicle.

George Carlin's 1970 Pontiac Trans Am

By Patrick Smith

When comedian George Carlin passed away in 2008, the world lost an original who wasn't afraid to try new things and push the boundaries further than ever in stand-up comedy. Carlin had a long career in showbiz after jumping from the U.S. Air Force into radio broadcasting. His Air Force stint wasn't the best one going. Although fit and able, he didn't blend in well with the Air Force mentality and was demoted and promoted so often they should have put rotating stripes on his uniform. After moving into broadcasting while in the service, George hooked up with Jack Burns and formed a duo act that proved to be popular.

Eventually Carlin went solo, and during the 1960s he developed his craft, moving slowly away from mainstream routines into an edgier, controversial style. It was in the late 1960s that George started getting a name for being hip and FM oriented. FM radio in the 1960s wasn't as commercially oriented as AM stations. FM was more likely to spin the longer album songs and air comedians with routines that were too

George & Pat Carlin
actor & friend

George Carlin poses with his brother, Pat, who was a car salesman at Livingston Pontiac at the time. The car was leased, meaning that it was likely returned and resold to the general public. (Photo Courtesy Kenny Gregrich)

spicy for television. FM was more underground, and the nighttime drive was when hipsters tuned in for freak-out songs and acts.

Carlin became famous for his "Seven Words You Can't Say on Television" sketch. He used this along with observations on the earthier side of life, including those about bodily functions, sex, and other stuff. He was following in the footsteps of the late Lenny Bruce, who was not only one of his friends, but also an early admirer and supporter before heroin addiction took him out of the picture. Carlin's new style of comedy was a hit with the younger generation and his albums were selling well. Sales weren't as hot compared to mainstream comedians, but thanks to regular gigs and guest hosting spots on late-night TV, Carlin was well known and making all the right noises.

The 1970

As a result of his success, George was able to indulge in a nice car for driving. Long drives between tour dates were a reality back then and George wanted a fast, comfortable set of wheels. He chose a 1970 Pontiac Trans Am coupe. His car was bought new at Livingston Pontiac in Woodland Hills, California. George's car was finished in Polar White with blue stripes and blue interior. One picture shows George with his brother, Pat, standing together at the Livingston Pontiac dealership lot. Pat Carlin was a salesman at Livingston and he leased the car to George. This turned out to be a significant detail.

Although George neglected to tell the details of his car, such as the color, I did learn that the poor car was badly damaged at a nightclub where he was performing. George described the carnage vividly: "I began to do sets at a folk night called the Ice House in Pasadena. The very first night I was there, I parked my Trans Am along the curb instead of in the parking lot. When I came out, someone had sideswiped it and the driver's side was just demolished and messed up. I remember thinking, 'This is the price I'm paying. This is a message that this material thing, this symbol of what I'm philosophically rejecting, is behind me. It's irrelevant. This affirms why I am here. I must follow through on it.'"

George's Zen-like attitude makes sense if you look at what he was going through at the time. He'd changed his whole approach to stand-up comedy and it was so outside the mainstream that some hotels in the lucrative Las Vegas circuit dropped him. He had no assurances yet that his brand of comedy was going to take off. George took the wreck as a sign to commit fully to his vision. It was a "Put your money where your mouth is" deal and George pursued his edgy routines with a vengeance.

This leads me to an interesting detail previously mentioned about George's 1970 Trans Am. A Trans Am owner in California read my article on Carlin's car and discovered from his PHS documentation *his* 1970 car was sold new at Livingston Pontiac and was finished with the same color, interior, and engine driveline as George's car. Because both were California vehicles, the engines were Ram Air III 4-speeds. (The Ram Air IV wasn't available in California.) The owner of the Trans Am was able to contact Pat Carlin, who recalled that George's car was a lease deal. That meant two things: It had collision insurance on it and was likely repaired instead of totaled. The residual value on a one-year-old car is quite high so it received all-new skins and panels.

I asked the owner to check his panels for date codes on the stampings and compare them with the passenger side. He said it was a project car missing its interior but is otherwise complete. No build sheet was found. It remains to be seen whether this is George's car or not. Because Livingston was a large dealer in a populated area, it's almost certain more than two 1970 Polar White Trans Ams were sold there. The search continues for these cars.

A Rental Car Crash

Carlin had another casualty from a life on the road. He managed to destroy a rental car while driving in Dayton, Ohio, en route to a performance in 1979. George was addicted to drugs and well on the way to alcohol addiction when he had an accident. He passed out while negotiating his way through one of Dayton's project areas and the car went straight down a massive construction crater, several feet deep.

Carlin suffered a nasty gash, which almost sliced his nose right off. To make matters worse, a cop who was ambitious and not above planting evidence, wanted to frame Carlin with a dope bust since the crash happened in a high drug-trafficking area. Fortunately, this didn't happen because another cop took charge of the scene and nixed the drug plant. He had Carlin taken to a hospital and arranged for a top plastic surgeon to repair his face. He also wrote up the crash report as a single-car accident with no alcohol involved.

Carlin was very lucky. His career was salvaged and he took the break to heart and turned his life around. The rental car was turned into a refrigerator before the year was over.

The Comeback

Carlin worked hard and his comeback decade was the 1980s. A series of comedy albums, a change in management, and several shows on HBO developed a new audience and regained some of his original followers.

By 1990 he was still relevant and inspiring others. Yet, the fate of George's 1970 Trans Am and BMW 3.0 CS remains unknown.

By Wes Eisenschenk

Alan Page is Minnesota sports royalty. Page, Carl Eller, Jim Marshall, and Gary Larsen, formed the Purple People Eaters, a quartet of run-stuffing and quarterback-pursuing bandits who dominated the defensive line of the Minnesota Vikings, culminating with four Super Bowl appearances in the 1960s and 1970s. Although Page never hoisted the Lombardi Trophy with the Vikings, he did something in 1971 that only one other defensive player has ever done: He was the league's MVP.

However, Page may owe his hard-charging MVP award to something else from the summer of 1971: drag racing. Huh? Alan Page, the former associate justice of the Minnesota Supreme Court, enjoyed revving up his engine for something other than pursuing Bart Starr and Gale Sayers? Yes, he did!

It all came together after the 1970 NFL season. White Bear Dodge was a large car dealership in White Bear Lake, Minnesota, sponsoring Funny Car driver and local NHRA drag racer Tom Hoover and his 1971 Dodge Charger. With Hoover campaigning nationally, White Bear Dodge approached Page about running one of its street cars at the local dragstrips for a little regional exposure. Page seemed eager at the opportunity and leased a 1971 Dodge Charger Superbee powered by a 383 Magnum.

Alan Page launches his 383 Magnum 1971 Charger Superbee at Minnesota Dragways in the familiar purple and gold colors. Page leased this machine from White Bear Dodge. (Photo Courtesy John Foster Jr. Collection)

Page's first foray into the world of drag racing came in early May 1971. A best-of-three drag racing competition was arranged against Minnesota North Stars' defensive specialist Barry Gibbs at Minnesota Dragways. Page's reaction? "It was unlike anything I ever felt in football. It's just about as much fun as squashing a quarterback," he said. Gibbs had a similar reaction. Although after North Stars General Manager Wren Blair read about the outing in the morning paper, his drag racing career would be one and done. Page campaigned the Superbee throughout the summer of 1971 in Class J Pure Stock Automatic, and according to reports, he set a track record in it by running 14.67 at 97.08 mph.

Of course this Superbee was adorned in none other than C-7 Plum Crazy with gold lettering (Vikings colors) that read "Freedom" across the doors. Mopar color assortments played right into the purple and gold sported by the Minnesota Vikings. On the rear quarter panel of the Superbee, White Bear Dodge placed its sponsorship logo, letting everyone know who provided the flashy Mopar. On the C-pillar, lettering also read "Alan Page Enterprises Inc" with a square logo noting "Alan Page" with a helmet and his number.

The Bee's interior was stitched in white; additions to the exterior included black stripes and the Power Bulge hood with a functioning Air Grabber hood scoop. Overall, the car had a very nice profile, and if you disagreed, you could take it up with the 255-pound defensive tackle.

Page returned the Charger Superbee to White Bear Dodge after the summer's racing season. Drag racing was just a fun hobby for Alan. "I'd like to go faster," he noted to AP writer Pat Thompson. "That's what I think of mainly when I'm driving in a race. I see the other car just ahead of me and it can become very frustrating if you're not able to catch it. The thrill is getting to the front."

It goes without saying that offensive linemen on opposing teams in the NFC North probably wished that Mr. Page would have stuck to drag racing.

By Chris Collard

The Nevada landscape streamed past my passenger-side window like a roll of newspaper off a printing press. It wasn't an actual window, but a mesh safety net. A concoction of sage, powder-fine dust, racing fuel, and fresh paint burning off the headers permeated the air. The smell was sweet, of victory from another era. Inside my helmet, every chuckhole, divot, and boulder launched a symphony of thuds, rattles, and clanks. Approaching a sweeping bend in the canyon, the driver lifted his right foot slightly from the throttle, slid his left over the brake, slowed to about 50 mph, and threw the car into a slight drift. He held the car in perfect symmetry to the arc of the turn, his feet dancing over the pedals. Every movement was that of a seasoned thoroughbred.

This wasn't your run-of-the-mill driver. Rod Hall is the winningest off-road racer in the United States, and at age 72, he seemed to be just getting into his groove. The hood stretched out before me also had a pedigree. White and yellow stripes slipped over the scoops to a 40-year-old emblem that formed the number 442. As in James Garner's Grabber Oldsmobile 442, the real thing that was raced by the actor, and others, in off-road events from 1969 to 1972.

I was originally invited to join the Grabber 442 team for the National Off Road Racing Association (NORRA) Mexican 1000 vintage race down the Baja peninsula in early 2010. When the Olds' engine blew during a pre-run two days before race day, Hall looked at me and

It's not everyday you find James Garner's famed Grabber Olds. This car has since undergone a thorough restoration. (Photo Courtesy Ron Johnson Collection)

said, "If we can get this car in another race, I want you to ride with me."

My job today: Watch the gauges and make sure we don't cook the engine again. An hour earlier, we'd pulled away from the Grand Sierra Resort in Reno, Nevada, with 70 buggies, trophy trucks, and Class 1 race cars in our rearview mirror. It was the ceremonial start of the inaugural Valley Off Road Racing Association (VORRA) Extreme Outlaws 250 desert race, and thousands of spectators lined up to witness this restored slice of automotive history roll under the green flag.

The official start was in front of the world-famous Mustang Ranch, and now we were in the actual race. Fist-sized boulders were skipping off the undercarriage and rocker panels, and I couldn't help but think, "Why in God's name would anyone spend two years and $60,000 restoring this car . . . then subject it to this hell?"

Behind the Madness

The man behind it all was Ron Johnson of Tacoma, Washington, a classic-car curator and aficionado of Vic Hickey–built race cars. In 2008, Johnson queried an ad in *Hemmings Motor News* for an Oldsmobile race car with a Vic Hickey roll cage. The vehicle, which did have said roll cage, could at best be called a basket case. It had no engine or tranny, was rusting from tailpipe to grille, and sported thick layers of cobwebs and dust. It wasn't until after he pushed it off the trailer at his shop that he realized he'd found the lost Jim Garner 1970 Goodyear Grabber 442. He knew what he must do.

James Garner, well known for *Maverick* long before he was famous for *The Rockford Files*, was an avid racer in the late 1960s. He even had his own fab shop and team, American International Racers,

Taking up racing was a common activity among the leading actors of the 1960s. One of the celebrities behind the wheel in competition was none other than James Garner. (Photo Courtesy Ron Johnson Collection)

which built cars for Daytona, Sebring, and other races. He was also an off-road racer from the start and even fabbed the famous fleet of AMC Ramblers that ran in the 1969 Baja 500. In the 1969 Mexican 1000, Garner piloted the 1970 Grabber 442, which was one of three preproduction cars built by off-road guru Vic Hickey, who had also created the Hurst *Baja Boot*, among many others.

The Olds seems an unusual choice, especially when you realize that the project was not factory backed. It has been assumed that it may have been influenced by Hickey's alliance with George Hurst, who was tight with Olds.

The car was ahead of its time, and Garner was an inherently skilled driver. In its first 1000, Garner was an hour ahead of his class when a sharp rock put him on the sidelines for a tire change. An oil leak had developed early in the race, and when Garner forgot to tie down the damaged tire (or it came loose), it thrashed around in the trunk and destroyed the spare oil cans. When the car was out of oil and on the sidelines again, it took 90 minutes to source additional oil and get moving. When the dust settled, Garner finessed the 442 under the checkered flag just 23 minutes behind the lead vehicle, landing a second-place finish.

Garner spent two more years behind the wheel while he waited for Vic Hickey to build the Olds Banshee, the tube-chassis predecessor to today's trophy trucks. Racin "Slick" Gardner then raced the Grabber 442 until he wadded it up. It was rebuilt and then retired from the Hickey fleet. New owners Mark and Jack Mendenhall raced the old girl on the tracks of Baja and Southern California until 1974. Its whereabouts became a mystery for the following 34 years, and it was considered to have vanished for eternity. Then Johnson found the two-line ad in *Hemmings*.

Getting the car into race-ready condition after extensive neglect became a project of biblical proportion. Extensive Internet research led to the discovery of some of the original, but now missing, components. The hood, which had been removed before the vehicle was barrel-rolled six times, showed up in Ventura, California. The original aluminum-block V-8 surfaced on the East Coast. Other hard parts, such as the rear axle and brakes, were beyond repair and required full replacement.

With a pile of new parts in hand and a bunch more coming in, Johnson began to patch together the old 442. Rusted quarter panels, cracked sheet-metal seams, and an array of dents were replaced, mended, or filled, and the body was prepped for paint. The undercarriage needed thorough sandblasting, and anything plastic or rubber found its way to the recycle bin.

From the Inside Out

Because the car was destined for the dirt again, what remained of the interior was gutted, and everything else was stripped to the metal, primed, and repainted. Johnson's goal was to keep the car basically original with upgrades for current racing.

The roll cage was inspected and improved where needed, and a Schneider Simpson 50-gallon fuel cell was fabbed to original specs, fitted with an ATL bladder, and remounted between the C-pillars. Dual Optima batteries were slipped behind a pair of new Mastercraft Safety Pro 4 racing seats and two spare BFGoodrich Mud-Terrains were shoehorned into the trunk.

The original air cleaner box, aluminum dash, tachometer, and factory speedometer were removed and refurbished, and the 1970s Stewart Warner gauges were updated with new Stewart Warner units. The car retained its original steering wheel, pedals, and Hurst Dual-Gate shifter, all of which James Garner used to finesse the 442 down the Baja peninsula.

Out Back and Up Front

With the original rear axle damaged beyond repair, a replacement Olds-style 12-bolt unit was sourced and fitted with a Moser spool, Yukon 4.11:1 gears, and a pair of Moser 35-spline axles mated to a Speedway Engineering full-floater setup. Capping each end were Wilwood billet calipers and rotors. Maintaining the original suspension and shock configuration, Johnson replicated the upper and lower shock mounts, fitted them with King bypass units at each corner, and replaced the aging rear control arms with C3 Fab Racing parts. Mastercraft limiting straps eliminated the possibility of hyperextending the shocks and losing a coil spring when the 442 left the ground.

Up front, the original Hickey-modified A-arms were inspected for structural integrity, treated to new rubber and ball joints, and the shock mounts were modified to accept new dual King bypass shocks. To keep the 442 between the flags, steering links were upgraded. Wilwood calipers and rotors controlled braking.

Under the Bonnet

When Vic Hickey received the car from Detroit in 1969, it sported an all-aluminum Olds 350. That mill went south shortly after and was replaced with a Dale Smith–built aluminum-block 410-ci V-8, one of only four built. Hoping to find an engine similar to the original, Johnson went back to the numerous Internet race-junkie forums. The research paid off when he received a note that one of the 410s was sitting in a warehouse on the East Coast. Further inquiry revealed it was the exact block originally in the car. A price was negotiated, Johnson laid down the coin, and in a few weeks the vintage mill was sitting in his shop.

After 34 years of grime was stripped from its core, the 410 was treated to a full overhaul: new crank and rods, Probe Racing 10.5:1 pistons, aluminum heads, and Comp Cams roller rockers and cam. Up top, the OEM air cleaner haloed an Edelbrock carburetor and Edelbrock Performer intake manifold. Spark plugs received their pulse via MSD's Pro-Billet aluminum distributor, plug wires, and dual coils. A pair of Hedman headers and a Flowmaster 3-inch system channeled the fumes. While the 410 was being resurrected, Destry Scott at A-Plus Transmissions was rebuilding a TH400 transmission and Victory Performance was turning a new driveshaft. When the engine was finally put on a dyno, Johnson says the old 442 pegged the needle at 508 hp.

Back on the Track

The temperature gauge was heading into the red zone as Rod Hall and I rounded the corner for the first pit stop. I didn't want to be the guy at the gauges if this second (and very expensive) engine melted down. I made the call for a full-stop inspection. The Flex-a-Lite aluminum radiator and dual fans were up to the task, but the 140-amp alternator gave up the ghost and the fans ceased to function as the batteries died. The guys from Samco-Hall's pit crew grabbed another alternator and slipped it in. It also died after a few miles.

Our race was over. As we rolled back to the pits, Hall flipped off the ignition toggles, I shut down the primary power, and a small crowd gathered. At that moment, crossing the checkered flag didn't really matter. James Garner's Grabber Oldsmobile was alive and mostly well. I'd spent the day in one of the most notable cars of its day, and with the most winning off-roader in history. It was a moment I'll never forget.

James Garner

June 28, 2010

Dear Ron,

I've just been looking at the YouTube video that Cliff Coleman sent and I just can't believe my ol' eyes! You guys have done such a remarkable job, I was just about ready to reach for my racing gear.

Those photos certainly brought back a rush of memories for me and I am in total awe of your accomplishment. I know the restoration took a lot of patience, love and persistent dedication; not to mention a few bucks too.

Rod, I sure am envious that you can still get out there and race it. It's got to be a remarkable experience. Déjà vu all over again!

I just can't thank all of you guys at Hickey Racing enough for executing perfection. The 442 rules!

Your friend always,

James Garner

Ron Johnson
Hickey Racing Team
1625 S. Adams Street
Tacoma, WA 98405

Does it get any cooler than a personalized letter from James Garner gloating over how great a job you did restoring one of his old Baja rides? No. (Photo Courtesy Ron Johnson Collection)

As we loaded the car to return to Reno, I asked Johnson about the time and cost involved with the restoration. "It wasn't cheap, but this car is a piece of history. I couldn't let it die in a pile of cobwebs," he responded. "I never could have taken this project on if it were not for the help of my brothers Rick and Dick, my dad, and all of the amazing sponsors who shared my vision."

When asked about being sponsored by Los Valientes Tequila and the famous Mustang Ranch, he said, "They are both big Baja race fans and provide . . . uh . . . moral support. At the end of the day, the money wasn't important. I wanted James Garner to know how much his car means to his fans and the racing public and that it should once again see the two dirt tracks of Baja."

By Mike Satterfield

In 1964, *Playboy* magazine started a tradition of gifting the Playmate of the Year a car. From 1964 to 1975 those cars were painted in the magazine's signature color, Playboy Pink. Some of the iconic cars that were painted in this hue include a 1964½ Ford Mustang convertible, a Porsche 911S, and a DeTomaso Pantera. For 1969, Playmate of the Year Connie Kreski received one of the coolest muscle cars ever built, a 1969 Shelby GT500 Fastback. And yes, this Shelby was the only one ever painted pink. Standard attire under the hood of the GT500 was the 428-ci Cobra Jet, making this car one mean machine for the dainty playmate.

Connie Kreski, 1969 Playboy *Playmate of the Year, poses with her 1969 Shelby GT500 Mustang. Hugh Hefner gave the pink pony to her for receiving the honor. (Copyright 1969* Playboy. *Reprinted with permission. All rights reserved)*

Connie was *Playboy* magazine's Playmate of the Month in January 1968 and landed the honor of becoming Playmate of the Year in 1969. She was known to run in Hollywood circles and had landed a few small roles in films and commercials. *Los Angeles Times* Writer Joyce Haber mentioned Kreski in a story about the murder of actress Sharon Tate. As a member of Tate's social circle, Connie had been invited to the infamous party at the home Tate shared with her husband, director Roman Polanski. Kreski had declined the invitation for an unknown reason the night that followers of Charles Manson paid a deadly visit to the mansion on Cielo Drive.

Over the years, searches for the Playboy Pink Shelby led enthusiasts to Connie's hometown of Wyandotte, Michigan. Before being discovered at a University of Michigan football game by a *Playboy* sports reporter, Connie had graduated from Mercy College of Nursing and had just started working at an Ann Arbor, Michigan, hospital. According to a cousin, her choice to become a Playboy Playmate did not sit well with her conservative Catholic family.

The title of a story published on April 30, 1969, in *The Daily Times News* sums up the relationship with her parents over her choice to appear in *Playboy*: "She's On Her Way to Stardom, But Mom's On Tranquilizers." The family had little to no contact after she moved away from Michigan and it seems that the car and Connie never went back to Michigan.

I turned my attention to Connie's life in California. She had a big year in 1969. She not only was named Playmate of the Year, but she also began her acting career. Kreski was a rising star in Hollywood and soon was dating famed actor James Caan in the early 1970s. It seems that Connie never married, and after her high-profile romance with Caan ended in 1976, she stepped back from the spotlight. She returned temporarily to take part in a documentary in 1992 and then drifted back into obscurity. Sadly, she died just three years later at the age of 48 from a blocked carotid artery. With her death, almost any chance of finding the real story behind her Shelby Mustang was lost.

Carroll Shelby's versions of the Ford Mustang have become some of the most sought-after cars, with Shelby Mustangs regularly selling at auction in the high six figures. A one-of-a kind GT500 would surely set an auction record. The only problem is that the car has not been seen since the 1970s and no one seems to know where it went. A pink muscle car, you would think, would attract a lot of attention, but only a few photos of the pink Shelby are known to exist.

Carroll Shelby, Bobby Unser, and Connie Kreski pay a visit to one of the largest Ford dealerships east of the Mississippi, Phil Long Ford. (Photo Courtesy Colorado Spring Gazette)

Shelby and *Playboy* had a long history of working together. Shelby often placed ads in *Playboy*, and in 1968 10 Shelby Mustang convertibles were ordered to serve as house cars for the Playboy Mansion at Lake Geneva. Carroll Shelby was there for the opening and rode in a 427 Cobra as part of the parade of Shelby's convertibles. All 10 of the Lake Geneva cars are accounted for; some are restored, others still awaiting restoration. Connie's 1969 GT500 has yet to surface.

The car remains unaccounted for in the Shelby registry. What I do know is that serial number 1027 left the factory in Pastel Grey and was repainted Playboy Pink before being delivered to Chaffe Motors in California. It was a regular production GT500 with an automatic and no air conditioning. After the repaint, Kreski took delivery of the car, and by all accounts it seems that there were just a few sightings of it around the Los Angeles area during the time she owned it. However, those cannot be confirmed. To date, not one picture of her or anyone else actually driving this fabled Mustang has surfaced.

Members of the Mustang community have been looking for Connie's GT500 for years and many rumors of the car's whereabouts have now reached the level of urban legend. Some say that Connie sold the car in the early 1970s and it was repainted and ultimately wrecked by the new owner; others claim that she kept the car until her death in 1995 and that the car is in storage somewhere in the Los Angeles area.

Could it be out there? Stranger things have been found in the garages of Los Angeles, such as Phil Spector's Shelby Daytona, languishing away in storage for nearly 30 years.

Jim Morrison's
1967 Shelby GT500 Mustang, *The Blue Lady*

By Daniel Fehn

Like Jim Morrison himself, many legends and mysteries surround the history and whereabouts of his 1967 Mustang Shelby GT500. Shelby fans have long sought this car, with every few years reports surfacing of it being found, but the reports have never turned out to be true.

Jim's Reward

The Blue Lady, as Morrison named the car, was a gift from Elektra President Jac Holtzman in 1967 after The Doors' self-titled debut album was released and "Light My Fire" hit number 1 on the music charts. Holtzman asked each band member what they wanted as a thank-you gift. Robby Krieger and John Densmore requested recording equipment and Ray Manzarek asked for a thoroughbred horse. Morrison thought the Shelby GT350 his hair stylist (Jay Sebring) had was the coolest car he had ever seen and requested a GT500 equipped exactly like Jay's.

The car was a 1967 Ford Mustang Shelby GT500, Nightmist Blue in color, build number 939. The interior was a parchment color rather than the typical black that was usually ordered with the Nightmist

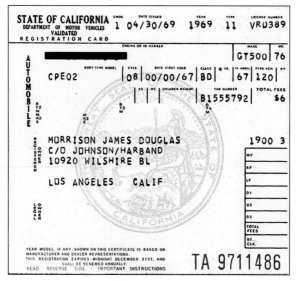

One of the few surviving relics pertaining to Jim Morrison's lost Shelby Mustang is this registration card. This card, along with the video shot by Paul Ferrara, remain two of the best resources for documenting The Blue Lady. *(Photo Courtesy Bret Mattison Collection)*

Blue exterior. According to Marti Reports (the licensee of Ford Motor Company's entire production database for the 1967–1993 model years), only 47 cars with this color combination were built.

It was delivered in late 1967, which means that it had the rarer close-set driving lights in the middle of the grille, which were changed to small rectangular lights shortly after to abide by federal regulations. The Shelby was not a Super Snake, so it did not have any stripes (which were still an option) and had the rarer optional 10-spoke wheels. The engine was a 428 Police Interceptor with dual quad Holley carbs teamed with a 4-speed manual transmission.

Although Jim dubbed the car *The Blue Lady* and was said by many to love the car, he did not baby it at all. It was the only car he ever owned, and he beat and destroyed it as he did with many of his rental cars. Although he crashed it multiple times, he had it repaired each time. He had at least five documented severe crashes. In Jim Morrison's biography, *No One Here Gets Out Alive* by Danny Sugarman and Jerry Hopkins, the authors document that *The Blue Lady* was involved in multiple major accidents, including one on La Cienega Boulevard, which leveled five young trees.

Each time, the car was repaired but sheet metal can only be bent and repaired so much.

HWY: An American Pastoral

In early 1969, Jim Morrison wrote a 10-page screenplay that was filmed and directed by Paul Ferrara. Jim plays a hitchhiker who kills the driver of the Mustang and takes the car for some "hard" rides. This film was never released. The first clips visible to the public were first shown in the 2009 Doors documentary *When You're Strange.*

This video has been digitally restored for the documentary, and quite a few videos on YouTube show different parts of this movie. The following website has some great details on this film if you want to know more: mildequator.com/filmhistory/hwy.html.

Speculation Stories

Unfortunately the true story of what happened to the car was buried with Jim. Many stories are floating around Hollywood about what happened to the car. Three of the most popular are:

1. He wrapped it around a telephone pole on his way to the Whisky a Go Go, a bar he frequented and where The Doors played many shows. Frustrated with the extensive damage, he walked the short distance to the bar and got his drink on for the night. When he returned to the scene later that night (or morning), the car had been towed away and he never followed up on it.

2. The car was towed from the Los Angeles Airport, where he parked it for an extended time during tours. It was then sold at auction and lost. Some stories mention the car was resold many times in California, and after multiple accidents, it was crushed in the early 1980s.

3. He wrapped the car around a light pole near a police station much later than the Whisky a Go Go incident.

No recorded documentation has been found to prove or disprove any of these stories. The Whisky a Go Go accident possibly happened much earlier, likely the spring 1969 filming of the *HWY* movie. It could be mentioned frequently only because it is a popular story, not the actual cause of losing the car. It's very possible number 3 happened with the accident, and the car was taken to the airport where it was eventually towed. We will likely never find out. Multiple writers have asked The Doors' surviving members, but no one knows.

Search Leads

I will make full disclosure here that I am *not* looking for the lost Shelby, for a number of reasons. I likely couldn't afford it, plus it seems that a number of people are searching for it and they may already have some knowledge that put them far ahead of me.

Brett Matteson, owner of shelbymustang.com and a classic car business, was able to purchase the original registration card of the car. He has written some detailed information about it at shelbymustang.com/morrison.php. He is currently looking for the car and seems to have some good leads, which he hasn't shared.

Patrick Smith, a blogger and car fan, wrote about contacting Johnson/Harbrand, the C/O on the registration card, a few years back. It is the accounting firm that managed Jim Morrison's assets. He simply asked about a company car from 1969. Instantly the person on the other end asked if it was a Mustang and whether he could verify it.

When Patrick mentioned that he was simply doing some research for a blog post, the person on the other end turned disinterested and basically ended the conversation. Obviously they know about the car, and they are likely contacted quite a bit about it. You can read about that at: http://phscollectorcarworld.blogspot.com/2012/05/lost-star-cars-jim-morrisons-1967.html#!/2012/05/lost-star-cars-jim-morrisons-1967.html.

Gone for Good?

Supposedly, the Shelby Registry has checked against the California DMV database, and the car has not been registered in California since 1969. This can mean only a few things. Either the car was moved to another state, it was immediately put in storage and never reregistered, or it was crushed and destroyed.

My personal hunch is that the car is lost for good, likely crushed and destroyed long ago. The car was involved in many major accidents, possibly damaging the frame. It may have been repairable the first few times, but if the account is correct that Jim wrapped it around a telephone pole and never saw it again, this would be the likely scenario.

These cars were expensive at the time (double the price of a standard Mustang), but it was only two years old and not yet collectible. I can't see someone buying it to fix it with frame damage, possibly having multiple issues from the previous accidents. Also, Jim Morrison was not the "legend" then that he is now, so I don't think anyone would have kept the car just because it was Morrison's.

If someone did have the Shelby in storage knowing it was Jim Morrison's, and waiting for the right time to sell a celebrity car, I believe it would have been long ago. Interest in Jim Morrison and The Doors was rekindled after Oliver Stone's movie *The Doors* was released in 1991, and this would have been a perfect time to sell the car at its highest value.

Here's a question: Who actually still owns the car? Although Brett Matteson was able to purchase the original registration card, he only owns the piece of paper and not the car itself. The car was last registered to James Douglas Morrison, C/O Johnson/Harband. Because no records show the car being reregistered or purchased after October 1969, I have to think the car legally still belongs to the Morrison estate or the firm listed on the registration title.

A legal battle could develop between the two because this car is easily worth more than $1 million. Maybe the possessor of the car does not want to release it because it would have to be turned over to the rightful owner decided by the courts.

If the car was scrapped, as I believe, the engine and other parts may still be out there. Although the body and frame were likely destroyed, the engine was probably in okay shape and was worth some money.

If you have information regarding Morrison's lost 1967 Shelby, please contact me at timelessrides.com.

By Matt Hardigree

Iknow the sound of money. It's the shaking voice of Erin Slone Pope at the other end of the phone, increasingly aware that she has the golden ticket: a gold and black 1971 Chevrolet Camaro Z28 once owned by "Papa John" Schnatter with a $250,000 bounty on its hood.

There was only one problem: Her brother had recently sold the car.

The reason that Pope was calling me at all was because she'd seen Schnatter on a television show talking about the car and thought it sounded a little bit like the Camaro her brother had purchased in 1983. A quick web search led them to an article I'd written for the car website Jalopnik, describing the afternoon I'd spent driving around with the pizza magnate in a nearly identical version of his beloved Z28 that he had built as a sort of placeholder until he could get the real thing.

Thanks to Jalopnik, "Papa John" Schnatter was able to find and repurchase his Z28 Camaro that he reluctantly sold to start his pizza chain. (Photo Courtesy "Papa John" Schnatter)

My Ride-Along

It was a few months prior to Pope's call on a typically hot Houston summer day when Schnatter rolled into town. His replica Camaro was puking out coolant like crazy. Our drive was short, but Papa John was nice enough to tell me a little bit about the car he so desperately wanted back.

He shared clues and details that he hoped would spark recognition in someone reading about the car. "It had the split-bumper, sunroof, BFGoodrich tires with steel wheels. I swapped out the rear end with a Posi-Traction differential, and now the speedometer reads 10 mph over the actual speed. It had a velvet interior, unlike the vinyl one in this car; it didn't have A/C, and the ashtray in back is falling off."

I thought it was curious how he kept switching between present and past tense for the car. The odds that a split-bumper Camaro hadn't been scrapped or, worse, wrapped around some tree on a snaky rural road leading up to a Kentucky holler seemed slight. I took it to mean that Schnatter, despite the unfavorable odds, still believed the car existed.

This wasn't just some emotionally manipulative stunt to get a lot of free PR. Schnatter didn't just want the car back, he needed it back.

We were tooling around in a replica that was probably better than the original in every way (except for maybe the cooling system) and all he could think about was the one that got away. He dismissed the replica he was sitting in, saying the original car was "the truth."

It's so fundamental to his story. Faith can get you far, but even the most fervent believer isn't going to snub his nose at a little proof. It's why there are enough pieces of the "true cross" in reliquaries in old European churches to build an ark. At the time, I could imagine him on his deathbed mumbling "Zee twenty-eight" instead of "Rosebud."

Setting the Bait

Because Jalopnik is so large, and because I'm a bit of an optimist myself, I kept a few of the details out of the original story on the off chance someone who read my article had the car. I'd used these details to dismiss a few people who thought they might have the Golden Camaro and reached out to me in the months after publishing the story.

I'd had no bites that seemed legitimate and had largely moved on from the hunt when I received a note from Mrs. Pope.

That message caught my interest because she said her brother purchased the car from Schnatter while their father was working in Indiana and then brought the car back to Kentucky at around the same time I'd heard described.

I'd guessed that if the Z28 still existed the only reason it had eluded private investigators was because it had changed hands so many times. I was wrong. In reality, it had only traveled a short distance across the border. For most of its life it had been owned by the people he sold it to. Life is in the details, and two details are key here:

1. The car was purchased on the Indiana side of the border and in 1983 they didn't keep electronic records, so Schnatter couldn't look up who had the car.

2. Schnatter, understandably more concerned with saving the family business than with cars, remembered the Camaro being a 1972 Z28 and not a 1971½ Z28, as it actually is.

Mrs. Pope's Story

I told Mrs. Pope to call me and that's when she explained the story of buying the car. She told me how Schnatter was broken up at the time, how he could barely watch the car drive away. Her timeline and the details of the car perfectly matched everything I'd been told a few months earlier. Their car was Papa John's car!

Well, actually, it was Jeff Robinson's car. Robinson purchased the Camaro from the Slones and drove it back to his home in Flatwoods, Kentucky, where he'd converted it into a monster 850-hp dragster.

It's remarkably good luck to end up buying the beloved car of a man who is about to turn the paltry $2,800 you just handed him into a worldwide pizza chain worth many times that. It's remarkably bad luck to hold on to that car for a quarter of a century only to hand it over to someone else around the time you realize that the kid in the red shorts who sold it to you is willing to pay so much to get his car back.

Success!

Once I was convinced that they might have the right car, I connected the Slones with Papa John's people and they eventually got in touch with Jeff Robinson, who was aware of the hunt for the car but didn't think he had the right one because his car was a 1971½.

I remember that, at the time, there was some confusion as to exactly who was owed what. That was eventually resolved when the Slones were offered a $25,000 finder's fee on top of the $250,000 Schnatter paid to Jeff Robinson.

Think about it for a second. That's nearly $300,000 exchanged between three people over the course of about three decades for an early-1970s Camaro that's far from the most coveted muscle car of the era and is, by the most charitable description, kind of ugly.

I was just an interlocutor in this whole process who happened to help connect some of the dots. There was no finder's fee for me, but I wasn't left empty handed. It's a rare and wonderful thing when you can help a fellow gearhead get back his first car.

By Danny Reed

In 1971, I was driving by a GMAC used car lot in downtown Austin when an unusual gold and black 1969 Corvette caught my eye. As a huge fan of the space program and a Corvette enthusiast, I knew about the General Motors Courtesy Lease program for astronauts. In fact, I had kept a December 1969 *Life* magazine that had a picture of the three Apollo XII astronauts sitting on their matching Corvettes. And there, right in front of me, was one of those special cars. When I asked about the car, the dealer had no information except that it was for sale on a "closed" bid. Keeping details to myself, I didn't discuss it further and immediately turned in a written bid for $3,230. Several weeks later, I was notified the car had been sold; but then fate intervened and soon after, I was called and offered the car if I were still interested.

The top bid had been $13,000, obviously from someone who also recognized the history and value of the car. For some reason, he did not come up with the money and I was the second highest bidder. That was my lucky day, and the beginning of the story of the lost Apollo XII Corvettes.

This very car, Alan Bean's 1969 gold and black Corvette Coupe, may be the only survivor of the original three Apollo XII Corvettes.

GM's Courtesy Lease Program

It all started in 1961 with Alan Shepard, the first man in space. When Shepard returned from his historic mission, General Motors presented him with a 1962 Corvette. The idea initiated by Jim

The Apollo XII astronauts pose proudly with their matching Corvettes. The astronaut/Corvette marriage dates back to 1961 when Alan Shepard received a 1962 'Vette as a gift from General Motors after his historic space flight. (Dottie Cole Collection, Courtesy Danny Reed)

Rathmann and Ed Cole developed into GM's Courtesy Lease program. This was the beginning of an incredible journey for the American astronauts and the Corvette, America's sports car.

Jim Rathmann, winner of the 1960 Indy 500, owned a Chevrolet-Cadillac dealership just south of Cocoa Beach in Melbourne, Florida. Cape Canaveral (renamed Cape Kennedy in November 1963) was close to the dealership, and Rathmann soon became friends with many of the astronauts. Ed Cole, president of General Motors, worked with Rathmann to negotiate the Chevrolet Courtesy Lease program that allowed astronauts to lease cars for $1 per year. At the end of that lease, each astronaut turned in their car and received the new GM car of their choice, again, for $1 per year.

In the early 1960s, an astronaut was considered the new American hero, and many of the astronauts drove Corvettes. From an advertising viewpoint, Rathmann believed the astronauts would indirectly provide the perfect marketing for the Corvette. Rathmann, with the help of Ed Cole, was able to place six of the original Mercury astronauts in Corvettes; soon, Rathmann's dealership became known as "The Dealership to the Stars."

As the Courtesy Lease program developed, astronauts were allowed to choose any General Motors vehicle for $1 per year. However, because many of the astronauts had families, they often chose a sedan or station wagon over the sporty Corvette.

Not Quite Identical

When the Apollo XII crew was assigned their Apollo flight, which was to be the second lunar landing, Pete Conrad, Dick Gordon, and Alan Bean decided to get really creative. They not only wanted Corvettes; they wanted something unique.

Bean said, "Let's get 'em all the same!" The crew discussed their ideas, finally agreeing on gold with black trim. According to Bean in later years, the crew, all being naval pilots, often wondered why they didn't pick blue and gold. Renowned industrial and automotive designer Alex Tremulis, stylist behind the iconic Tucker Torpedo, presented the paint design with the unusual black wings for the rear of the cars signifying flight, and a small red, white, and blue emblem for the front fenders.

The three identical 1969 Corvette sport coupes were delivered to Rathmann's dealership. Each came equipped with a 390-hp 427 V-8 Turbo-Jet, 4-speed wide-range transmission, 3.08 Posi-Traction rear axle, air-conditioning, black vinyl interior, special PO2 wheel covers, and three-point seat belts.

After delivery, at Bean's request, Rathmann added a little white stripe between the black and the gold, the final touch for the three identical Corvettes. But to make the cars unique to each of the highly competitive pilots, a small touch was added to identify the astronauts. Every personal item in the spacecraft was color-coded.

Conrad's food and towels had small red Velcro tabs. Gordon's tabs were white. Bean's were blue. So in the rectangular red, white, and blue emblems on the front fenders, Conrad's car had "CDR" over the red square in the emblem, which stood for mission commander. Gordon's had "CMP" over the white square for command module pilot. And Bean's had "LMP" over the blue for lunar module pilot.

NASA Ends the Program

Alan Bean wasn't a car guy when he joined NASA in 1963. "I couldn't afford to be a car aficionado," he says. "I was an airplane aficionado. All I did was concentrate on flying planes for the navy." But like the original seven astronauts, which included Alan Shepard, Gus Grissom, and Gordon Cooper, Alan Bean was offered a new car every year for a measly dollar.

In 1969, Bean was 37, driving around in a GM Courtesy Lease gold and black Corvette. The astronauts appeared on the three television networks, in *Life* magazine, and enjoyed ticker-tape parades. In appearances to this day, you always hear Bean say, "Wow! It was great! It was fun! What could be better?"

Sadly, in the early 1970s, NASA bowed to outside pressure and concern that the public might believe that the astronauts had actually purchased the cars and they (along with NASA) were formally endorsing Chevrolet and Corvettes. General Motors was forced to end the Courtesy Lease program.

Alan Bean's Astrovette

I know that the history, documentation, originality, and condition determine a collector car's value. The car I accidentally found sitting on a GMAC lot was Alan Bean's "Astrovette." Documentation? It had it all: 28,000 original miles, Protect-O-Plate, owner's manual with handwritten notes to the dealer from Alan Bean.

Shortly after purchasing his historic Corvette, I photographed the car that once belonged to astronaut Alan Bean. The sister cars leased by Pete Conrad and Dick Gordon are still MIA. (Photo Courtesy Danny Reed Collection)

Since then, I have been able to secure the order sheet, build sheet, and shipping order. And Alan Bean's name is actually on the tank sticker. I have never seen another tank sticker that included the owner's name. In addition, Tremulis' nephew sent me copies of his uncle's original design and the envelope and letter with Alan Bean's approval. Documentation should never end.

True value includes verifying the documentation and getting the car judged by others or outside sources. With Corvettes, the National Corvette Restorers Society (NCRS) is a good place to start. I chose Bean's car to be judged only at NCRS regional or national events, where standards are held to the highest level.

In preparation, I hired one of the top Corvette restorers around, Ray Repczynski of Corvettes by Ray in Houston. He is one of the founding members of the Texas NCRS. He was instrumental in reconditioning the car to the highest standards, while retaining the car's originality. With his help and attention to detail, the car achieved Top Flight at every event entered.

And now, Alan Bean's car has achieved the NCRS Duntov Award of Excellence *and* the most coveted NCRS American Heritage Award. It is the first and only Corvette to receive both awards.

Exposure builds value. Alan Bean's car has been featured in major magazines including *Life*, *Vette*, *Collector Car*, *Vette Vues*, *Corvette*,

Motor Trend, and *Motor Trend Classic*. It has appeared on television shows including the U.K.'s *Top Gear with James May, Wheeler Dealers with Mike Brewer*, and *Classic Car Rescue*. It has been on display at the National Corvette Museum, the Cosmosphere, multiple Johnson Space Center open houses, the Houston Space Center. It has also appeared as the feature Corvette at major car shows such as the Dallas and Houston Corvette Chevy Expos.

The Other Apollo XII Corvettes

I have always dreamed of owning all three Apollo XII Corvettes. In the mid-1970s I began my search. I have the serial numbers, and no, they are not consecutive. In fact I have the numbers of most, if not all, of the cars in the GM Special Lease program. I have spent years searching through engine vehicle records with help from law enforcement, investigators, insurance companies, and the NCRS.

To my knowledge and findings, the two missing Apollo XII Corvettes have not been registered in any of the 50 states in the past 40 years. Special Lease cars were never titled in the astronauts' names, making it more difficult.

In 2001, working with the National Corvette Museum, I tried to find all astronauts' Corvettes for the museum display celebration of the 40th anniversary of the first man in space. Once again, I was unsuccessful at locating the two cars.

Pete Conrad's widow, Nancy Conrad, was at the celebration, and she too has been searching for Pete's car for years. My advertising agency handles advertising and public relations for the Texas NCRS. Every year, NCRS refers people and questions about the possible finds, all to no avail. I search *Hemmings* and other magazines and request VINs on every 1969 Corvette coupe for sale, regardless of condition.

I have been contacted many times over the years, but so far, no one has found Conrad's or Gordon's car. I will continue my search, but unless it is tucked away in someone's barn or overseas, it is very likely the cars are gone . . . but not forgotten.

But beware when you buy a historical or collector car. If you aren't careful, it will soon own you. I always say, "My car has a better life and resume than I do."

If you know of the location of the two remaining Apollo XII Corvettes, please contact me at danny@dannyreed.net.

By Corey Owens

Big Willie Robinson, a Vietnam veteran, is perhaps the most legendary street racer this world has ever known. He and his wife Tomiko were the unquestioned rulers of the West Coast street racing scene, and his name is synonymous with Chrysler performance cars. Their Dodge Charger Daytonas, three in all, became famous from coast to coast, appearing in national advertisements ads for performance parts and attending various appearances all across the country. If you were into street racing in the 1960s and 1970s, you know about Big Willie and Street Racers Inc.

Big Willie and Tomiko started an organization called Street Racers Inc., National & International. At one time they had 80,000 members in 38 states and 9 countries. Big Willie wanted to help keep kids off the streets and off drugs and he did it through the promotion of street racing. With his hulking 6-foot 6-inch frame and bulging biceps, Big Willie was often found standing between two rival gang members negotiating a treaty for the evening and offering an avenue to settle a beef. If you were coming to watch the races, you played by Big Willie's rules.

Gary French (pictured) purchased the **Duke & Duchess** *Daytona directly from Big Willie Robinson. Note the surviving T-bolt-style hood that was featured on* **King Daytona** *in the movie* **Two-Lane Blacktop***; it was transplanted onto this car. (Photo by Gary Emord-Netzley,* **Messenger-Inquirer***)*

When Willie returned from Vietnam, he began to work with the Los Angeles Police Department, an unlikely pairing, but fixing race relations after the Watts Riots was needed. The relationship remained fruitful for years. With the LAPD's cooperation, certain areas of Los Angeles were shut down for racing, which allowed for safer racing conditions.

Legend has it that on the first night of this arrangement an estimated 10,000 people were in attendance to witness organized street racing. On the second night, 20,000 people showed up as word of mouth spread quickly and participating and watching these events became the thing to do. The LAPD reported that crime rates were down and everyone with a brain knew why. Through these very positive results, Terminal Island became known as Brotherhood Raceway Park and featured street racing for years.

The Cars

The first two Daytonas campaigned by Willie and Tomiko were Hemi cars. Willie campaigned *King Daytona* and Tomiko drove *Queen Daytona*. The *Duke & Duchess* Daytona, the third in the stable, is thought to have been built as a public relations vehicle, although the car does have scars showing some racing history.

King Daytona and Big Willie were very popular in the Los Angeles area. He and other members of Street Racers Inc. had cameos in the movie *Two-Lane Blacktop*, a car culture classic filmed in 1971. The fate of *King Daytona* came via too many dips in the acid tank, damaging the car beyond saving. Willie did this to lighten the car for drag racing.

Queen Daytona met its fate on a dragstrip in Arizona, where it hit the wall and rolled numerous times, which destroyed the car.

Although no pictures or documentation show that Big Willie raced the *Duke & Duchess* Daytona, the car has many hints that he did. It retains the *King Daytona* hood, and the firewall had been beaten up, allowing a rod to go through for the famous ClutchFlite transmission that Big Willie always ran. The bottom of the floor where the pinion snubber hit was mangled, and a piece of 3/8-inch-thick plated steel was welded in place for more support. The pinion snubber was modified to be taller, the lips on the quarters were rolled to accommodate larger tires, and the rear axle was bent slightly. Moreover, there are all the telltale signs of him running his high-powered Hemi engine in this car. Enough signs to clearly show that this wasn't just a PR car.

The Survivor

Big Willie was alleged to have parked the lone surviving Daytona in 1979, shortly after Keith Black freshened up the original 440 block. The car sat in his back yard next to his swimming pool until he sold it in 2003 to Gary French in Kentucky. Gary was a longtime fan of Big Willie and maintained a positive line of communication with him for years before buying the car, earning Willie's trust and friendship. Gary took the car home and got it running again and drove it.

He drove the Daytona to shows and enjoyed it for many years until he sold it to a collector in New Jersey, who had the intention of restoring the car but never found the time.

The car then was sold to Corey Owens and Jim Ripka in central Minnesota. Corey owns a body and restoration business in Ogilvie, and has always been a muscle car and Mopar fanatic. The car was in fairly good shape, but weathered from sitting in Big Willie's back yard for years, so the decision was made to restore the *Duke & Duchess* Daytona to a concours day-2 car.

Restoration Results

A period-correct restoration began in the summer of 2012, and Big Willie and Tomiko's Daytona was totally disassembled and documented. More than 1,200 hours were put into bringing the old muscle car back to its former glory. Every small detail on the car was restored to concours specifications, including the R4 red paint it wore when it rolled off the assembly line. The Daytona was then painted the off-white cream color that it sported when Willie ran it. All the small details were addressed, including applying a little overspray into the engine bay and trunk jamb. No stone was left unturned when restoring the car.

The car was completed in the spring of 2014 and has been seen and shown at some of the larger Mopar shows across the United States. The Daytona attracts huge crowds of spectators that would make Big Willie and Tomiko proud. Unfortunately, Tomiko passed away in 2007 and Willie in 2012; they never saw their *Duke & Duchess* Daytona completed.

If you have any photographic history of the *Duke & Duchess* Daytona, please contact me at cudacorey@hotmail.com.